Portraying
'the Jew' in
First World War Britain

For Betty Herbert

Portraying 'the Jew' in First World War Britain

ALYSON PENDLEBURY

Foreword by MARK LEVENE
University of Southampton

LONDON • PORTLAND, OR

First published in 2006 in Great Britain by
VALLENTINE MITCHELL
Suite 314, Premier House,
112–114 Station Road,
Edgware, Middlesex, HA8 7BJ

and in the United States of America by
VALLENTINE MITCHELL
c/o International Specialized Book Services, Inc.,
920 NE 58th Avenue, Suite 300
Portland, Oregon, 97213-3786

Website: www.vmbooks.com

British Library Cataloguing in Publication Data

A catalogue record for this book has been applied for

ISBN 0-85303-614-4 (cloth)
ISBN 0-85303-615-2 (paper)

Library of Congress Cataloging-in-Publication Data

A catalog record for this book has been applied for

Typeset by FiSH Books, London
Printed in Great Britain by MPG Books Ltd, Bodmin, Cornwall

Contents

List of Plates

Foreword

Until one actually starts living in a time of acute societal crisis the ability to empathise with dead and buried people who responded to their own catastrophes in ways we might consider – for want of a better word – 'mad' is a problematic one. If things around us are, in the most general sense, functioning and if our understanding of the broader political and economic environment points to the likelihood that the world as we know it will continue along its merry course, with our own lives, and those of our progeny, set to be purposeful and happy ones, how could we possibly imagine human responses to a world in which that certitude has been blown to shreds?

It begs the question, of course, how far we have descended into our own contemporary crisis. Or to what degree our response is mad – or perhaps just plain maddening. But most of us would agree that the world turned on 9/11, generating levels of anxiety and hysteria, certainly in the United States and much of the Western world, that arguably were never reached throughout the long darkness of the Cold War. More surprising, perhaps, is the way it has generated at high political as well as deeper societal levels, an arguably inherent tendency towards Manicheism. The doctrines of the third-century Persian gnostic and dualist, Mani, were, of course, treated as heresy by the Christian Church. But the struggle between the forces of light and the forces of darkness, or, put into more familiar biblical terminology, between good and evil, God and Satan, is a facet of the human condition. Throw a spanner into the works of our everyday optimism and the tendency is likely to surge. Add a teleological dimension, again specifically inherent in the Abrahamic world-views, and we have the potential for lift-off.

But surely all that stuff about the end being nigh, or that we are now witnessing the Last Days – foretold in those dread works of Judeo-Christian Apocalypse, above all in the Book of Revelation – while music to the ears of millenarians, dispensationalists and Bible bashers, is hardly going to be relevant to a UK mainstream whose God is Tesco, whose level of religiosity might be lighting a candle in memory of Princess Di, and whose religious knowledge, otherwise, is zilch. Or is this to somehow miss the point? Just because we live in a profoundly, even abysmally secular and ahistorical age, does this imply that the deep, two-millennia-old strata of essentially Christian-informed motifs, myths and mores are not waiting in the wings to take their traditional place on the stage just at the moment when, with nothing else to fill the void, a populace is crying out culturally, psychologically and emotionally for spiritual suste-nance and succour? 'It is just at the point in the development of culture, when a myth is renounced on the conscious level, that it take hold even more strongly on the unconscious one,' remarked the late Hyam Maccoby.

The fact that Maccoby, especially along with Norman Cohn, is clearly a critical influence on Alyson Pendlebury's work should be persuasion enough to read on. Their many studies, from slightly different starting points, have searchingly charted the problematic and disturbing legacy of Christian dualism – the potency of its message, certainly, but also its tendency to arrive at 'closure', as Pendlebury puts it, through an all-or-nothing conflict with some identifiably illegitimate and false purveyor of the 'truth'. From a Christological perspective that can only really mean one of two cosmic enemies, Judaism or Islam, although one might argue that the early modern fracture of Catholic Latin Christianity provided, for Protestant break-away states such as England, the occasion for the Pope to fulfil the Antichrist role.

Alyson Pendlebury's book is thus timely, provocative and compelling for the very reason that while looking at a moment when all this came to a fissile matrix in England's green and pleasant land not so long ago, it really stands as a warning to *us* now. Her historical subject is the crisis of British national identity in the vortex of that first truly apocalyptic military struggle of the last century, which we now remember as the First World War but which contemporaries more appropriately spoke of as 'the Great War'. What, moreover, is truly frightening is the way she draws up the whole arsenal of Christian 'holy war', 'crusade' and 'Armageddon' polemic, rhetoric and representation ultimately not as an instrument with which to combat a tangible Prussian-German enemy but as one that can be used against a supposedly much more insidious but actually wholly indefinable 'Jewish' one.

Remember, this is not the conspiracy-laden, phobically antisemitic society *we know*, that is, Nazi Germany. This is supposedly that land of freedom, fairness and tolerance: Britain.

Actually, that 'myth' has been increasingly eroded through judicious and often quite brilliant historical and literary studies over recent decades. Far from Britain standing as some offshore island, immune, for instance, to the worst aspects of continental antisemitism, the works of Colin Holmes, Tony Kushner, Bryan Cheyette, David Cesarani and others have confirmed that the disease was much more prevalent among British political, ecclesiastical, academic and opinion-forming elites, not to mention literati, media tycoons and court circles, than previously acknowledged. It was, in short, not simply the preserve of cranks and lunatics: it pervaded polite and indeed serious elite discourse.

What Pendlebury does here is show how, in conditions of escalating extremity, a morbid and vengeful representation, invoking (correctly or incorrectly) the Christian message, was repeatedly deployed in ways that increasingly threatened to turn polity and society into a mirror image of what the country imagined it was opposing. The newspaper accounts of the crucified Canadian soldier that began to circulate in May 1915 may or may not have been true, but they served for those such as A. F. Winnington-Ingram, the Bishop of London, who sought to whip up a Protestant fervour and send young men on a moral crusade as a conscious 'sacrifice' against a 'pagan' Prussian enemy. But what if the 'sacrifice' does not work, and there is no salvation? After all, what, might one ask, had 'the Jews' to do with any of this business, this war created by European elites, including Britons themselves? The fact that within 18 months of the crucifixion story, the papers were becoming increasingly fixated on some other 'Unseen Hand', hence the *real* explanation for why the war, far from being won was actually being 'betrayed,' not least from within, provides us with our clue.

On one level, of course, this is at the very heart of a flawed humanity. If you cannot face up to your own failings, your own responsibility for disaster, blame somebody else. But it speaks volumes that the accused so many turned to in their desperation was not simply the sizeable British-domiciled German community, nor, God forbid, the obviously very unBritish-sounding Saxe-Coburg royal family but rather an archetypal Judas enemy.

Christ without Judas makes no sense. Airbrush the latter out of the Gospel story and you lose the very thing – the hatred, the malice, the envy – that Jesus is up against. So when, soon after the war, Britain's most front-ranking papers, *The Times* and the *Morning Post*, were reporting that the Russian Bolsheviks had put up a statue in Moscow to none other than Judas Iscariot himself (a complete nonsense, of course) the pieces all began to fall into

place. The notion that Bolshevism was actually a Jewish plot –
linked certainly in turn to the Kaiser's Germany – to pulverise and
defeat Britain was *not* some marginal one. On the contrary, it
links directly to the portrayal of the late 1917 Balfour Declaration
decision to support a Jewish national home in Palestine as an
entirely misconceived government effort to deflect the *perceived*
Jewish leaders of Bolshevism from making peace with Germany,
just as it does to the repeated newspaper columns and official
government reports at the end of the war, regurgitating the story
that the Christ-like 'sacrifice' of the tsar was at the hands of the
Jews and, too, to the story of an international Jewish conspiracy
to undermine Western civilisation – Christianity of course
included – which by then was doing the rounds in the various,
newly published editions of *The Protocols of the Elders of Zion*.

Should we be relieved that in many of these accusations the
distinction was made between 'good' Jews and 'bad' Jews as in
Winston Churchill's (in)famous 1920 article in the *Illustrated
Sunday Herald*? Or that Jewish bigwigs from the established
community were allowed to stand up on Gentile platforms and
distance themselves from their anarchist-tainted immigrant
fellows, or that, more often than not, their wives were encouraged
to do the same, when it came to matters of 'the white slave trade'?
That prostitution, like syphilis, like, for that matter, tuberculosis
were all part of the same sexual and bodily assault and
contamination for which Jews were held primarily responsible in
the early twentieth century is likely to sound familiar. It's only the
geographical location that may be less so.

One might, argue, of course, that as none of this came to a
head in Britain, unlike in Germany, the tendency could not have
been quite so toxic or alarming as is being suggested. But then,
of course, Britain won the Great War, or, put another way, its
salvation, at least in a very temporal and unsatisfactory way, was
accomplished. What is surely alarming, however, is the very close
resonance between what happened then, in Britain, and what is
happening now, admittedly with regard not to Jews but to
Muslims. The same requirement for the establishment within this
community to distance itself from its 'fanatical' elements, to
(repeatedly) demonstrate loyalty and the capability to be 'good'
Britons, to denounce 'Islamic' terrorism, Saddam, or, for that
matter, Hamas, and to disavow an allegedly perverse, 'oriental'
and uncivilised culture that treats its women as worse than chattel.

Plus ça change, plus c'est la même chose. Whether the Christian
or post-Christian mythologies and motifs with regard to Muslims
will quite follow those made about Jews is debatable. The

Christian–Muslim trajectory, despite its history of 'infidel' accusation, conflict and venom, is noticeably different from the more intense, competitive rivalry between Judaism and Christianity, borne out what in effect was the rupture between the practices of 'father–mother' and their intensely alienated but eventually politically dominant 'son'. Then, too, the British society into which most Muslims were coming as immigrants, in the1960s and 1970s, was going through a rapid, more general transition not quite so evident (or at least not the same way) as in the era of mass Jewish immigration a half-century and more earlier.

With regard to the latter, what is particularly discerning and thought-provoking about Pendlebury's study is the way she weaves around her central Jewish–Christian dialectic a much broader canvas of *fin-de-siècle* British culture and society. In this way we discover that Christian imagery, often of a quite millenarian flavour, suffused – intentionally or unintentionally – all manner of controversies and debates of the time, including those within the suffragette movement. In some ways it was thus bound to shape not just mainstream attitudes to Jews, including those articulated in published prose, but also those among the literati within the established Jewish community, a response that could not but respond to overt or covert conversionist pressures.

Fortunately, Pendlebury's story is not entirely one of doom and gloom. The young men, both Jew and Gentile, who volunteered for war and went off to the western front, or Mesopotamia, or indeed Palestine, with poetry books in their knapsacks, were a good deal more literate on the whole than those in our own society. And they knew their Bible, too, often intimately and profoundly. But while leading High Church clerics were extolling them to lay down their lives in a crusading zeal, the Owens, Sassoons or, for that matter, Rosenbergs, who were experiencing the reality of the front in all its bleak pointlessness, were articulating their rejection of 'holy war' in no uncertain terms. Against the grain of the misinformation, disinformation and downright lies the British public is now having to endure from its political masters in order to pump up a climate of perpetual fear, not to say great swathes of a media and film industry that seems to excel at nothing better than regurgitating notions of civilisational clash, Islamophobia or just plain ignorance about Muslims, I am convinced that the stories and memoirs of returning soldiers from Iraq and Afghanistan will point to a very different reality. At least, this time, we should expect them to be supported by the majority of religious leaders, of whatever denomination, keenly aware of their broad responsibilities. For the rest of us, understanding the dread biblical warnings of apocalypse and Armageddon are reasons for us to reflect, resist and overcome – not to embrace.

Mark Levene
Parkes Institute,
University of Southampton
2005

Acknowledgements

One of the key influences upon the research for and the writing of this book has been Professor Bryan Cheyette's work *Constructions of 'the Jew' in English Literature and Society: Racial Representations, 1875–1945* (1993). Other influences include works by Professor Norman Cohn, particularly *The Pursuit of the Millennium* (1957), and *Warrant for Genocide: The Myth of the Jewish World-Conspiracy and the Protocols of the Elders of Zion* (1967). In addition, Alan Wilkinson's *The Church of England and the First World War* (1978) gives a detailed and informative account of the position of the Anglican Church in national life during the First World War, and has been very helpful in this study.

The research project was supervised by Professor Cora Kaplan, whose guidance, enthusiasm and encouragement has been invaluable and very much appreciated. I would also like to thank Dr Nadia Valman, for her genuine interest in and continuing support for my work, and my editor at Vallentine Mitchell, Sian Mills. I am grateful to the Arts and Humanities Research Board for the award that enabled me to undertake and complete this project, and for the use of the resources of the Hartley Library, especially the Parkes Collection, at the University of Southampton, and those of the British Library.

My friends and family have provided me with constant support, and I would like to thank my sister, Anne Nevill, my parents and various friends, including Sue Cross, Sue Blackwood, Jackie Furby, Rebecca Rogers, David Freemantle, Peter Lawson, Michelle Whiteside, George Slater and Tony Archdeacon for their patience and encouragement during the course of this project. Thanks also to Jason Philpott, for making me smile during the last stages of preparing for publication. Finally, thanks to my dear and much missed friend Betty Herbert, for her good company and the use of her chalet in Cornwall. This book is dedicated to her.

Abbreviations

AAMC	Australian Army Medical Corps
BEF	British Expeditionary Force
BUF	British Union of Fascists
EEF	Egyptian Expeditionary Force
EES	Eugenics Education Society
FJPC	Foreign Jews' Protection Committee
ILP	International Labour Party
JTO	Jewish Territorial Organisation
JAPGW	Jewish Association for the Protection of Girls and Women
JLWS	Jewish League for Woman Suffrage
NUWSS	National Union of Women's Suffrage Societies
NVA	National Vigilance Association
Okhrana	Tsarist secret police
PIS	Prophecy Investigation Society
SPCK	Society for the Promotion of Christian Knowledge
WSPU	Women's Social and Political Union

1

Introduction

While researching this book, I was focused on the use of the rhetoric of 'crusade' in Britain during the First World War, and I thought of such rhetoric as a thing of the past. I did not expect the notion of a Christian force for 'good' and a non-Christian force for 'evil' to suddenly enter into popular usage in the twenty-first century, but it has. Since the events of 11 September 2001, the idea of a Western 'crusade' against Islam has once more entered into political discourse, with Osama Bin Laden referring to the Bush–Blair alliance in these terms, and calling upon Muslims worldwide to wage 'holy war' or *jihad* in response to events in Afghanistan and Iraq. Western politicians, in turn, have adopted a crude political language of 'good' versus 'evil', and George W. Bush in particular has spoken repeatedly of an 'axis of evil' that must be defeated at all costs.

There are other parallels with the early twentieth-century context that this book sets out. Trafficking in prostitution has hit the headlines recently, with concerns over the number of immigrants from Eastern European countries who are working in the sex industry in Britain. In the early twentieth century, Jewish migrants were the focus of much of the anxiety over 'white slavery'. Whereas in the First World War it was Jews in Britain who were put under pressure to demonstrate their loyalty to the country, now British Muslims have become the focus of suspicion, and have been since the destruction of the World Trade Centre. In November 2003, Denis McShane, Minister for Europe in Tony Blair's cabinet, urged Muslims to choose between the 'British way' of political dialogue or terrorist tactics. Muslim leaders are understandably angry at this, and as Massoud Shadjareh, chairman of the Islamic Human Rights Commission, put it with reference to McShane's remarks, 'What does he want us to do? Apologise, to give an indication that somehow we are responsible, when we are not?' (Massoud Shadjareh, quoted in the *Guardian*, 22 November 2003).

In many of the texts discussed in this book, there is an identifiable fantasy that history was, in some senses, 'repeating itself' during the First World War. This is especially clear in relation to the British campaign in Palestine in 1917 and the excitement that this generated, which was most frequently expressed through the idea of the 'last crusade'. Certainly, Muslims in Britain are encountering levels of suspicion similar to those experienced by Jews living in Britain throughout the war and afterwards. But history does not repeat itself; rather, historical and religious narratives are mobilised as a means of justifying prejudices and enabling them to persist, and, sadly, they are effective in this.

Writing in 1909, the Liberal MP Charles Frederick George Masterman (1873–1927) observed that 'Religions which appear dead are so often discovered to be only sleeping.'[1] In his view Christian doctrine in modern Britain was being superseded by 'a non-dogmatic affirmation of general kindliness and good fellowship, with an emphasis rather on the service of men than the fulfilment of the will of God'.[2] This he regarded as progress, although he acknowledged that the rational, tolerant society was always potentially threatened by outbursts of religious fanaticism, through which 'the vision of blood and fire' might enter into everyday life.[3] In a sense this was what happened during the First World War, when Germany and Britain, two Protestant nations whose monarchs were related, and who shared a sense of historical and cultural connection, entered into armed conflict. In this context, it was imperative that the similarities between the two countries should be put aside, and a clear differentiation made between them for the duration of the hostilities. Religious language, or 'the vision of blood and fire', became one of the means by which this differentiation was made. In Britain, religious rhetoric was used in order to demonise Germany and glorify the Allies, as leading clergymen and politicians spoke of the conflict as a 'holy war' against the 'pagan' forces of 'Prussianism'. In political speeches and pamphlets, and in the British national press, Germany was charged with having renounced Christianity, replacing the worship of God with, in the view of the former diplomat Viscount Bryce, the worship of the state.[4] Britain, by contrast, was imagined as a devoutly Christian nation, despite the process of secularisation that Masterman had commented on in 1909, and the fact that the pre-war decline in church attendance had been a matter of concern to the higher Anglican clergy. It should be noted, however, that despite the efforts of the clergy, there was no religious revival to accompany the rhetoric of a Christian Britain engaged in a 'holy war'; rather, this was a revival of religious notions of national identity. The idea of Britain as a nation united by the Christian faith was itself old-fashioned in 1914. Church attendance was in decline, and the emancipation of Catholics in 1829 and Jews in 1858 meant that religious minorities had gained civil rights, and that full participation in national life was no longer dependent upon swearing Protestant affiliation. Nevertheless, the rhetoric of the First World War as a Christian 'crusade' against the 'evil' forces of 'Prussianism' seemed to capture the public imagination, and was widely taken up.

The notion of 'holy war' was far from unique to the First World War, but during this period it became tied to Christian representations and interpretations of international politics and national identities. Both Christians and Jews were redefining nationhood at the time: Christians in relation to a war between rival imperial powers, and Jews with regard to both Palestine and Britain. Not only were Jews in Britain under pressure from the wartime reassertion of a retrograde Protestant national identity, but also political Zionism had, for strategic reasons, gained the interest of the French, German and British governments. Support for Jewish nationalism became politically expedient for non-Jewish politicians, both during and after the war, yet to many assimilated British Jews the idea of Jewish nationalism was itself old-fashioned. Nevertheless, biblical allegory was used in the press and in popular discourse with regard to the formation of the Jewish Legion in 1917, and its deployment in Palestine in 1918, and examples of this are given in Chapter 5.

The focus of this book is on constructions and representations of British and Jewish identities during the early and mid-twentieth century, their interrelation and dissemination in popular discourse, and in particular the role of biblical imagery in those representations. Much of the discussion focuses on ideas about Jews and Jewish identity, rather than Jews as an historical group or as individuals, and inverted commas have been used throughout to signal clearly that the 'Jew' referred to is a representation, based on popular perception and prejudice rather than on fact.

Chapter 3 examines the wartime representations of the British as a Christian nation united in divinely sanctioned warfare against a 'godless' enemy. This imagery proliferated through tales of 'miracles' on the battlefield, such as the story of 'The Angels of Mons', in which it was claimed that the English bowmen of Agincourt, led by St George, had provided cover for British troops retreating from the Battle of Mons in 1914. The fact that this story (publicly acknowledged as fiction by its author, Arthur Machen) and others like it were widely circulated suggests that the notion of Christian warfare prompted a desire for evidence of an interventionist God, one who would give manifest support for the 'holy war' and the Allied cause. The God of the New Testament, however, is not interventionist, unlike Yahweh of the Old Testament, who is portrayed as deeply connected to his people and alternately benign and punitive, depending on their observation of the covenant. And the Old Testament, of course, concerns the Jews as the 'chosen' people, a small problem in the context of wartime claims that God was on the side of the (Christian) British, and the Evangelical rhetoric of the British as 'chosen' to lead the nations in creating the kingdom of God on earth. Ultimately, therefore, Old Testament imagery was not compatible with constructions of Britain as a Christian nation engaged in 'holy war', and New Testament tropes, chiefly those of 'crucifixion' and 'apocalypse', were mobilised instead.

The widespread use of religious language with regard to the British nation, the nature of the enemy, and the purpose of the war, meant that not only did Christian idealism enter into public discourse – in the rhetoric of self-sacrifice for the good of others and of the war as a purging and renewing process for Britain – but also that aspects of religious antisemitism came to the fore. The Christian narratives of 'crucifixion' and 'apocalypse', particularly that of 'crucifixion', have an antisemitic component which, I argue, is necessary to their dramatic impact, coherence and completion. These stories allocate a specific role to 'unbelieving' Jews, and portray them as hostile towards Christians and Christianity: as Judas the betrayer of Christ in the crucifixion story, and as the followers of Antichrist (or potential converts to Christianity) in the Revelation narrative and in exegetical work on this text. The Christian concept of the Jewish 'threat', then, is embedded in the New Testament, in the figures of Judas and Antichrist, and also in early Christian theology, in which Antichrist was in some cases aligned with Jews and Judaism.

The books of the New Testament were written during a period in which the new Christian faith and Judaism were engaged in a struggle over religious identity and authority in Palestine, and they reflect this rivalry. Thus in the crucifixion story, it is the Jewish high priest, Caiaphas, whose authority Jesus threatens, who is portrayed as scheming for his death, and it is Judas who facilitates it. In Revelation it is 'those who profess to be Jews, but are liars, because they are no such thing' (3: 9) – that is, Jews who deny the divinity of Christ – who will bow to the two witnesses of the Antichrist (11: 3–9) and perish in the apocalypse, along with everyone else 'of false speech and false life' (22: 15). In the context of the First World War, the figures of Antichrist and Judas entered into popular discourse with regard to both Germany and Bolshevik Russia. These two representations of anti-Christian 'evil' were central to rhetorical constructions of 'Prussianism' and Bolshevism, and provided the narrative of Christian warfare with its necessary components for completion. Such emotive and familiar narratives as 'crucifixion' and 'apocalypse' could not be used selectively or mobilised in isolation from their other essential components. If one has a rhetorical 'Christ' then a 'Judas' is required to complete the analogy and make it recognisable. Similarly, where there is a construction of 'Antichrist' there must also be his followers, the 'anti-Christian hordes', and Christian apocalyptic tradition clearly identifies 'unbelieving' Jews in this regard. Without Judas the betrayer the crucifixion narrative loses some of its dramatic impact, and becomes a story of the punishment of a dissident by the Roman occupying powers. Without 'unbelievers', or non-Christians, Antichrist has no followers in the battle of the 'last days'. The narratives of crucifixion and apocalypse are reliant upon these malevolent 'Jewish' figures for their coherence and dramatic effect, and this book aims to show how modern versions of those figures emerged in Britain during and after the First World War.

Once the language of 'crucifixion' and 'apocalypse' had been launched into public discourse in relation to the war, it was impossible to control its uptake, and the anti-Jewish components that are integral to these familiar Christian stories were provided by popular interpretation and expansion of these themes. Whether or not the intention was to arouse hostility towards Britain's Jewish population, both immigrant and British-born, the narratives of crucifixion and apocalypse, with the distinct and adversarial role they ascribe to unconverted Jews, found their completion in popular discourse of the period. Like Vladimir Propp's analysis of the folk tale, in which certain components and characters will always combine to create predictable narrative outcomes, these Christian stories found their familiar and necessary antisemitic closure in the context in which they were launched – that of modern 'total war' and the political turmoil of the immediate post-war period.[5]

Yet there are links between Judaism and Christianity that cannot be overlooked, and these were ironically revealed in rhetoric that sought to assert a stable and independent Christian national identity. One obvious link, of course, is the fact that Jesus was a Jew, but in addition to this, the New Testament clearly draws on the Old for some of its most dramatic components. Revelation borrows from Daniel's vision, and from the imagery of the Fall and the Flood in Genesis. The crucifixion trope – the sacrifice of a son according to the will of God – has a precedent in the story of Abraham and Isaac, although in that case the command to sacrifice was ultimately withdrawn. Similarly, the trope of 'crusade' or 'holy war', used in various contexts to promote a collective and embattled Christian identity, carries echoes of the Pentateuch, as the writer Karen Armstrong has pointed out. Armstrong argues that the concept of the spiritual journey that becomes a holy war is found in all three of the monotheistic faiths, and that the paradigm for this is the Exodus story, in which the migration of the Israelites was followed by the conquest and invasion of Canaan, and ultimately the establishment of the Jewish faith and nation.[6] Just as Christianity is theologically indebted to Judaism, then, so aspects of the Exodus story can be seen to inform the idea of the Christian 'crusade', and particularly popular accounts of the First Crusade, which resulted in the capture of Jerusalem by Christians. It was the story of the First Crusade, with its themes of Christian knighthood and the expansion of 'Christian' territory that was most commonly evoked in the popular rhetoric of the First World War as 'holy war'. This is discussed in detail in Chapter 3.

Pope Urban II's call to crusade, made at Clermont in 1095, linked pilgrimage, traditionally undertaken without arms, to warfare, and thus sanctioned violence against 'unbelievers' in the name of Christianity. Through the idea of 'crusade', Christian identity was presented as simultaneously authoritative and embattled, and an urgent call for its consolidation and defence was made. Although the enemy was ostensibly Muslim, popular interpretation of the crusade frequently translated into attacks upon Jewish communities in

Europe. The violence was at its worst in the Rhineland, where the entire Jewish community at Mainz was murdered between 25 and 29 May 1096. The Jews of Mainz had the support of some of the Christian townspeople, but when a crusader was killed during a confrontation, Jews were blamed for dividing the Christians against each other, and were attacked.[7] Beneath the image of Christian piety and unity associated with the crusades, then, lay a current of antisemitism, its expression facilitated by the idea of 'holy war'. Hatred and fear of Jews during and after the crusades became sufficiently widespread to produce legislative changes that restricted their freedom and brought their expulsion from most European countries from the twelfth century onwards.[8] By the late Middle Ages, as Gavin Langmuir observes, '"The Jews" had become the great symbol of hidden menaces of all kinds within Christendom.'[9]

This book examines some of the constructions of 'the enemy', as political and religious 'other', that circulated in Britain during and after the First World War. It is structured around four rhetorical themes that circulated widely in Britain during the war years: those of 'crusade', 'conversion', 'crucifixion' and 'apocalypse'. These are all interrelated, but it has been necessary, in order to set out the argument, to keep them apart through the use of themed sections. This is an artificial device, and it will be seen, for example, that the narrative of 'crusade' implies conversion, as does that of 'apocalypse', but this structure has been adopted for the purposes of clarity. Chapters 2–5 engage with the themes of 'crusade' and 'conversion', giving examples of their usage before and during the war, and show how, in the contexts described, these narratives found the antisemitic closure that is crucial to their impact. Chapter 2 explores the pre-war use of 'crusade' imagery, focusing on the purity crusades against 'white slavery', and the campaign for women's suffrage, and examines the imagery used in these campaigns in the context of the mass migration of Jews from eastern Europe during the late nineteenth and early twentieth centuries. Chapter 3 discusses the 'call to crusade' in wartime Britain, and the development of its antisemitic subtext. As in the First Crusade, the Church's sanction of religious warfare provided an outlet for popular antisemitism, and once the rhetoric of collective Christian self-defence had been unleashed it could not be fully controlled. Jews living in Britain during the First World War became subject to hostility even though the conflict was with German and Turkish forces. Unlike the medieval 'holy wars', this was a 'crusade' in which Jews participated, enlisting in the British army in a higher proportion (in terms of the size of this group) than did gentiles, but despite this, their loyalty remained under suspicion from some quarters as the war progressed.[10] During the early years of the war there were accusations in the national press that 'Jews' were working in league with the Germans, and after the revolutions in Russia in 1917, Bolshevism was represented as a politics that attracted and was dominated by 'Jews'.

All this was consistent with the tradition, originating in the New Testament and developed in Christian theology, in which the threat to Christianity has been identified as coming from 'unbelieving' Jews. The rhetoric used by the press, politicians and clergy portrayed the conflict as the 'war to end war', a moral struggle between the forces of 'good' and 'evil', with the forces of 'good' characterised as Christian. Although the British forces, which included Jews, were fighting the Turks and Germans, anti-alien feeling in Britain was often directed towards the Jewish community. Wartime anti-Jewish hostility lacked the violence of the attacks that occurred during the First Crusade, and the aim here is not to try to establish direct parallels, as though history 'repeats itself' (a fantasy that is identifiable in many of the texts discussed below), but to explore the function of religious and historical imagery as the basis of constructions of national identity, and to trace patterns of hostility towards Jews and representations of Jewish identity in relation to this.

Similarly, Chapters 4 and 5, on the theme of 'conversion' in wartime discourse, do not list forced conversions of Jews by Christians, as these did not occur. Rather, they examine religious and political expressions of the desire to transform the threat of 'Jewish' difference during the war years, and thereby construct a reassuring homogeneity. Chapter 4 examines the effects of the war on the Anglican Church, and suggests that the internal conflicts that arose over the wartime Anglo-Catholic revival may be viewed as a form of 'conversion anxiety' among members of the higher Anglican clergy, reflecting concerns that religious worship would 'revert' to a more ritualised form. There is also a discussion of the use of religious imagery in soldiers' writing, and the impact of war upon the religious faith of combatants. This is followed by an account of religious conversion discourse, which remained at the margins of Protestantism during the war, and the efforts of some Jewish writers to define a British-Jewish identity at that time. Chapter 5 explores the then contemporary view that Judaism and revolutionary politics were connected, the perception among gentiles that Jewish people had an inherent capacity for self-transformation, and the idea that this should be mobilised in accordance with the values and concerns of the non-Jewish majority. Conversion, or the transformation of 'the Jew' in some way has long been the gentile 'solution' to the 'Jewish question', and represents the impulse to homogenise and absorb threatening difference, yet retain elements of that difference so that full equality is impossible. Jews have been aware of this, what might be termed the price of assimilation, and it is a recurrent theme in Anglo-Jewish writing of the period.

Because the idea of Christian nationhood was a popular response to the war, this book focuses on expressions of and responses to this in popular literature and discourse. The tropes examined – 'crusade', 'conversion', 'crucifixion' and 'apocalypse' – extended into almost all areas of textual production, and are found in press articles, sermons, political speeches and pamphlets, poetry, novels and cartoons. The range of texts has been selected in order to demonstrate just how widespread the adoption of religious imagery was in relation to the war and the changes it brought about. The emphasis is on 'realist' rather than modernist writers, partly because while there are plenty of 'Jewish' characters in modernist texts, Anglo-Jewish writers are under-represented in literary modernism.[11] In addition, I wanted to focus on popular fiction, to examine how Jewish writers in Britain engaged with wartime anti-alienism, and to see how those writers working in the 'realist' literary tradition attempted to represent Jews and Jewish identity. The writers discussed below – Gilbert Frankau, Gladys Bronwyn Stern, Isaac Rosenberg, Leonard Woolf, Moshe Oved and others – directly engaged with the experiences of Jews in wartime Britain, and their work both upholds and challenges some of the popular representations of Jewish identity of the period. Fiction may have provided a space in which popular ideas about 'Jews' could be interrogated, challenged, and in some cases, resolved, and this is explored in several of the following chapters.

Bryan Cheyette's analysis of the dual nature of images of 'the Jew' and the use of this figure as a repository for various fears and fantasies has been an important influence on this book, which undertakes to show how this duality was represented during the war and the years immediately following it. In the preface to *Constructions of 'the Jew' in English Literature and Society: Racial*

Representations, 1875–1945 (1993), Cheyette argues that 'race-thinking' is integral to the formation of modern British cultural identity, and that racialised images of 'the Jew' are central to liberal self-construction. I examine this dynamic in the context of the First World War, and suggest that the formation of a Christian national identity during this period was dependent upon a rhetorically constructed 'other'. Initially this was Germany, but reactions to the Bolshevik Revolution of October 1917 combined images of the religious and political enemy, in which the 'apostate Bolshevik Jew' was cast as the political enemy of the Christian state. As Cheyette observes, 'the Jew', far from being an unchanging, historically transcendent signifier, is one that shifts in relation to specific political and social anxieties, and as these change, so does the representation of the threat.[12] The construction of a Christian national identity in Britain during and after the war appeared to generate a reworking of biblical representations of the 'Jewish' threat to Christianity, particularly in the rhetorical figures of 'Judas' and 'Antichrist'. These representations are undeniably modern, and specific to the war, yet they are also insistently biblical, and it is this combination that the book explores. Such reworkings, or reconstructions of 'the Jew' are not necessarily overt in some of the examples given, but they are always there by implication, and sometimes emerge in relief, as a result of the strongly Christian rhetoric that was being used with regard to the nation. There was a general climate of xenophobia, exacerbated by the crisis of the war, which created the conditions for hostility to develop towards Britain's Jewish population, and facilitated their portrayal and perception as a threatening group. Fears regarding pre-war immigration, and exaggeration of the influence of assimilated Jews in the post-war period, helped to create a context of suspicion and mistrust in which the Christian narratives discussed below readily found their necessary antisemitic components and closure.

It has been argued that gentile use of biblical metaphors in relation to Jews should not be regarded as negative or ironic, but as an acknowledgement of the connections between Judaism and Christianity, modern Jews and Old Testament figures.[13] While it is true that Old Testament imagery was one of the more positive ways through which Jewish identity was constructed during the period discussed, in some cases it was used to draw unflattering comparisons between the Jews of antiquity and those of the early twentieth century. The implications of the ubiquitous use of biblical imagery during the First World War – with regard to both Jews and Christians – are complex, subtle and revealing. This book seeks to demonstrate that complexity, and its significance with regard to the changing ideas of national identity and rapid political developments of the period. The Christian identity that was being constructed and promoted during the First World War was embattled, vulnerable and insufficiently grounded in fact to serve as an authentic representation of the British nation at that time. Yet I have been struck by the persistent use of biblical themes with regard to the nation and the war in a wide variety of texts produced during that period. As Alan Wilkinson has observed in *The Church of England and the First World War* (1978), 'Perhaps the most powerful (and ambiguous) contribution which the Churches made to the nation during the Great War was in the realm of imagery'.[14] It is that realm of imagery and its ironic capacity to reveal the links between Christianity and Judaism, Christians and Jews, when its purpose was to differentiate and distinguish, which is the subject of this book.

NOTES

1   C. G. F. Masterman, *The Condition of England* (London: Methuen, 1909), p. 264.
2   Masterman, *Condition*, p. 268.
3   Masterman, *Condition*, p. 276. Masterman was head of the secret wartime bureau for propaganda at Wellington House in London during the First World War.
4   Viscount James Bryce, *Neutral Nations and the War* (London: Macmillan, 1914), p. 6.
5   Vladimir Yakovelich Propp, *Morphology of the Folk Tale* (London and Austin, TX: University of Texas Press, 1968).
6   Karen Armstrong, *Holy War: The Crusades and their Impact on Today's World* (London: Macmillan, 1988), pp. 5–6.
7   Jonathan Riley-Smith, 'The First Crusade and the persecution of the Jews', in W. J. Shields (ed.), *Persecution and Toleration: Papers Read at the 22nd Summer Meeting and the 23rd Winter Meeting of the Ecclesiastical History Society* (Oxford: Blackwell for the Ecclesiastical Society, 1984), pp. 51–2.
8   Jews were expelled from England in 1209, France in 1306, Germany in 1348, Spain in 1492 and Portugal in 1496.
9   Gavin I. Langmuir, *History, Religion, and Antisemitism* (London and New York: I. B. Tauris, 1990), p. 303.
10   Figures in the *British Jewry Book of Honour* (1922) indicate a higher proportion of enlistment among Jews than in other social groups. See Sharman Kadish, *'A Good Jew and a Good Englishman': The Jewish Lads' and Girls' Brigade 1895–1995* (London: Vallentine Mitchell, 1995), p. 60.
11   There is extensive work on the use of the image of 'the Jew' by modernist writers. See, for example, Bryan Cheyette, *Constructions of 'the Jew' in English Literature and Society: Racial Representations 1875–1945* (Cambridge: Cambridge University Press, 1993); Anthony Julius, *T. S. Eliot, Antisemitism and Literary Form* (Cambridge University Press, 1995); Jean Moorcroft Wilson, *Virginia Woolf and Antisemitism* (London: Cecil Woolf, 1995), and Neil R. Davidson, *James Joyce, Ulysses, and the Construction of Jewish Identity. Culture, Biography, and 'the Jew' in Modernist Europe*

(Cambridge: Cambridge University Press, 1998).

12   See Cheyette, *Constructions of 'the Jew'*, p. 3.
13   See W. D. Rubinstein, *A History of the Jews in the English-Speaking World: Great Britain* (Basingstoke: Macmillan, 1996), p. 146.
14   Alan Wilkinson, *The Church of England and the First World War* (London: SPCK, 1978), p. 11.

2

The Imagery of 'Crusade', 1880–1914

The language and imagery of 'crusade' was by no means peculiar to the First World War, but was adopted by various reform movements of the late nineteenth and early twentieth centuries, groups ranging from the anti-vice and social purity associations to the broad campaign for women's suffrage. The crusade theme enabled campaigners to claim moral superiority over those who opposed their aims, and to represent themselves as a righteous and embattled minority engaged in a struggle with the forces of 'evil', however these were defined. The idea of 'crusade' that these groups mobilised was based on popular rather than historically accurate accounts of the crusading period, however, and it is necessary to briefly set out the context of the historical crusades before discussing the later rhetorical use of this narrative.

The crusades that began in the eleventh century CE and ended in the thirteenth were part of an attempt to create a new order in which Jerusalem would be under Christian control. The First Crusade, which began in 1096, was an attempt to reverse the loss of territories and thereby authority that the Church had been suffering for some time. In the early eighth century CE, Christians had lost control of North Africa, Palestine, Syria and much of Spain to Muslim forces. Pope Urban II's call for Christians to defend their co-religionists in Palestine, made at Clermont in 1095, met with an enthusiastic response, in part because the venture represented a form of penance, for which the clergy granted the remission of sins, and offered Christians a means of salvation.[1] Those who answered the call were encouraged to believe that as Christian pilgrims and warriors they were fulfilling the will of God and hence would be victorious, and Christians from all over Europe took part in armed pilgrimages to the Holy Land.

Violence was, strictly speaking, counter to Christian teaching, but there were circumstances in which it could be morally justified. These had been outlined by Augustine in *The City of God*, written in the fifth century CE, in which it was stated that war could be 'just' if fought out of necessity only; in self-defence, for example. This idea was later expanded to include the concept of 'holy war', a struggle between 'good' and 'evil' in which Christians would defend their faith against heresy, and under Pope Gregory I (590–604 CE), this idea was extended further, to include missionary warfare and territorial expansion through military aggression.[2] By 1096, when the First Crusade to the Holy Land began, this more complex idea of 'holy war', combining Christian self-defence and expansionism, was established. The venture was a success: Christian forces gained control of Jerusalem in 1099, along with territories in Palestine and Syria. It was the First Crusade, culminating in victory for the crusaders, which was subsequently evoked in the rhetoric of 'crusade' and 'holy war' that is examined in this book. Christians held Jerusalem and the new territories for 88 years, until 1187, when Saladin's forces were victorious at the battle of Hattin. This defeat prompted further crusades, and during 1227–29 Christians regained control of Jerusalem, only to lose it again in 1244, after which Palestine remained part of the Turkish empire until late 1917.

The use of the crusade narrative in popular rhetoric has, however, been selective. Whilst the First Crusade is associated with Christian victory, it is also associated with the persecution of Jews throughout Europe. Although the enemy was ostensibly the Muslim forces that held Jerusalem and other formerly Christian territories, the First Crusade is notorious for attacks upon Jews, by crusaders en route to the Holy Land. Outbreaks of antisemitic violence continued throughout the period of the crusades, until eventually Jews were expelled from most European countries.[3] Yet these historical facts – that Christians ultimately lost control of Jerusalem, and that the crusades prompted violence against Jews – were largely overlooked in the popular imagery of 'crusade' that is discussed below. In the rhetoric of the purity and suffrage campaigns, and during the First World War, the idea of 'crusade' represented a struggle between the forces of 'good' and 'evil', and the establishment of a new order after the conflict. This new order was variously imagined: as the kingdom of God on earth described in the Apocrypha, the new moral order sought by the anti-vice movement, the women's franchise, or the regeneration of the British nation and empire that many hoped the First World War would bring about. In all these contexts, the idea of 'crusade' was used to promote a sense of collective identity and unity of purpose in the face of crisis, its participants engaged in a moral struggle with powerful forces, over which, with God's help, they would eventually triumph. This chapter examines the use of the 'crusade' theme in relation to the social purity and women's suffrage campaigns in particular, and considers these modern 'crusades' in the social and political context of the late nineteenth and early twentieth centuries.

THE ANTI-VICE AND SUFFRAGE 'CRUSADES'

One of the uses of the crusade theme has been to express concerns regarding the nation and its moral, physical and political health. In *Myth and National Identity in Nineteenth-Century Britain* (2000), Stephanie L. Barczewski examines medievalism in Victorian society, as it was mediated through the legends of King Arthur and Robin Hood. Barczewski observes that prominent imperial figures such as Lord Curzon and Sir James Outram were often compared to medieval knights, and that by this means imperialism could be framed as an heroic quest. Yet the crusade context could also provide a vehicle for criticism of the imperial venture. At the time in which the Robin Hood legend is set, Richard I was away on the crusade. Although in some versions of the story, Robin Hood serves in the crusade, for the most part, the crusade context applies to the king, as it is in his absence that Robin Hood and his followers emerge to counter the lawlessness that has ensued. Barczewski suggests that Victorian writers used the prolonged absence of the king and the subsequent social decline in this legend as a metaphor for an excess of imperial zeal, to the detriment of the domestic life of the nation.[4] As she points out, the crusade context is also used to represent misguided imperial activity in some of the children's literature of the period, with crusaders being portrayed as an elite and self-indulgent group, motivated by material greed rather than religious piety.[5]

It was in the context of the anti-vice and women's suffrage campaigns of the late nineteenth and early twentieth centuries, and during the First World War, that the crusade was once more portrayed as a noble and selfless venture. Groups such as the White Cross Army, the National Social Purity Crusade, the National

Vigilance Association (NVA) and the Women's Social and Political Union all adopted the imagery of 'crusade' and the rhetoric of Christian warfare in their attempts to establish a new moral and social order. The social purity and anti-vice campaigns, although mostly interdenominational, were initiated and led by Evangelical Christians, and this was reflected in their campaign rhetoric, which drew on religious imagery for much of its dramatic effect. These modern 'crusades' were concerned with social and political conflicts – issues of morality, gender politics and national identity – but the idea of divine sanction underpinning the venture was retained, as was the notion of righteous warfare against an enemy that was sometimes clearly defined, sometimes not.

The anti-vice and social purity campaigns took place in the context of relatively high levels of immigration to Britain from the 1880s to 1914, and some of their rhetoric was influenced by the fears that were associated with this. Most of the migrants were Jews from eastern Europe, who were fleeing tsarist pogroms.[6] Despite widespread condemnation of tsarist antisemitism in Britain, there was also alarm at the numbers of refugees entering the country (around 120,000 settled in major British cities, particularly London), and the concentration of immigrants in the East End fuelled fears among some sections of society of an 'alien invasion'. Gradually, the migration of Jews became linked to existing concerns over the international trade in prostitution, or 'white slavery' as it was then called. This gave rise to exaggerated accounts of the involvement of Jewish migrants in vice, and a popular perception that the trade was organised by Jews from eastern Europe. Although this view was undoubtedly informed by antisemitism and exacerbated by immigration, there was also a small amount of justification for it, as some migrants, faced with economic difficulties, did become involved in the trade, both as procurers and prostitutes. Jewish women were sometimes tricked into prostitution through false job offers or secret marriages before emigration, and were then sold to brothels or forced into the trade through poverty. Argentina and Constantinople were the two main centres for traffic in prostitution during the late nineteenth and early twentieth centuries, and large Jewish communities existed in both places.[7] But the extent of Jewish involvement in the international vice traffic was exaggerated, and in fact many of the prostitutes involved were Japanese and Chinese. Nevertheless, as Edward J. Bristow has shown, the popular image of the 'trafficker' was predominantly associated with the Yiddish-speaking Jew.[8]

Provocatively entitled pamphlets such as Alfred Dyer's *The European Slave Trade in English Girls*, published in 1880,[9] fuelled alarm over international prostitution, and various movements were formed in order to counter the vice trade. The social purity movement which developed in Britain during the late nineteenth century was made up of a number of organisations, including the Women's Total Abstinence Union, the Church of England Temperance Society, the Church of England Purity Society and the White Cross League, also known as the Bishop of Durham's Movement. All of these groups participated in the anti-vice 'crusade', campaigning for chastity and the closure of brothels, but it was the White Cross League, co-founded in 1883 by Ellice Hopkins and J. B. Lightfoot, D.D., then Bishop of Durham, that came to dominate the social purity movement. Ellice Hopkins (1836–1904), the daughter of a Cambridge mathematician, had previously been active in campaigning for the closure of brothels and the rehabilitation of prostitutes in Brighton during the 1870s. Turning her attention now to the chastity of the nation's young men, she became a key speaker and pamphlet writer for the White Cross movement.

Working within an existing tradition of constructions of 'knightly' masculinity that was disseminated through public schools and movements such as the Scouts, the White Cross League used the language of chivalry and the imagery of Christian knighthood to appeal to its potential recruits.[10] The following passage, an extract from an address made by the Bishop of Durham to an audience of young men in Gateshead in 1883, is typical. Lightfoot told his listeners

> you are an Army of God. You are enlisted in a holy campaign; you are called to do battle with the most malignant and insidious of foes; you will fight shoulder to shoulder and foot to foot in this glorious crusade; you will feel the strength of numbers; you will be inspired by an honourable rivalry; you will be fired by a noble ambition; you will go forth, like those knights of old, to do battle for the weak. Woman's honour, woman's purity, will ever find in you a jealous and a valiant companion.[11]

The imagery is of righteous warfare against an unspecified enemy. In a sense the 'enemy' was within, and young men joining the White

Cross League were encouraged to take pledges of chastity and temperance, as well as a vow to defend women from the threat of corruption and entrapment. Ellice Hopkins, like the Bishop of Durham, appealed to notions of chivalry, but extended her rhetoric to include a comparison of the young purity crusader with Christ himself. Hopkins described the aims of the movement as being to teach men that their relationship to women was one of self-sacrifice, 'even as Christ loved the Church and gave Himself for it'. This sacrifice related to abstention from pre-marital sexual activity, and the promotion of male chastity was one of the movement's chief strategies for reducing the demand for prostitutes.[12] Other approaches included campaigning for the closure of brothels and the provision of safe, affordable accommodation for young single women in the cities. In another pamphlet, entitled *Touching Pitch*, Hopkins developed her theme, declaring that those who took the purity pledge seriously would remain uncontaminated by the vice around them, developing 'magical' powers, and becoming the healers of society:

> And then the marvellous promise will be fulfilled to you as to us; you will be able to take up serpents, and the serpent will turn into a rod of wonders which will enable you to smite through this dead sea, and open a path through its waters of death for yourself and others to a higher and purer life. And you will be able to drink of any deadly thing, and the cup of poison as it touches your lips shall turn into the 'cup of blessing', filled not with the poison of sin, but the wine of Love that overcame sin by the sacrifice of itself; and you shall lay your hands on the sin-sick and they shall recover.[13]

As was customary in a variety of nineteenth-century reform campaigns, the language draws on biblical imagery for dramatic effect. Hopkins alludes to both Old and New Testaments, invoking the Fall, the Exodus story and the parting of the Red Sea, as well as the miracles attributed to Jesus. The purity crusader is portrayed almost as a divine figure, gaining, through his asceticism and chastity, the ability to resist temptation, lead and redeem others, and work 'miracles' of a moral nature that would cleanse and transform society.

The White Cross movement was concerned with social purity and the health of the nation, and accordingly there was an occasional appeal to nationalism and xenophobia in its campaign rhetoric. In a pamphlet entitled *Ten Reasons Why I Should Join* (*c.*1885), Hopkins described the international scale of the vice trade and the threat it represented to English women, and asked readers, 'Will you submit to your English girls being bought and sold to gratify the lusts of foreigners?'[14] In another pamphlet, she suggested that the sexual degradation of women through prostitution had a detrimental effect on national life, and that this was why 'Eastern and Mahommedan nations, like Turkey and Egypt, where the woman is looked upon as the slave of man's passions...cannot be reformed, and are hopelessly rotten'.[15] The tendency among nineteenth-century women writers to characterise unpalatable attitudes and behaviour on the part of men as 'Eastern' has been termed 'feminist orientalism' by one critic.[16] Joyce Zonana argues that this is a rhetorical means of neutralising the threat inherent in any calls for change in attitudes to and treatment of women in Western countries. As she puts it,

> If the lives of women in England or France or the United States can be compared to the lives of women in 'Arabia', then the Western feminist's desire to change the status quo can be represented not as a radical attempt to restructure the West but as a conservative effort to make the West more like itself.[17]

Examples include Charlotte Brontë's use of the imagery of the sultan and the slave in chapter 24 of *Jane Eyre* (1847), but Zonana also traces this theme to Mary Wollstonecraft's *A Vindication of the Rights of Woman* (1792).[18] Ellice Hopkins appears to have drawn on this tradition of feminist orientalist discourse, and in the pamphlet *Saved At Last!* (1886), she argued that Christianity was the only religion that offered women any protection or salvation:

> The Mahommedan has but one remedy for the woman who has lost her virtue – to tie her up in a sack and fling her into the midnight river. The Jew and the Pharisaic Christian leave her to corruption in her living grave. Thank God, both are wrong. There is one power and one only that can restore her – the power of Christianity.[19]

But the purity crusade was an interdenominational movement, and one that attracted support from diverse groups with opposing views on politics, 'race' and women's rights. The tension between its various supporters is apparent in the movement's publications. In 1908, the National Social Purity Crusade published a collection of essays on vice under the title *The Cleansing of a City*. The book included forewords by the Bishop of Hereford, the Archbishop of Westminster, the President of the Free Churches, and the Chief Rabbi, Hermann Adler. It also included a contribution by the antisemitic propagandist Arnold White, entitled 'The Foreign Bully'.[20] In his foreword, the Chief Rabbi set about establishing Judaism's moral credentials, stating that 'obedience to the Divine precepts of self-restraint and continence [had] proved a powerful preservative of the Jewish race during thousands of years of oppression and persecution'. It seemed to him, therefore, 'passing strange' that Arnold White considered Jews to have an 'Oriental view' of women as a sexual commodity. Adler admitted that while there were Jews involved in 'the abominable White Slave Traffic', there were reasons for this, and that

> However deeply we may grieve, we dare not be surprised if ill-treatment, defective education, persistent exclusion from honourable pursuits, and consequent fear of starvation drive men and women to reprehensible means of earning a living. But we do not view any action which encourages vice and immorality with indulgent toleration.[21]

Arnold White's contribution to the conference asserted that London was a hotbed of vice, and that 'foreign bullies' had organised themselves into a syndicate and were carving up the capital into districts of immorality. He identified most of the 'bullies' as 'Jews' from eastern Europe, noting that this was entirely consistent with the situation in Russia and the Near East, in which, he claimed, 'the exploitation of vice is mainly in the hands of Jews'. White acknowledged that enforced segregation had contributed to this situation, and suggested that Jews had, out of hardship and necessity, 'exploited the sensual vices of their Christian fellow citizens'. Nevertheless, Jews were 'Oriental', and therefore had an 'Asiatic view of womanhood', and it was this, rather than poverty, that in his view explained the involvement of 'Jews' in vice.[22] According to Arnold White, the essentially 'oriental' nature of the 'Jew' overrode the moral teachings of Judaism, and thus, he implied, 'nature' overcame culture. Like much antisemitic propaganda,

White's arguments were confused and confusing. He acknowledged, for example, that under English law, a married woman was considered her husband's 'chattel', but he did not accuse the English of showing an 'Oriental' attitude towards women. His 'foreign bullies' were identified as impoverished 'Jewish' immigrants from eastern Europe, yet they were also well dressed, and spoke English perfectly, which was how they were able to trick young women into trusting them. They targeted white Christian women for sexual exploitation, yet they also brought large numbers of 'foreign' prostitutes into the country through advertisements in the press. White's rhetoric focused more on making accusations than finding solutions: he shared with his fellow delegates a sense that there was a moral and social crisis at hand, but differed in his view of its causes and perpetrators. His 'foreign bullies' represented a variety of threats; national, sexual and 'racial'. Not only were they attacking the nation by entrapping and corrupting British women, they were also prospering by this activity, 'passing' as British, and then gaining control of districts of the capital.

The sexual anxieties associated with the figure of 'the Jew' have been a persistent theme in British antisemitic discourse. In *Skin Shows* (1995), Judith Halberstam discusses the embodiment of monstrosity and the attribution of a perverse and threatening sexuality to the figure of the 'foreigner', with regard to Bram Stoker's *Dracula* (1897).[23] Count Dracula, she argues, embodies late nineteenth-century fears regarding decadence, degeneracy and invasion, and the idea that a nation is vulnerable to attack through its women. Many of the characteristics of the vampire, she argues, match those of antisemitic caricature: both vampire and 'Jew' are constructed as animalistic and predatory; their anatomy and physiognomy repellent, their gaze compelling. Both are from the east, creatures of excessive sensual appetite, preoccupied with money and the blood of others, and there is a further parallel between the unpleasant smell associated with the vampire and the medieval antisemitic notion of *foetor judaicus*. Each of these monsters reproduces in its own likeness: Dracula creates more vampires through feeding, and the 'Jewish' vice trafficker spreads corruption and moral degeneracy through the entrapment and sexual exploitation of English women. Even before the 'white slavery' scares, there was an antisemitic tradition that held that Jewish men were bent on seducing Christian women.[24] Both vampire and 'Jew', then, are portrayed as the sites of the reproduction of disease and degeneracy, marginal but powerful figures that threaten the health of the 'race' and nation. They also threaten to disrupt the boundaries of class: the vampire is a corrupt eastern European aristocrat, and the 'Jew' has been portrayed as a class usurper, gaining control of powerful institutions within national life, such as finance and the media. Both vampire and 'Jew' act as repositories for a variety of fears and it is their constructed monstrosity that is used to justify their denigration. The difference, however, is that although both are constructs, only the 'Jew' is likely to be confused with actual Jews. Accusations of blood libel – the ritual use of the blood of Christians – are not levelled against vampires, since vampires are constructs and do not exist, but such allegations have been made against 'Jews' even into the twentieth century. Although Arnold White made no direct comparison between the 'Jewish' vice trafficker and the vampire, the characteristics he ascribed to the former were comparable with those associated with Dracula in Bram Stoker's novel. White's 'foreign bully' dressed well and was wealthy; he had the ability to lure decent English women into prostitution, and, in drawing them into the vice trade, he in a sense recreated them in his own image, thereby increasing his number. White's construction of the 'Jewish foreign bully', therefore, drew on familiar representations of the corruption of society, specifically through women, by outsiders.

It was partly in response to views like those of Arnold White that Jews in Britain became involved in the anti-vice movement. Although Jewish traffickers generally recruited Jewish women, this did not prevent rumours that they targeted Christians, and in this respect, the medieval fear of the Jewish attack on the Christian body took a new form, focusing on the perceived threat of the corruption and enslavement of British Christian womanhood by immigrant 'Jewish' procurers. It was this that prompted Anglo-Jewry to act, recognising the issue as, in Edward Bristow's words, 'the sexualization of blood libel'.[25] After some debate over whether participation in the anti-vice movement would appear to confirm the popular view that Jews dominated the trade, and thereby provoke more antisemitism, Anglo-Jewry joined the campaign. British Jews participated out of philanthropic concern for immigrants, and in order to counter the antisemitism that was aroused by 'white slavery', and their support was central to the spread and success of the anti-vice movement.[26]

In fact, it was Jewish women who initiated and led Anglo-Jewry's campaign against prostitution. In 1885 Constance Rothschild Battersea founded the Jewish Ladies' Society for

Preventive and Rescue Work, which later became the Jewish Association for the Protection of Girls and Women (JAPGW). This organisation modelled itself on the Christian anti-vice groups, providing religious education and domestic training for 'fallen women', but its function was also partly anti-conversionist: existing Jewish philanthropy did not address prostitution, thus Jewish prostitutes were obliged to approach Christian societies for assistance, or remain in the trade.[27]

Despite the formation of the JAPGW and the participation of British Jews in the broader purity movement, there was a continuing need for Jews to defend themselves against popular prejudices relating to the vice trade. At the Conference on Public Morality organised by the National Social Purity Crusade in London in 1910, Rabbi Professor Hermann Gollancz, representing the Chief Rabbi, felt it necessary to point out once again that Judaism was neither immoral nor pagan. Gollancz described himself as a member of 'a race and religion whose greatest claims rest upon social purity'. He also remarked that the laws given in the Pentateuch

> all had but one object in view: to make the people 'a kingdom of priests and a *holy* nation', the word 'holy' in the original meaning 'separated', removed from the impure and demoralising worship, from the moral degradation of the surrounding peoples, those with which the Israelites came into contact'.[28]

This was one of the ways in which Jews involved in the purity movement countered the excesses of Christian rhetoric in campaign literature and debate – they reminded Christians of the origins of their faith. Gollancz pointed out that Jews had created the first monotheism, which had formed the basis of Christianity, and that in fact, the Christian model for morality and social purity was derived from Judaism. Nevertheless, some conference speakers remained insensitive to the interdenominational nature of the purity crusade, and repeatedly defined the movement as Christian. Father Bernard Vaughan, for example, gave a paper entitled 'The Nation's Warning', in which he asserted that 'the true greatness of a nation depends upon the number of its pure, bright and simple Christian homes', a point he reiterated in his closing remarks.[29]

One purity organisation that co-operated with British Jews to combat vice trafficking and acknowledged the contributions of the Jewish community to its success was the National Vigilance Association, formed in Britain in 1885. W. T. Stead, editor of the *Pall Mall Gazette*, initiated the venture, and early supporters included Millicent Fawcett, Ellice Hopkins and Josephine Butler. William Coote was appointed secretary, and in 1910 he published a memoir entitled *A Vision and its Fulfilment* (1910), in which he used military metaphors to describe his sense of mission, feeling himself constrained 'To enlist in the army of those who would wage war against the men and women who, for the greed of gain, seek victims to satisfy the insatiable lust of men, of whom it might truly be said that their appetite grows with eating.[30]

Coote claimed to have received divine inspiration for furthering the cause in a 'day-dream' he experienced in September 1898.[31] God, he stated, was working through his conscience, and through this 'revelation' it became clear that the movement against vice must become international, as was the trade itself.[32] Coote's account of the NVA and its work draws upon the imagery of 'crusade' and 'Exodus'; using 'crusade' to express the chivalric fantasies and sense of religious mission associated with the movement, and 'Exodus' as a metaphor for the liberation of society from vice.[33] Coote extended the Exodus analogy, declaring that his 'revelation' to expand the movement internationally was 'as direct a Divine Command to go forward as any that Moses received when he was leading the children of Israel from the bondage of Egypt to the freedom of Canaan', thus implicitly casting himself as the Christian 'Moses' who would lead the 'Hebrews' to the Promised Land of a life free from prostitution.

It is important here to consider Coote's use of the term 'Hebrews'; to whom it refers, and whether any differentiation between 'Hebrews' and Jews is implied. The Hebrew–British analogy originated in eighteenth-century millennialism, and identifies the British with the biblical story of the Hebrew slaves in Egypt. It is based on the idea of the small and righteous nation whose destiny it is to lead the others, and when used in relation to the British, the 'Hebrews' metaphor is most frequently concerned with Protestant and Evangelical notions of 'chosenness' and embattlement. Its function is to claim for the British the privileged relation to the deity that is ascribed to the Jews of the Old Testament, but not necessarily to create an association with the Jews of the present. In this respect it is similar to British Israelism, which identifies the British as the direct descendants of the lost tribes of Israel who were dispersed as a result of the Assyrian invasion.[34]

William Coote's self-comparison with Moses in the context of the 'white slavery' scares, then, drew on existing ideas of the 'Hebrew' British, and attempted to claim for the NVA the moral superiority associated with the biblical Hebrew slaves, through the idea that the British had been 'chosen' to lead the nations against vice. This and his account of divine inspiration for the NVA implied a new, Christian 'covenant', the observation of which would secure for the British the protection of the deity and the fulfilment of the promises made to the Jews in the Old Testament. The background of slavery and the lapses into depravity that are also components of the Exodus story become, in the context of early twentieth-century 'white slavery', the threat that the 'chosen' are fighting, and in this context, these characteristics are implicitly conferred onto prostitutes and procurers.

But who was responsible for the enslavement of women through prostitution? Here, Coote's use of the Exodus theme becomes more ambiguous, and takes on a different significance, in the context of the migration of Jews to Britain and the perceived link between this and the vice trade. The number of Jews in Britain who were involved in prostitution was exaggerated, but the association between Jewish immigrants and prostitutes prevailed.[35] Coote's rhetoric of 'Exodus', therefore, may have appealed to popular prejudices in ways that he did not anticipate. In this respect, his reference to 'Hebrews' may have had another resonance, reinforcing the perceived connection between 'Jews' and vice. At the same time his rhetoric of 'slavery' could be taken to apply to prostitutes, thereby introducing a note of compassion into attitudes towards 'fallen' women. The portrayal of prostitutes as 'Hebrew slaves' would render them not fearful but powerless figures, to whom the Christian could safely offer charity and guidance.[36] As 'Hebrews', however, prostitutes would remain a group distinct from Christian society, and even when rehabilitated through the NVA's rescue homes, would be unlikely to completely shed the taint of their former profession. It is difficult to be certain exactly how Coote was using the Exodus metaphor, although the notion of 'chosenness' seems most likely. The purpose of this extended discussion of his analogy, however, is to show how, in the context of the promotion of Christian unity under conditions of real or perceived crisis, biblical metaphors can become subject to multiple

and sometimes conflicting interpretations. Whether taken from the
Old Testament or the New, their meaning cannot be fixed and
although ostensibly religious images, they may feed into and
exacerbate existing social and political tensions.

Some biblical rhetoric was to be expected in a movement
initiated and led by revivalist Christians, Evangelicals and
Nonconformists, as the anti-vice 'crusade' was. But the campaign
against international prostitution was not confined to the churches.
Broad secular support for the purity 'crusade' was demonstrated in
1911, through the National Council for Public Morality's 'Manifesto
on Public Morals'. This document, which expressed concern over
the declining birth rate, 'degeneration' and the effects of sexual
incontinence on the future health of the British nation was signed
by, among others, Ramsay MacDonald, leader of the Labour Party,
and the socialist writer and campaigner Beatrice Webb.[37] In
addition, Coote's international crusade against prostitution
received support from powerful figures throughout the world,
including the Empress of Germany, whose enthusiasm prompted
Coote to draw another analogy with Exodus, observing that 'Here
certainly was the Pillar of Cloud by day'.[38] For Coote, the support of
a European monarch seemed to confirm his belief that the cause
was divinely sanctioned.

The NVA was an interdenominational movement, and therefore
concerned that Jews should participate in its campaigns. Some of
the campaigners used biblical rhetoric in appealing to Jewry for
support, as in this exhortation from John Cameron Grant, author of
The Heart of Hell, a booklet on 'white slavery' published in 1913:

> O Children of the Orient, where I first saw the light, Sons of
> far-off Isles and Continents, arise for the honour of your great
> religious leaders, the great souls that you have given to the
> ages, and with us in the name of, and for the sake of, our
> common humanity, strike down for ever and abolish this
> accursed thing.[39]

Such appeals to the prophets were not lost upon Jews involved in the
purity campaigns. In his contribution to Coote's book, Chief Rabbi
Hermann Adler stated that fighting vice was indeed in obedience to
the will of God as described by the prophet Ezekiel, which he quoted
as 'That which is lost I will seek again; that which has gone astray, I
will bring back'.[40] In making this assertion he avoided any

implication that Jewish anti-vice campaigners were following a Christian revelation, and drew authority for the movement from a far earlier source than Coote's 'day-dream' inspired by the Holy Ghost, suggesting that Jews who fought against vice were fulfilling their own religious duty by obeying the prophets.

Jewish women were active against vice, as previously noted, through the JAPGW. In addition, and in common with many of the anti-vice organisations, the JAPGW had links with the temperance and suffrage movements, as Jewish women saw the connection between sexual, economic, religious and political inequality, and began to seek change.[41] The twin concerns of prostitution and women's inequality brought Jewish feminists into contact with the broader women's movement, and Millicent Garrett Fawcett, leader of the National Union of Women's Suffrage Societies (NUWSS), was a guest at the first Conference of Jewish Women, held in London in 1902. Delegates sought a compromise between tradition and reform, discussing ways to expand the existing women's 'sphere' of activity (traditionally education, domestic matters, religious reform and philanthropy), while keeping it within recognisable parameters, and advocated social work and continuing religious reform.[42]

It was not until November 1912, however, that a specifically Jewish suffrage organisation was founded, in the Jewish League for Woman Suffrage (JLWS). This group sought both religious and political equality for women, and members sometimes adopted controversial tactics. In October 1913, women campaigners inter-rupted a synagogue service in order to protest at the support of the Anglo-Jewish politicians Herbert Samuel and Rufus Isaacs, then Postmaster-General and Attorney-General respectively, for the forcible feeding of suffragette hunger strikers. The women were thrown out of the building.[43] Like the JAPGW, the JLWS addressed the involvement of Jews in 'white slavery', but in more direct terms, describing its aims as 'to influence Jewish thought about women... and thus to remove from the Jewish name the reproach of an oriental attitude towards women'.[44] It was perhaps statements such as this that aroused hostility in the Anglo-Jewish press towards the JLWS. In the context of exaggerated accounts of the involvement of 'Jews' in 'white slavery', this statement could be construed as a tacit admission that Jews regarded women as commodities and a confirmation, therefore, of the antisemitic viewpoint. The *Jewish Chronicle* repeatedly criticised the JLWS, fearing its activities would fuel perceptions of Jews as 'troublemakers'. The group had powerful allies among Anglo-Jewry, however, being led by Lily Montagu, sister of the politician Edwin Montagu, and having the support of the well-known writer Israel Zangwill, who regularly spoke on its behalf, and whose wife Edith was a member of the Women's Social and Political Union (WSPU).

These overlapping concerns – immigration, antisemitism, the involvement of Jews in prostitution and sexual inequality within Jewry – are also found in some of the literature of the period, and a more or less contemporary novel that engages with all these themes is Celia Anna Nicholson's *The First Good Joy* (1923).[45] Nicholson's novels make it clear that if not Jewish herself, she was certainly conversant with the issues of assimilation and Jewish nationalism, feminism and Jewish tradition, and antisemitism and ambivalence that were faced by Jews living in Britain during the early twentieth century. *The First Good Joy* is a sympathetic account, written from the perspective of the 'white slave' herself, which gives a complex and imaginative rendering of the issues of prostitution and the inequality of Jewish women. Written shortly after the First World War, when the vice traffic and the campaigns against it were reviving, *The First Good Joy* attempts to show the reasons why young Jewish women might become involved in prostitution and interrogates the idea of 'rescue' through marriage as a solution. Zosia, the daughter of a Polish-Jewish woman and a French aristocrat, is tricked into the trade in Brussels after escaping from the convent in which she has lived since her mother's suicide. She is rescued by Justin Davis, a young Anglo-Jewish man who is on a tour of Europe in the company of Harry Grossmann, a vulgar and lecherous family acquaintance. On the instruction of Justin's father, the tour is to include his son's sexual initiation before he goes to Cambridge. Grossmann embodies the predatory sexuality popularly ascribed by antisemites to the 'Jewish' immigrant procurer, while Justin is the equivalent of the Jewish purity campaigner. When Grossmann takes him to Brussels' red light district, therefore, Justin is repelled. He encounters Zosia, rescues her and takes her to England, where they are married. Zosia becomes pregnant, but the baby dies, and Justin goes to Cambridge while his wife lives alone in the country. In her isolation she begins to consider Jewish nationalism as the solution to her feelings of displacement and loss, feelings that are linked not only to the death of her child but also to a profound sense of deracination. Justin mistakes her interest in Palestine for political idealism, and dismisses this with scorn, arguing that the exploitation of the poor by the rich would continue even in a

Jewish state. But Zosia's identification with Palestine stems more from the alienation generated by the dual experience of sexual inequality and antisemitism. She argues that the only solution to antisemitism is the formation of a Jewish state, and challenges Justin to tell his Cambridge friends that he is Jewish, something he has so far avoided. When Justin does this and experiences rejection he decides Zosia is right and that they will emigrate to Palestine, where he will write 'big, serious plays' for a National Jewish Theatre (p. 137). Finding Zosia has left him, however, he returns to London and the wealthy, middle-class Anglo-Jewish community from which he originated.

Zosia, meanwhile, has drifted back into prostitution, as a result of poverty. Her upbringing and experience have not equipped her to support herself in any other way and as a prostitute she is an outcast, her estranged husband being her only contact with Jews in Britain. The novel makes no mention of the Jewish anti-vice and rescue organisations, which has the perhaps intentional effect of making the situation of the Jewish prostitute appear all the more desperate and therefore deserving of compassion. Justin eventually finds Zosia wandering along the Thames embankment in contemplation of suicide, and they resolve their differences, move to the country and start a family. Having briefly explored Jewish nationalism as a means of escape from sexual exploitation and antisemitism, the novel ends on an assimilationist note, as Zosia finds 'Zion' in family life, and Justin turns to culture rather than nationalist politics to express his Jewish identity, writing successful plays for Anglo-Jewish audiences. In this way, the novel suggests that Jewish identity is cultural, rather than political or 'racial', and that because of this, British and Jewish identifications can be negotiated with relative ease, particularly in Justin's case. The narrative offers a sympathetic and intelligent engagement with the issues of migration, vice, Jewish nationalism and antisemitism that confronted Anglo-Jewry in the early twentieth century. Nicholson's young Jewish characters have considered all these matters, particularly Jewish nationalism, and have opted for assimilation, their collective identification as Jews now depoliticised and 'safely' channelled into art and community life. They do not, therefore, represent a radical political threat, nor are they 'a nation within a nation', and any involvement with 'white slavery' on their part is prompted either by poverty or philanthropy. Those Jewish characters who have an 'oriental' attitude towards women, namely Harry Grossmann and Justin's father, are of the older generation, whose influence is depicted as waning.

While it retreats from a utopian view of Jewish nationalism, *The First Good Joy* retains a strong feminist note. Ultimately, Zosia decides that her suffering is the result not so much of 'racial' or religious persecution as sexual economics: women, like animals, will be treated as commodities because there is a market for women and therefore they will be exploited in order to meet that demand. The concept of the Promised Land is briefly considered as a solution – as a place of potential sexual equality – but dismissed, and eventually a compromise is reached, in which the couple's needs are met through family life and the Anglo-Jewish community. Nicholson's novel uses the image of the Jewish prostitute to explore the racial and sexual politics of the period and to highlight the antisemitism in British society. As Alan Mintz has pointed out, the trope of the abused woman is used to represent the sufferings of the Jewish people in sections of Second Isaiah or the Book of the Consolation of Israel, which is read in synagogue on the 9th of Ab, the day on which the destruction of the Temple is mourned.[46] In this text Zion is portrayed as a woman violated by gentiles, grieving over the loss of husband and son, when God intervenes and promises to restore all that she has lost.[47] Mintz argues that the resonance of this image as a metaphor for the condition of Jews lies in its suggestion of continuing victimisation.[48] Nicholson's character Zosia functions in a similar way, but she represents not so much the prolonged suffering of Jewry as that of women, and Jewish women in particular, who must deal with both antisemitism and inequality. *The First Good Joy*, therefore, places the image of the abused Jewish woman in a modern feminist context. Although she is proud of her Jewish ancestry, Zosia realises that Jewish nationalism cannot free her, since she sees women's inequality as part of Jewish culture. In this novel, it is not an 'exodus' to Palestine that is called for, but rather, a re-negotiation of the balance of power between Jewish women and men.

THE 'CRUSADE' FOR THE VOTE

The inequality of women was, of course, common to both Jewish and Christian cultures, and the Anglican Church acknowledged the need for change, lending its support to calls for the women's franchise. Whereas the anti-vice campaigns had been widely represented as a 'crusade' against prostitution, the linked campaign for the vote was not explicitly portrayed in these terms, although some of the more moderate suffrage groups did use religious imagery in their campaigns. The NUWSS, for example, organised a Women's Pilgrimage during June and July 1913, in which women from all over the country marched to London to demand the vote.[49] It was the militant suffragettes of the WSPU, however, that most enthusiastically adopted the rhetoric of 'enslavement' and 'crusade', applying the language of slavery to themselves,[50] and adopting Joan of Arc as their icon. Joan was beatified by the Catholic Church in 1909 and although she was not canonised until 1920, she became the 'patron saint' of the WSPU and suffragette processions were often led by a woman in armour mounted on a white horse, in emulation of her.

The suffragettes clearly saw a connection between Joan of Arc and the crusades, in their adoption of the former as their icon and the latter as a theme in their campaign imagery, but is there any historical basis for an association between Joan of Arc and the crusades? Marina Warner notes that Godfrey de Bouillon, who was elected King of Jerusalem at the end of the First Crusade, was Duke of Lower Lorraine, and that during Joan's lifetime, the crusades retained their appeal in that region as an example of dedication to the service of God.[51] The image of the pious crusader provided a model for others seeking to emulate the knightly ideal, and may, therefore, have informed Joan's own self-construction as a 'knight'. Joan used the theme of crusade in her speeches and letters, dictated to a scribe, and in 1430, in a letter to the Hussite leader Jan Hus, she threatened to launch a crusade against his sect.[52] But what was more important about Joan was that, as Cheryl Jorgensen-Earp argues, her image as a warrior provided the WSPU with a means of countering the popular stereotype of the suffragette as 'hysterical'. The representations of Joan mobilised by the WSPU combined an historical example of female militancy with the familiar allegorical figures of Liberty and Justice, to produce an image of purity, militancy and moral superiority, and above all, strategy.[53] Small wonder, then, that Christabel Pankhurst described suffragettes as the 'spiritual descendants' of Joan of Arc.[54] Joan had transcended the constraints of femininity in her time to become leader of the French army, but she was also betrayed and condemned to death for heresy, thus as Lisa Tickner points out, for the suffragettes, Joan represented both the liberated and the oppressed woman.[55]

The themes of battle and martyrdom associated with Joan appeared frequently in suffragette literature. Christabel Pankhurst compared suffragettes to the 'saints and martyrs of the past' and portrayed their campaigns as a struggle between the forces of 'good' and 'evil', in which the victims would eventually triumph.[56] Front covers of *The Suffragette*, which she edited, portrayed the suffrage campaigner as a female knight, wearing chain mail and leading the march to freedom. *The Suffragette* frequently used biblical imagery, and the cover of the issue dated 27 December 1912 (see Plate 1) featured verses from Charles Kingsley's poem 'The Day of the Lord', used to suggest 1913 as the year of redemption, or the gaining of the vote. In this context the lines

> True hearts will leap up at the trumpet of God,
> And those who can suffer, can dare

related not to the second coming of Christ, but the battle for women's equality.[57]

The use of biblical metaphors was characteristic of a number of Edwardian reform movements, which, like their Victorian predecessors, frequently couched their radicalism in religious language. Religion was still a fairly strong force in national life at the time and the widespread use of biblical allusion suggests that a greater proportion of the population was biblically literate than in today's society. Both Old and New Testaments provided a source of metaphors for oppression and resistance, and the same imagery was applied to women across the social spectrum. William Coote of the NVA used the story of the Israelites' escape from bondage in Egypt in relation to the campaign to free society from vice, and the writer and critic Laurence Housman used the same imagery with regard to the removal of legal and political disabilities against women. Writing in *Votes for Women* in 1912, Housman focused on the theme of divine retribution in the Exodus story and the plagues as Egypt's punishment for the oppression of the slaves, justifying by analogy the WSPU's attacks on private property as part of their campaign.[58] Comparisons were also made between the suffragette and Christ, in terms of the rejection and persecution suffered by both. An example of this appeared on the cover of *The Suffragette* in 1913, in a reference to 'Judas' in verses from a poem entitled 'The Present Crisis' by the American poet James Russell Lowell (1819–1891) (see Plate 2). The verse that concerns 'Judas' reads as follows:

For Humanity sweeps onward; where to-day the martyr stands,
On the morrow crouches Judas with the silver in his hands;
Far in front the cross stands ready and the crackling faggots burn,
While the hooting mob of yesterday in silent awe return
To glean up the scattered ashes into History's golden urn.[59]

The effect of this is to portray the suffragette as a Christian martyr: she becomes a Christ-figure and her enemy becomes Judas, thus the crucifixion of Jesus is mapped onto the struggle for the women's franchise. Exactly who or what 'Judas' represented in Lowell's poem is not clear, nor is it clear who Christabel Pankhurst saw as the betrayer, but mention of 'Judas' in *The Suffragette* in 1913 indicates that the battle for the vote was intensifying. Hopes for parliamentary support had begun to fade, as it became clear that Liberals and Conservatives feared women's suffrage would benefit their political opponents, and the Labour Party believed working-class men should gain the franchise before women did. Frustrated by the prevarications of the political parties, members of the WSPU adopted more violent strategies, and in February 1913 burned down Lloyd George's new country house. The government retaliated, passing the Prisoners' Temporary Discharge for Ill-Health Act, known as the 'Cat and Mouse Act', in April 1913, in response to hunger strikes by suffragettes.

The more militant approach of the WSPU alienated some of the membership, and as public hostility towards the cause grew, the rhetoric of martyrdom in *The Suffragette* increased. On 4 June 1913 the WSPU found its 'Christ' figure, in Emily Wilding Davison, who was trampled under the king's horse while demonstrating at the Epsom races and died four days later. Shortly before her death, Davison had written an article (published posthumously in the *Daily Sketch* on 28 May 1914) entitled 'The Price of Liberty', in which she described the role of the militant suffragette as 'to re-enact the tragedy of Calvary for generations yet unborn'.[60] Her death gave the suffrage movement a sacrificial figure and after her funeral *The Suffragette* published a collection of tributes under the heading 'A Christian Martyr'.[61] Throughout the rest of 1913, *The Suffragette* continued to wage its own 'holy war' against vice and inequality, and published articles of an apocalyptic tone that described prostitution and venereal disease as poisoning the nation 'morally, mentally, and physically'.[62] The cure for this was for women to avoid marriage and its accompanying risk of venereal infection;

votes for women, which would lessen their economic reliance upon men, and male chastity, and the WSPU initiated a moral crusade in support of this.[63]

Given the popular and exaggerated association of Jews with vice during the early twentieth century, Christabel Pankhurst's rhetoric of the poisoning of the nation through prostitution fitted neatly into antisemitic discourse. It was not, however, antisemitic in itself. She did not blame women's exploitation and inequality on 'Jews' or immigrants, but attributed this to men generally, and the semitic discourses found elsewhere at the time are lacking in her engagement with these issues.[64] In fact, despite its emphasis on the idea of the suffrage and anti-vice campaigner as defender of the health of future generations, suffrage propaganda in general avoided racism, although there is one early exception. A postcard designed by Edward Llewellyn in 1907 and entitled 'This is Allowed to Vote' compared the position of the British middle-class woman with that of immigrants to the United States, using racialised images which included that of a 'Jewish' man (see Plate 3). The postcard is thought to have been independently produced, and has not been directly linked to any particular suffrage group.[65]

Similarly, Christabel Pankhurst's increasingly millennialist perspective on the suffrage campaign might prompt one to expect some blame to be allocated to the 'Jew', but again, this is not the case. Traditionally, millennialists have attacked Jews rhetorically for their alleged role in the death of Christ, in the belief that this had prevented the establishment of the kingdom of God on earth, for which they must now wait. Their arguments, therefore, frequently end not with a description of the utopia that will follow the second coming, but with the denunciation of the Jews for 'deicide' (see Chapter 4 for examples). Yet despite the millennial rhetoric, James Russell Lowell's figure of Judas is the only 'Jewish' threat identified in the pages of *The Suffragette*, and exactly what he represents is unclear. Although the WSPU used similar imagery to millennialists and purity campaigners, then, it did not rely upon antisemitism to explain the oppression of women or the delay of the feminist utopia.

After the First World War, the focus of Christabel Pankhurst's millennialism shifted away from feminism and became increasingly 'orthodox' in its expression. From 1921 to 1940 she travelled and preached on the subject of the second coming, and published a number of millennialist texts, with titles such as *'The Lord Cometh!'* (1923), *Pressing Problems of the Closing Age* (1924), *The World's Unrest:*

The Suffragette

Greetings to All.

EDITED BY CHRISTABEL PANKHURST.

The Official Organ of the Women's Social and Political Union.

VOL. I.—No. 11.   FRIDAY, DECEMBER 27, 1912.   Price 1d. Weekly (⌐¹⌐)

THE DAY OF THE LORD.

The Day of the Lord is at hand, at hand :
  Its storms roll up the sky :
The nations sleep starving on heaps of gold ;
  All dreamers toss and sigh ;
The night is darkest before the morn ;
When the pain is sorest the child is born,
  And the Day of the Lord at hand.

Gather you, gather you, angels of God
  Freedom, and Mercy, and Truth ;
Come ! for the Earth is grown coward and old,
  Come down and renew us her youth.

Wisdom, Self-sacrifice, Daring, and Love,
Haste to the battlefield, stoop from above,
  To the Day of the Lord at hand.

*   *   *   *   *   *

Who would sit down and sigh for a lost age of gold,
  While the Lord of all ages is here ?
True hearts will leap up at the trumpet of God,
  And those who can suffer, can dare.
Each old age of gold was an iron age too ;
And the meekest of saints may find stern work to do,
  In the Day of the Lord at hand
           By CHARLES KINGSLEY.

1. 'The Day of the Lord', front cover of *The Suffragette*, 27 December 1912. By permission of the British Library.

2. 'The Sword of the Spirit', front cover of *The Suffragette*, 21 March 1913. By permission of the British Library.

3. '*This* is Allowed to Vote', Edward Llewellyn, 1907. Bodleian Library, University of Oxford, John Johnson Collection; Postcards, Women's Suffrage.

4. Girls operating cranes in a shell-filling factory at Chilwell, Nottingham, 1917. Photograph courtesy of the Imperial War Museum, London. (Q30038)

BETRAYED.

The Pander. "COME ON; COME AND BE KISSED BY HIM."

5. 'Betrayed', cartoon published in *Punch*, 12 December 1917. Reproduced by permission of the *Punch* Cartoon Library and Archive.

Visions of the Dawn (1926) and *Seeing the Future* (1929). Even in this capacity she did not denounce Jews, unlike other millennialists, but imagined their conversion to Christianity as a simple matter of persuasion and agreement. In *The Lord Cometh!* (1923) Christabel wrote that the 'Jewish Question' would be resolved by 'the simple condition of faith in Jesus Christ – whereupon all distinction between Jew and Gentile disappears'.[66] For her, the 'Jewish Question' seemed to arise only in the context of millennialism, and not in relation to the anti-vice and women's suffrage campaigns, despite her frequent use of Christian imagery in *The Suffragette*. Within the WSPU's campaign for the vote, the themes of crusade, crucifixion and millennium seem to have been adopted more for their emotive appeal and rich metaphorical content than out of any direct hostility towards Jewish people. In addition, Anglo-Jewish writers on feminism were well received by the WSPU: Walter Lionel George's book *Woman and To-Morrow* (1912) was described by one suffragette reviewer as 'a splendid bit of suffrage propaganda',[67] and Israel Zangwill, whose wife Edith was a member of the Union, spoke frequently in support of the cause.

To summarise, although the White Cross League, the National Social Purity Crusade, the National Vigilance Association and the Women's Social and Political Union all made use of the 'crusade' trope with regard to vice and the vote, the function of these themes within their propaganda differed considerably, as did the relation of their campaigns to contemporary antisemitism. As a leading figure in the NVA, William Coote, a Christian, repeatedly referred to the movement as a 'world-wide crusade' prompted by 'a Divine impulse'.[68] He combined this with themes from Exodus, casting himself as 'Moses' and implying that the British were a modern version of the biblical 'Hebrews', a people chosen by God to be the moral leaders of the nations. His 'Hebrews' analogy was ambiguous, however, since there was a popular perception that the vice traffic was controlled by Yiddish-speaking Jews. The social purity campaign was largely a male-led 'crusade' against immorality that portrayed women as vulnerable to corruption by 'outsiders' and became linked to existing fears concerning immigration. In suffragette language and iconography, however, women were the 'crusaders' – their own deliverers. The WSPU regarded vice as a direct result of women's inequality, and their enemy was the legal establishment that denied women the vote that could empower them. Despite drawing on the imagery of crucifixion and millennium – Christian narratives that allocate a specific, adversarial role to 'unbelieving Jews' – and the contemporary concerns over vice and immigration, the WSPU 'crusade' did not invoke the 'Jew' for its completion. There was an absence of nationalism in the WSPU campaigns that the NVA, despite leading an international movement, retained, in the theme of the British as 'chosen' to lead the nations against vice.

Jewish feminists, already part of a minority, drew attention to sexual inequality within Jewry itself. The actions of the JLWS in particular aroused hostility within a community that was already embattled, and it was feared their campaigns would bring reprisals for Jews in Britain. More broadly, Jews participated in the anti-vice movement partly to counter antisemitism, and where they gave religious significance to their involvement it was in response to the rhetorical excesses of the Christian majority. Mindful of the antisemitism that was aroused by immigration and prostitution, they were of necessity more circumspect than their Christian counterparts, and focused their approach on philanthropy rather than religiosity.

The anti-vice and suffrage campaigns were interrupted by the outbreak of war in 1914 and the language of 'crusade' found a new focus, being applied to the nation at war. The international vice trade declined during the war years, and the role of women in British society underwent dramatic changes.

WOMEN AND WAR

On 24 October 1914, Christabel Pankhurst explained to an audience at Carnegie Hall, New York, why suffragettes were co-operating with the government that had so vigorously opposed their aims. She referred to Belgium as 'the suffragette country' and portrayed the German invasion of Belgium as a violation on a par with the pre-war 'torture' of British women by the government, by which she meant the forcible feeding of suffragette prisoners on hunger strike.[69] Belgium's neutrality had been guaranteed by a treaty between Prussia, France and Britain, ratified in 1839 and renewed in 1870. German forces, however, had invaded Belgium on 2/3 August 1914. Christabel characterised German expansionism, or 'Prussianism', as male violence on an international scale, and described the war as a battle for the future of women's rights, arguing that Germany was hostile to women's equality, and that although they still lacked the vote, British women were better off than their German counterparts, who were 'unduly subordinated to the men'. A German victory, Christabel declared, would be 'a disastrous blow' to the women's movement in all countries, and she added 'we will not allow a male nation to dominate the earth'. The war, then, was part of the international gender struggle, in which, if necessary, former suffragettes were willing to take up arms, in emulation of Joan of Arc. In response to a question from the audience concerning 'a revival of the spirit and mission of Joan d'Arc', Christabel replied that women would fight if necessary.[70] The suffragette image of Joan as both victim and warrior now appeared to become divided: in identifying Belgium as 'the suffragette country', the element of martyrdom was conferred onto a feminised Belgium and the warrior aspect of Joan became more pronounced and linked to Britain, as former militants postponed their pursuit of the women's franchise and campaigned vigorously in support of the new militarist 'crusade'.

The outbreak of war had split the suffrage movement in Britain. The United Suffragists, established by the Pethwick-Lawrences in February 1914, continued to campaign for suffrage and pacifism throughout the war, and a group of former suffragists launched a Women's Peace Crusade in 1915, which undertook relief work among Germans in Britain.[71] The majority of the NUWSS, led by Millicent Garrett Fawcett, supported the war and took up morale-boosting activities. *The Suffragette* was renamed *Britannia* in 1915, and the WSPU became the Women's Party. Some of the members objected to this and the movement's new militarist stance. As Annie Kenney, a key figure in the WSPU noted, 'They were quite prepared to receive instructions about the Vote, but they were not going to be told what they were to do in a world war.'[72] Sylvia Pankhurst joined the anti-conscription movement, while Christabel and her mother Emmeline embraced militarism, their supporters distributing white feathers to unenlisted men while they travelled the country campaigning to dissuade workers from industrial action.[73]

This abrupt transition from militancy to unequivocal militarism was not always approved of, and to some, the former suffragettes' enthusiasm for the war was simply another example of their 'unladylike' behaviour.[74] Women were generally expected to embody the principles of piety and self-denial, and to accept bereavement with patriotic pride, leaving militarism to the men. Patient suffering was their role in the 'crusade' against

'Prussianism', an idea that was disseminated by women as well as men. Elma Paget, wife of the Bishop of Stepney, published a pamphlet in late 1914 entitled *The Woman's Part*, in which she urged women to take comfort in the knowledge that their loved ones had died in the service of God.[75]

Beside pamphlets, poetry provided another means of promoting or contesting the notion of the 'woman's part' in the war as one of patient suffering and resignation to the loss of loved ones. Women writers in particular, used poetry to examine the role of women in relation to the conflict. In 1916, the year of huge losses at the Somme, the Irish novelist and poet Katharine Tynan published a collection of poetry entitled *The Holy War*, dedicated to 'the mourners of the War... who praise your God although he slay'.[76] Tynan (1861–1931) also published fiction and autobiography, and was associated with a number of Irish nationalist writers, including William Butler Yeats. Her wartime poems use the 'crusade' trope to signify male endeavour, solidarity and sacrifice, while women are allocated a passive and vicarious role in the 'holy war'. In the poem 'To the Others', the female speaker expresses excitement at the prospect of the spiritual regeneration of the soldier through battle, in the lines

> Your son and my son, clean as new swords,
> Your man and my man and now the Lord's!
> Your son and my son for the Great Crusade,
> With the banner of Christ over them – our knights, new-made.[77]

The image of 'knights' united under the 'banner of Christ' is a chivalric representation of war that also has feudal associations and appears to be nostalgic for a 'lost' model of society. These themes are found in another of Tynan's wartime poems, 'New Heaven', in which death in battle appears as a rite of passage, and 'Paradise' is reminiscent of a baronial hall in which the ghostly 'knights' bask in the approval of their 'lord':

> PARADISE now has many a Knight,
> Many a lordkin, many lords...
>
> Some have barely the down on the lip,
> Smiling yet from the new-won spurs,
> Their wounds are rubies, glowing and deep,
> Their scars amethyst – glorious scars...

> Paradise now is the soldiers' land,
> Their own country its shining sod,
> Comrades all in a merry band;
> And the little Knights' laughter pleaseth God.[78]

The paradise depicted in this poem is full of young people, who have won their 'spurs' through dying for their country. The line 'Comrades all in a merry band' suggests that the war dead enjoy a security and unity that the living cannot. Their struggles are over, and paradise the reward for their sacrifice. In this respect, the poem is similar to clerical representations of the war as a Christian 'crusade', with the prize a glorious death in the service of God. The relationship between the romanticised images of death in battle in Tynan's poems and clerical rhetoric of the time is of interest with regard to ideological production and reproduction in wartime. Arthur Foley Winnington-Ingram, then Bishop of London, enthusiastically preached the 'holy war', and urged his female listeners to support their men in what he termed 'this great and splendid crusade' and to bear their losses with dignity.[79] Katherine Tynan developed these themes into a poetic language of patriotism, sacrifice and regeneration, which reproduced the ideology of bereavement as 'the woman's part' in romantic and chivalric language. The cycle was completed when Bishop Winnington-Ingram quoted Tynan's poems in his sermons.[80] The fact that Tynan was a Catholic and an Irish nationalist, and that her poems were possibly ironic in their use of chivalric imagery, seems not to have deterred the Anglican and strongly imperialist bishop.

Another Catholic writer, Alice Meynell, who knew Katherine Tynan, took a different view of the role of women in the war, in her poem 'Parentage':

> Ah! No, not these!
> These, who were childless, are not they who gave
> So many dead unto the journeying wave,
> The helpless nurslings of the cradling seas;
> Not they who doomed by infallible decrees
> Unnumbered man to the innumerable grave.
>
> But those who slay
> Are fathers. Theirs are armies. Death is theirs –
> The death of innocences and despairs;

The dying of the golden and the grey.
The sentence, when these speak it, has no Nay.
And she who slays is she who bears, who bears.[81]

Alice Meynell (*née* Thompson, 1847–1922) was a British writer and feminist who published her first collection of poetry in 1875. She converted to Catholicism in 1868 and much of her poetry engages with religious themes. In 1877 she married the author Wilfred Meynell and they had eight children. Her daughter Viola asserted that her mother supported the war, but 'Parentage' suggests ambivalence. This poem insists that women's role in war is not passive: they bear the children who fight and die in conflicts initiated by men; thus men and women between them sentence their children to death in a world in which war seems inevitable. Meynell was involved in the suffrage movement, and in some respects 'Parentage' echoes Christabel Pankhurst's remedy for the spread of venereal disease and the exploitation of women in marriage – that they refuse to marry. The logic of Meynell's poem implies that if women truly want to stop war, they should stop bearing children. Neither 'solution' was possible or realistic, and in the case of Catholic women like Meynell, contraception was at odds with religious doctrine. What links these two analyses, though, is the idea that, however unlikely, a sexual embargo imposed by women could bring about the profound changes desired: in the one case, equality for women, in the other, an end to war.

Women contributed to the mass slaughter of the First World War not only through the sacrifice of their loved ones, but also through their war work. Many took over the jobs of their absent husbands, working in manual or service trades. Christabel Pankhurst and her mother led what Lloyd George termed the 'new crusade' for the 'industrial conscription' of women. This was highly successful, and by November 1918 over 1,587,300 women were employed in government work, many of them in munitions factories.[82] At the same time Sylvia Pankhurst was campaigning against military conscription, introduced in 1916. For a short time Jewish refugees in Britain were exempt from conscription because the then Home Secretary Herbert Samuel sympathised with their understandable reluctance to fight in alliance with tsarist Russia, the country from which many of them had fled. This exemption aroused hostility, however, and Jewish refugees in Britain were eventually faced with a choice between conscription and deportation, a development examined in more detail in Chapters 3 and 5. In this context it seems possible that the much-discussed entry of women into war work fuelled accusations that unlike women, Jews were not 'doing their bit' for the war effort. Yet women's contribution to the war prompted criticism among Jews and non-Jews alike. The writer Joseph Leftwich was of Dutch-Jewish descent. Born in The Netherlands in 1892, he moved to Britain in his youth, settled in the East End of London, and became part of a group of Jewish writers and artists that included David Bomberg, Mark Gertler and Isaac Rosenberg. He commented bitterly on the enthusiasm with which women had joined the militarist 'crusade' in the poem 'Song of the Women', written in 1914:

> We are women and mothers and mothers-to-be,
> And we work in this horrible factory,
> We are making munitions, we work with a will,
> We sing at our work, for our working will kill
> The fathers and sons of such women as we.
> We are women and mothers and mothers-to-be.[83]

The poem reveals the irony of the situation, whereby women, the biological producers of life, had gained the independence, recognition and financial security they wanted by becoming the industrial producers of death, manufacturing shells for the Front. They were not only sacrificing their own families to the war, but also producing the means by which the families of German women would be killed (see Plate 4).

Poetry provided a way of interrogating some of the changes in gender roles that the war had brought about, and the employment of women in munitions production was a popular subject with women writers in particular. Some expressed ambivalence, others horror, at women's contribution to the slaughter by this means. Madeline Ida Bedford's poem 'Munition Wages' depicts a working-class woman enjoying her prosperity and independence while she can, and giving no thought to the consequences of her labour:

> Earning high wages? Yus,
> Five quid a week.
> A woman, too, mind you,
> I calls it dim sweet.[84]

Any criticism of the woman munitions worker in this poem is implied, rather than stated, and the dialect style suggests that the speaker is uneducated, and unaware of or unwilling to recognise the irony of the matter. At a time when women were restricted in their employment options and paid less than men, it was important for many to grasp the opportunity of earning a decent wage. Mary Gabrielle Collins' poem 'Women at Munition Making', on the other hand, expressed the view that it was sacrilegious for women to do this work; the prospect of men destroying one another was familiar if tragic,

> But this goes further,
> Taints the fountain head,
> Mounts like a poison to the Creator's very heart.[85]

Women's poetry of the First World War examines the relationship of women to war, and gives an indication of the diverse attitudes that existed among women with regard to the war and war work. Katherine Tynan's poems appeared to celebrate the 'glorious' death of young men in battle, while Alice Meynell grieved over the seeming inevitability of war and the role of the mother in the cycle of birth and violent death that 'Parentage' describes. For some writers, the active and integral part taken by women munitions workers in the 'crusade' against 'Prussianism' was an affront to femininity itself, whereas others acknowledged the economic freedom that women gained through their war work. Like the suffrage 'crusade', the war generated debate and divided opinion over the nature of women's role in British society.

THE WOOLWICH 'CRUSADE'

It was in relation to munitions production that the Anglican Church brought the 'crusade' to civilians in 1917, having previously applied this rhetoric mainly to promoting enlistment and justifying the war. Despite the relatively high munitions wages (Christabel and Emmeline Pankhurst had negotiated a minimum wage for women with Lloyd George in 1915) there were occasional labour disputes at the armaments factories during the war. In the spring of 1915 King George V began visiting workplaces in order to boost morale and counter the threat of industrial unrest.[86] His visit to the Woolwich Arsenal in March that year was successful in this respect, in contrast to a similar effort made by the Church two years later. During the first two weeks of September 1917, the Anglican clergy mounted what it termed 'the Woolwich crusade', a simultaneous attempt to mediate in a dispute at the munitions factory and bring the gospel to the workers. Prior to the war, Anglican clergymen had been troubled by the failure of the Church to attract the working classes in significant numbers. This was not due to a lack of working-class religious feeling so much as perceptions of the Church as a class institution, reflected in the public-school background of most of the clergy and in practices such as pew-renting, which had continued until the late nineteenth century. Successive Anglican Convocations had attempted to address the situation, but church attendance among the working classes remained low.[87] The ill-fated Woolwich crusade was in part an effort by the Church to establish contact with this section of British society. It may also have been an attempt to dissuade workers from a revolution of the kind that had occurred in Russia in February 1917. After the abdication of Tsar Nicholas II a provisional government was formed, of which Alexander Kerensky became Prime Minister in July 1917. By September that year, the time of the Woolwich crusade, the Kerensky administration was faltering, and the Bolsheviks were gaining ground. Events in Russia, Britain's ally, were widely reported in the British press, and the situation aroused fears that Bolshevism would spread to Britain, through the labour movement. Church leaders attempted to mediate in various wartime and post-war labour disputes, possibly with Bolshevism's hostility to religion in mind. The Woolwich was not only an opportunity to bring the gospel to the workers, but also, perhaps, to avert any threat to Christian authority represented by political radicalism (as seen in recent events in Russia), and by doing so, to secure for the Church a role in post-war reconstruction. That the Church was concerned with its role in the post-war period was made clear in a report in *The Times*, which described the purpose of the Woolwich crusade as

> to persuade the workers to combine in a great effort to raise the whole moral tone of the social and industrial life, as a first stage in the reconstruction of modern conditions, in the belief that such a reconstruction can only be effectively achieved on a Christian foundation.[88]

As workers in a vital war industry, the munitions employees represented a means for the Church to gain influence among an important group, and one that included large numbers of women, who would soon receive the vote.

The 'crusade' was organised by the Bishop of Southwark and attended by the Archbishop of Canterbury, Randall Thomas Davidson, and numerous high-ranking clergymen, including Winnington-Ingram, Bishop of London. Events opened with a procession of clerical 'crusaders', who carried banners and wore the emblem of St George and the dragon, after which a letter of support from Prime Minister Lloyd George was read out. The workers were then addressed by the Reverend H. J. Warde, who stated that in 'the new England', Christ would settle employment disputes.[89] In his address on the last day of the 'crusade', Archbishop Davidson noted the many recent and rapid changes in British society – in industry, education and relations between men and women – and reminded his listeners that the Church could offer spiritual guidance, both during and after the war.[90] The Anglican journal *Christian Challenge* followed the progress of the Woolwich crusade, and reported that although the workers expressed interest in the clergy's message, church attendance remained low.[91] Nevertheless, the event enabled the Church to identify some of the reasons why it was losing authority. The matter was largely one of class: most of the leading clergy were Oxbridge-educated and the Church was perceived as hierarchical and therefore unsympathetic to the growing demand for full democratisation. If it was to lead the nation towards moral and spiritual regeneration after the war, significant changes were necessary. As the official report on the Woolwich crusade concluded, 'the need for ecclesiastical reform is overwhelming'.[92]

In all the 'crusades' discussed above, women were a linking theme. In the language of the NVA campaigns they were the victims or potential victims of international vice, to be protected or rescued by the purity 'crusaders'. Underlying this was the fear of moral and social deterioration and the effects of prostitution on the health and strength of the nation. NVA literature drew on Old Testament themes of enslavement, escape and the building of a new society in a 'Promised Land' free from vice. Jewish purity campaigners joined the cause out of philanthropy and self-defence, aware that the combined issues of immigration and prostitution aroused antisemitism. The NVA and affiliated groups focused on prevention, rescue and rehabilitation, but their literature did not explicitly address the poverty that was often the cause of prostitution and the legal inequality that facilitated the 'enslavement' of women through vice. This was addressed by writers such as Celia Anna Nicholson, in her novel *The First Good Joy*, and also by suffrage campaigners, particularly members of the WSPU, whose literature argued that society could not change for the better unless the balance of power between the sexes was shifted. Women, through activism and self-sacrifice if necessary, were to be their own 'rescuers', and the themes of female strength and chastity and the idealisation and exploitation of women were combined in the figure of Joan of Arc. The issue of women's political and sexual inequality was divisive, and the militant tactics of the WSPU and their confrontation of sexual inequality brought them under attack from the wider community. Similarly, members of the Jewish League for Woman Suffrage, some of whom emulated WSPU tactics, were regarded as potential troublemakers, and attracted criticism from British Jews.

The war and the need for a collective national effort alleviated some of the tension over women's inequality, albeit temporarily, by increasing women's employment opportunities. At the same time, sermons and pamphlets detailed 'the woman's part' in the war, encouraging women to bear the loss of their loved ones bravely and to embody the virtues of humility, temperance and chastity. Katherine Tynan's poems reflect this attitude, apparently celebrating the death of the 'knight' in battle, and portraying women as united in pride and sadness. In fact women took a far more active role in the war, making up a large percentage of the workforce, and replacing men in many occupations. The former WSPU was instrumental in this, and in co-operation with Lloyd George embarked upon the 'industrial crusade', which mobilised women for war work. This direct involvement of women in the war raised new concerns and these were explored in some of the poetry of the period. Male and female writers questioned the morality of women's participation in the war effort, particularly with regard to munitions, taking the view that it was wrong for women, as the biological creators of life, to produce the means of death and profit by it. There is a suggestion of betrayal in Joseph Leftwich's juxtaposition of 'women and mothers and mothers-to-be' with the woman munitions worker, which relates to pacifist constructions of femininity based on women's reproductive function. But pacifist womanhood was at odds with the needs of the nation at war, and, given the sheer numbers of women who undertook war work, unrealistic. Women had to replace the men who had left for the Front, and they took on a number of previously male roles. The mass entry of women into the workforce during the war helped to support arguments for the franchise, and by June 1917 preliminary suffrage legislation was being approved by parliament, despite the fact that the campaign for the vote had been generally postponed during the war itself.

Ironically, then, it was through the suspension of the suffrage 'crusade' that its aims were partially realised, and it was occupational change among women that paved the way for political reform.

NOTES

1   See Marcus Bull, 'The Roots of Lay Enthusiasm for the First Crusade', *History*, Vol. 78 (1993), pp. 353–372.
2   Carl Erdmann, *The Origin of the Idea of Crusade* (Princeton, NJ: Princeton University Press, 1977), pp. 8–10.
3   Jews were expelled from Britain, with a few exceptions, in 1290, 46 years after Jerusalem had been returned to Muslim control.
4   See Stephanie L. Barczeweski, *Myth and National Identity in Nineteenth-Century Britain: the legends of King Arthur and Robin Hood* (Oxford: Oxford University Press, 2000), p. 224.
5   See Barczewski, *Myth and National Identity*, pp. 226–27 for examples.
6   Lloyd Gartner puts the overall figure for Jewish migration during this period at 3,000,000. See Lloyd P. Gartner, *The Jewish Immigrant in England, 1870–1914*, Studies in Society No. 4 (London: George Allen & Unwin, 1960), pp. 270, 274.
7   The Zwi Migdal was an organisation of Jewish brothel-keepers which originated in Buenos Aires in 1906, and members of the large Ashkenazi community in Constantinople were involved in the vice trade. See Edward J. Bristow, *Prostitution and Prejudice: The Jewish Fight Against White Slavery 1870–1939* (Oxford: Clarendon Press, 1982), pp. 182–3.
8   See Edward J. Bristow, *Vice and Vigilance: Purity Movements in Britain since 1700* (Dublin: Gill & Macmillan, Rowman & Littlefield, 1977), pp. 46–7.
9   Alfred Stace Dyer, *The European Slave Trade in English Girls: A Narrative of Facts* (London: Dyer Bros., 1880).
10   On chivalric or 'knightly' constructions of masculinity during the nineteenth and early twentieth centuries, and their dissemination, see Mark Girouard, *The Return to Camelot: Chivalry and the English Gentleman* (New Haven, CT, and London: Yale University Press, 1981).
11   J. B. Lightfoot, Bishop of Durham, *An Address to Members of the White Cross Army*, at St Mary's Church, Gateshead, 20 May 1883 (London: Hatchards, 1883), p. 12.
12   Ellice Hopkins, *The White Cross Army: A Statement of the Bishop of Durham's movement* (London: Hatchards, 1883), p. 21.
13   Ellice Hopkins, *Touching Pitch* (c. 1883), p. 11, in *Ten Reasons Why I Should Join the White Cross Society* (Darton: Wells Gardner, 1890).
14   Ellice Hopkins, *Ten Reasons Why I Should Join* (London: Hatchards, Piccadilly, c. 1885).
15   Ellice Hopkins, *Man and Woman, or, the Christian Ideal* (1883), p. 13, in *Ten Reasons Why I Should Join the White Cross Society* (Darton: Wells Gardner, 1890).
16   See Joyce Zonana, 'The sultan and the slave: feminist orientalism and the structure of *Jane Eyre*', in *Signs: Journal of Women in Culture and Society*, Vol. 18, No. 3, (1993),

pp. 592–617.

17   Zonana, 'The Sultan and the Slave', p. 594.

18   Mary Wollstonecraft, *A Vindication of the Rights of Women*, ed. Mary Warnock (London: J. M. Dent, 1985) pp. 33, 39. See also *Jane Eyre* (1847, chapter 24). Having accepted Rochester's proposal of marriage, Jane is disconcerted by changes in his attitude towards her, buying her clothes and jewellery she does not want, and treating her as his possession in anticipation of their sexual union: 'He smiled; and I thought his smile was such as a sultan might, in a blissful and fond moment, bestow on a slave his gold and gems had enriched'. Jane uses Eastern imagery to portray his behaviour and missionary rhetoric to deflect his attentions.

19   Ellice Hopkins, *Saved At Last!* (London: Hatchards, 1886), p. 7.

20   *The Cleansing of a City*, published for the National Social Purity Crusade (London: Greening, 1908).

21   Chief Rabbi Hermann Adler, foreword to *The Cleansing of a City*, p. xii.

22   Arnold White, 'Foreign bullies', in *The Cleansing of a City*, p. 106.

23   See Michael Ragussis, *Figures of Conversion: 'The Jewish Question' and English National Identity* (Durham, NC, and London: Duke University Press, 1995), and Judith Halberstam, *Skin Shows: Gothic Horror and the Technology of Monsters* (Durham & London: Duke University Press, 1995).

24   See Ragussis, *Figures of Conversion*, for more on this.

25   See Bristow, *Prostitution and Prejudice*, p. 46. The Board of Jewish Deputies supported the work of the NVA.

26   Bristow, *Prostitution and Prejudice*, p. 5.

27   See Linda Gordon Kuzmack, *Woman's Cause: The Jewish Woman's Movement in England and the United States, 1881–1933* (Columbus, OH: Ohio State University Press, 1990), p. 53.

28   Hermann Gollancz, foreword to *The Nation's Morals: Being the Proceedings of the Public Morals Conference held in London on the 14th and 15th July, 1910* (National Social Crusade, London: Cassell, 1910), p. 8.

29   Father Bernard Vaughan, 'The warning of a nation', in *The Nation's Morals: Being the Proceedings of the Public Morals Conference held in London on the 14 and 15th July 1910* (London: Miscellaneous Institutions, Societies, and other bodies. National Social Purity Crusade, Cassell, 1920). (1910), p. 113.

30   William Alexander Coote, *A Vision and Its Fulfilment: Being the History of the Origin of the Work of the National Vigilance Association for the Suppression of the White Slave Traffic* (London: NVA, 1910), p. 19.

31   Coote, *A Vision*, p. 19.

32   Coote, *A Vision*, p. 19.

33   Coote, *A Vision*, p. 24.

34   It was Richard Brothers who, partly in response to millennial expectations aroused by the French Revolution, suggested that the descendants of the lost tribes could be found among Christians, in *A Revealed Knowledge*, published in 1794–95. Brothers, born in Newfoundland in 1757, promoted an international Christian Israelism, and identified himself as 'the Prince of the Hebrews' and 'the nephew of the Almighty'. The identification of the British with the lost tribe of Ephraim was a gradual development from this, in which the idea of 'chosenness' became imaginatively and rhetorically linked to British imperial success. It was John Wilson, whose date of birth is unknown, but who died in 1871, who disseminated the British–Israel theory through public lectures and his popular and influential book *Our Israelitish Origin*. The Association of British Israelites was formed in the 1870s. See John Wilson, 'British Israelism: the ideological restraints on sect organisation', in Bryan R. Wilson (ed.), *Patterns of Sectarianism: Organisation and Ideology in Social and Religious Movements* (London: Heinemann, 1967), pp. 345–76. On these particular points, see pp. 353–4, 360–3.

35   Edward J. Bristow observes that only a quarter of the arrests in London in the 1900s for trafficking involved foreigners, including not only Russian and Polish Jews but also French, German and Belgian nationals. See Bristow, *Vice and Vigilance*, p. 170.

36   After the First World War, the NVA became more sceptical regarding stories of

entrapment, and campaigned for responsible sex education for future generations. See Roy Porter and Lesley Hall, *The Facts of Life: The Creation of Sexual Knowledge in Britain, 1650–1950* (New Haven, CT and London: Yale University Press, 1995), pp. 264, 238.

37   Bristow, *Vice and Vigilance*, p. 145.
38   Coote, *A Vision*, p. 36.
39   John Cameron Grant, *The Heart of Hell: A Note Upon the White Slave Traffic* (London: New Constitutional Society for Women's Suffrage, printed by the Women's Printing Society, 1913), p. 17.
40   Dr Hermann Adler, in Coote, *A Vision*, p. 176. Adler seems to have been referring to Ezekiel 34:16, which reads 'I shall look for the lost one, bring back the stray, bandage the wounded and make the weak strong.'
41   The Jewish feminist Bertha Pappenheim discussed the role of Jewish women in religious reform, in a book entitled *The Jewish Woman in Religious Life* (London, 1913, reprinted from *The Jewish Review*, January 1913). Translated from the German by Margery Bentwick. (London: Miscellaneous Institutions, Societies, and other bodies. The Jewish League for Women suffrage, 1913).
42   See Kuzmack, *Woman's Cause*, p. 49.
43   Kuzmack, *Woman's Cause*, p. 134.
44   Leaflet issued by the Jewish League for Woman Suffrage, 1912.
45   Celia Anna Nicholson, *The First Good Joy* (London: Hutchinson, 1923).
46   Alan Mintz, *Hurban: Responses to Catastrophe in Hebrew Literature* (New York: Columbia University Press, 1984), p. 45.
47   See Isaiah 2.51:18 onwards. The image of Israel as an abused woman is also found in Lamentations 1:8.
48   Mintz, *Hurban*, p.24.
49   See Diane Atkinson, *Votes for Women*, Women in History Series (Cambridge: Cambridge University Press, 1988, reprinted 1989), pp. 34–5.
50   Christabel Pankhurst's autobiography, for example, is entitled *Unshackled: The Story of How We Won the Vote* (London: Hutchinson, 1959).
51   Marina Warner, *Joan of Arc* (London: Vintage Books, 1981), pp. 175–7.
52   Letter from Joan of Arc to Jan Hus, 3 March 1430, quoted in Warner, *Joan of Arc*, p. 178.
53   Cheryl Jorgenson-Earp, *'The Transfiguring Sword': The Just War of the Women's Social and Political Union* (Tuscaloosa, AL, and London: University of Alabama Press, 1997), pp. 96–8.
54   Christabel Pankhurst, 'Joan of Arc', in *The Suffragette*, 9 May 1913, p. 501.
55   Lisa Tickner, *The Spectacle of Women: Imagery of the Suffrage Campaign 1907-14* (London: Chatto & Windus, 1987), p. 290.
56   Christabel Pankhurst, *The Suffragette*, 11 April, 1913, quoted in Andrew Rosen, *Rise Up Women!: The Militant Campaign of the Women's Social and Political Union 1903–1914* (London: Routledge & Kegan Paul, 1974), p. 196.
57   Charles Kingsley, 'The Day of the Lord', in *The Works of Charles Kingsley*, Vol. 1. *Poems* (London: Macmillan, 1887), pp. 259–60.
58   Laurence Housman, 'Proper Lessons', in *Votes for Women*, 5 April 1912, p.429. Cited in Jorgensen-Earp, *'The Transfiguring Sword'*, pp. 118–19.
59   James Russell Lowell, 'The Present Crisis', December 1844, in *Poems I* (London: Macmillan, 1890), pp. 178–84. Verses 5 and 14 are used on the cover of *The Suffragette*, 21 March 1913.
60   See Rosen, *Rise Up Women!*, pp. 199–200.
61   *The Suffragette*, 13 June 1913, pp. 578–9.
62   *The Suffragette*, 11 April 1913.
63   See Rosen, *'Rise up, Women!'*, p. 207.
64   Bryan Cheyette's term 'semitic discourses' is useful here in conveying the ambivalence that the NVA literature, for example, displays. See Cheyette, *Constructions*, p. 8.
65   See Tickner, *Spectacle of Women*, p.37.
66   Christabel Pankhurst, *'The Lord Cometh': The World Crisis Explained* (London: Morgan & Scott, 1923), p. 91.

67   'A. H.', Review of W. L. George's *Woman and To-Morrow* (London: Herbert Jenkins, 1913), in *The Suffragette*, 15 November 1912, p. 7. Walter Lionel George (1882–1926) was born in Paris to Jewish parents. He trained as an analytical chemist, but was also a barrister, engineer, journalist and drama critic. He wrote short stories, essays and novels, and served in the French army during the First World War. He was a friend of the Anglo-Jewish writer G. B. Stern, whose work is discussed in Chapters 3 and 4.

68   Coote, *A Vision*, pp. 18, 17.

69   Christabel Pankhurst, *The Great War*, a speech given at Carnegie Hall, New York, 24 October 1914 (London: WSPU, 1914), pp. 8, 10.

70   Pankhurst, *The Great War*, pp. 15–16.

71   Jill Liddington and Jill Norris, *One Hand Tied Behind Us: The Rise of the Women's Suffrage Movement* (London: Virago, 1978), pp. 257–8.

72   Annie Kenney, *Memories of a Militant* (London: Edward Arnold, 1924), p. 255.

73   See Trevor Wilson, *The Myriad Faces of War: Britain and the Great War, 1914–1918* (Cambridge: Polity Press, 1986), pp. 706–7.

74   See, for example, Herbert Gray, *The War Spirit in our National Life*, Papers for War Time Series, No. 7 (London: Oxford University Press, 1914), in which the author expressed the hope that after the war, the 'unfeminine' behaviour of suffragette-militarists would cease (p. 15).

75   Elma K. Paget, *The Woman's Part*, Papers for War Time Series, No. 3 (London: Oxford University Press, 1914), p. 5.

76   Katherine Tynan, *The Holy War* (London: Sidgwick & Jackson, 1916).

77   Extract from Katherine Tynan, 'To the Others', in *The Holy War*, p. 11.

78   Extract from Katherine Tynan, 'New Heaven', dedicated to Sir William Haldane, in *The Holy War*, p. 14.

79   A. F. Winnington-Ingram, 'Women and the war', an address to 2,000 women at Church House, October 1914, in *A Day of God: Being Five Addresses on the Subject of the Present War* (London: Wells Gardner, Darton, 1914), p. 61.

80   See Alan Wilkinson, *The Church of England and the First World War* (London: SPCK,1978), p. 180.

81   Alice Meynell, 'Parentage', in *Collected Poems of Alice Meynell* (London: Burns & Oates, 1914), p. 86.

82   See David Lloyd George, *War Memoirs of David Lloyd George* (London: Ivor Nicholson & Watson, 1933, reprinted 1936), pp. 291, 292.

83   Joseph Leftwich, 'Song of the Women', in Leftwich, *Along the Years, Poems 1911–1937* (London: Robert Anscombe, 1937), p. 29. Joseph Leftwich was a journalist and writer who edited and translated anthologies of Yiddish poetry and was part of a group of East End Jewish writers and artists that included John Rodker, Isaac Rosenberg, David Bomberg, Mark Gertler, Simon Weinstein (later Stephen Winsten) and Paul Nash. He knew the gentile anarchist leader Rudolf Rocker, and wrote an introduction to Rocker's memoir, *The London Years* (London: Robert Anscombe, 1956).

84   Extract from Madeline Ida Bedford, 'Munition Wages', in *The Young Captain: Fragments of War and Love* (London: Erskine Macdonald, 1917), p. 7.

85   Extract from Mary Gabrielle Collins, 'Women at munition making', in *Branches Unto the Sea* (London: Erskine Macdonald, 1916), p. 24.

86   Lloyd George, *War Memoirs*, p. 318.

87   See E. R. Norman, *Church and Society in England 1770–1970: A Historical Study* (Oxford: Clarendon Press, 1976), pp. 160, 162, 165.

88   *The Times*, 29 August 1917, p. 8.

89   *Christian Challenge*, 7 September 1917, p. 296.

90   Archbishop Davidson, sermon reported in *The Times*, 17 September 1917, p. 5. Randall Thomas Davidson (1848–1930) was Archbishop of Canterbury from 1903 to 1928.

91   *Christian Challenge*, 14 September 1917, pp. 302–3.

92   *The Woolwich Crusade*, report issued by Southwark Diocesan Council (London: SPCK, 1918), discussed in *Challenge*, 31 May 1918, p. 67.

3

The First World War as 'Holy War'

By August 1914, the purity and suffrage campaigns were over-shadowed by another form of 'crusade', in the First World War, which was widely portrayed in Britain as a 'holy war' against 'pagan' Germany. Politicians, clergymen and the press made use of religious imagery to glorify the conflict, and the clergy in particular portrayed the soldier as defender of the faith, and encouraged civilians to join the 'crusade' through prayer. For some, however, the strongest link between the medieval crusades and the war was the Palestine campaign, and the capture of Jerusalem from the Turkish army by British forces in December 1917. This campaign was frequently referred to as the 'last crusade', and prompted the most explicit portrayals of the British soldier as an idealised medieval knight. Indeed, some of the soldiers who served in Palestine during the First World War made explicit connections between themselves and the medieval crusaders.

The use of the imagery of 'crusade' in the construction of ideals of 'Englishness' was already well established prior to the war. The code of chivalry and the image of the gentlemanly knight, which were revived in Britain during the late eighteenth century, became central to the construction of a romanticised upper-class masculinity that continued into the nineteenth century and was disseminated through public schools and institutions, art and literature.[1] In *The Return to Camelot* (1981), Mark Girouard traces the chivalric ideal in English culture throughout this period into the First World War, which, he suggests, provided both a climax and a 'natural termination' to Victorian and Edwardian notions of chivalry.[2] This chapter builds upon Girouard's analysis of the image of the 'knight' during the First World War, to include its significance with regard to the British campaign in Palestine, and the antisemitic subtext of the war as 'crusade' is explored. It demonstrates the ubiquity of the idea of 'holy war', and the popularity and the fragility of this concept, focusing on the xenophobia and religious hostility generated by the rhetoric of 'crusade' and its effects on Britain's Jewish population, both at home and at the Front.

'HUNS OF SATAN'[3]

Although there was a high level of popular support in Britain for the war, there was also unease, particularly in the Liberal press, at the outbreak of hostilities. Unlike their Tory counterparts, the Liberal papers were initially ambivalent with regard to Britain's involvement, and did not fully subscribe to Foreign Secretary Sir Edward Grey's view that participation in the conflict was in the nation's vital interest, as a means of maintaining the balance of power in Europe and protecting against German invasion. In *England's Holy War: A Study of English Liberal Idealism During the Great War* (1928), Irene Willis argued that much of the rhetoric of a 'just' war and a 'final battle' between 'good' and 'evil' was prompted by Liberal ambivalence, and that it was the conflict between abhorrence and acceptance that gave rise to the compensatory idea of 'holy war'.[4] The ambivalence Willis identified was evident in the national press. The *Daily News* and *Daily Chronicle* analysed responsibility for the war, and on 5 August 1914 the former published a full-page announcement by the Neutrality League, urging Englishmen to 'DO YOUR DUTY and Keep Your Country out of a WICKED AND STUPID WAR'.[5] *The Nation*, a popular liberal publication, reluctantly acknowledged that Britain was indeed bound to defend Belgian neutrality by the treaty made between France, Britain and Prussia in 1870, and began to justify British involvement on moral and religious grounds. The conflict now became a 'crusade' against war, and journalists used religious language for dramatic and emotive effect. In an article entitled 'The Holy War', G. Lowes Dickinson noted 'the dominance of the Power of Darkness' in Europe, and added 'the words of Jesus, spoken to redeem mankind from just such a desolating crime as this, are as if they had never been said'.[6] H. G. Wells published articles on the theme of 'The War to End War' in the *Daily News*, the *Daily Chronicle* and *The Nation*, in which he called for the moral regeneration of Germany rather than its destruction, and argued that if the Germans could be made to reject 'the idea of war', the rest of humanity would follow.[7] The present conflict, he suggested, was partly owing to the failure of the Church and the Christian must now become as ruthless 'as any evil doer' in the albeit rather paradoxical fight for peace.[8] It was, therefore, a Christian's duty to support the war.

The theme of Christian warfare also appeared in political speeches and pamphlets, in which Germany was charged with having renounced God for the worship of the state. In a speech delivered at London Guildhall in September 1914, Prime Minister Herbert Asquith announced that the Germans had 'made force their supreme divinity', and added 'This is not merely a material, it is also a spiritual conflict.'[9] No longer guided by Christian principles, he argued, Germany had become ruthlessly expansionist, as the invasion of Belgium showed. Britain, on the other hand, was portrayed as a benign imperial power, whose dominions might almost have volunteered for incorporation into the empire. In another speech, given at Cardiff in October 1914, Asquith, with no apparent irony, declared 'We do not covet any people's territory. We have no desire to impose our rule upon alien populations. The British Empire is enough for us.'[10] Asquith was careful, however, not to represent the 'spiritual conflict' as a solely British or Christian matter, and acknowledged the contribution of the Hindu and Muslim subjects of the empire to the war effort. David Lloyd George, then Chancellor of the Exchequer, was more explicit regarding the nature of the conflict, and in a speech entitled 'Honour and Dishonour', given in London on 19 September 1914, asserted that 'The new philosophy of Germany is to destroy Christianity.'[11]

A flurry of pamphlets, many of them written by Oxford academics, picked up the theme, arguing that since the invasion of 'little Belgium' Germany could no longer be regarded as Christian, and that Britain, therefore, was fighting a pagan power.[12] The more moderate pamphleteers suggested that there were, in effect, two Germanys; the nation that had produced Luther, Beethoven and Kant, and the Germany that had been temporarily seduced by Prussian militarism.[13] Most, however, focused on denouncing militarism as Germany's new 'creed', a 'gospel' of violence based on the ideas of the 'unholy trinity' of Nietzsche, Treitschke and Bernhardi, and a threat to Christianity.[14] Heinrich von Trietksche (1834–96) was an eminent German professor of political science. His book *Politik* (1899) argued that war was vital to the establishment and continuity of the State, and was often cited as the inspiration behind Germany's new 'paganism'. General Friedrich von Bernhardi's book *Deutschland und der nächste Krieg* (1911), which was based on Treitksche's writings, was regarded by some as a statement of German imperial policy. With hindsight, it was easy for those who wished to, to portray the writings of these three men as a threat to Christendom, and, in effect, a warning unheeded. A typical example, entitled *Nietzsche and Trietschke: The Worship of Power in Modern Germany*, was written by Ernest Barker, a member of the Faculty of Modern History at Oxford University. Barker traced the development of the new German 'paganism' through reductive accounts of Kant's ideas on the importance of duty; Hegel's views on the state as an absolute, and Nietzsche's attacks on Christianity, and concluded that this combination had produced the nationalistic heroism that had now gained the status of a religion in Germany.[15]

German theologians defended their country, and in September 1914 the *Westminster Gazette* published a document entitled *Address of the German Theologians to the Evangelical Christians Abroad*, which until then had been circulating mainly in the United States.[16] Bearing the signatures of a number of prominent German academics, this document expressed regret at the prospect of 'fratricidal war', and blamed Russia for the conflict, claiming that while Germany had striven for peace, the tsar had effectively declared war against 'Teutonism and Protestantism'.[17] The British were admonished for their alliance with 'heathen Japan', and the address ended with a reminder that by involving their dominions in the conflict, the British were endangering the international missionary enterprise, and that 'a war of white against white' would undermine the Christian message.[18] Twenty-five Oxford scholars put their names to a rejoinder that acknowledged the contributors to the German Address, but refuted their claim that Germany was not responsible for the war. In response to their criticism of Britain's alliance with non-Christian Japan, the Oxford group argued that Germany was no better, since as they put it, 'Turkey is religiously just as much of an Asiatic Power as Japan'.[19] Finally, the Oxford response suggested that the clamour of nationalism and militarism in Germany had rendered the Christian message of peace and brotherhood inaudible, and implied that this was not the case in Britain.

This was, of course, untrue. A belligerent Christian nationalism had developed in Britain since the outbreak of the war – to which clergymen, academics and politicians alike contributed – which was couched in the language of righteous warfare. Although the terms 'crusade' and 'holy war' were most frequently used by the Anglican clergy, the representation of the war as a cataclysmic struggle between 'good' and 'evil' was common to both religious and secular commentators. Ironically, prior to the war, attempts had been made to strengthen religious links between Britain and Germany, through an organisation with the rather lengthy title of 'The Associated Councils of Churches in the British and German Empires for Fostering Friendly Relations Between the Two Peoples', which was formed in 1911.[20] After August 1914, however, ecumenism gave way to Christian nationalism and the rhetoric of 'holy war' against a 'pagan' enemy, which, it was asserted, threatened the very existence of Christendom, and must, therefore, be fought without mercy.

The most outspoken proponent of this view was Arthur Foley Winnington-Ingram (1858–1946), Bishop of London 1901–39. Winnington-Ingram had previous experience of 'holy war', having been involved in the purity campaigns as chairman of the Public Morality Council since 1901. He now applied his evangelical and rhetorical skills to the 'crusade' against the Germans, describing them as a people in the grip of pagan and unchristian ideas.[21] Other clergymen who adopted a strongly militaristic tone during the war were Handley Carr Glyn Moule, Bishop of Durham 1901–20; Basil Wilberforce, Archdeacon of Westminster, Basil Bourchier, Vicar of St Jude's, Hampstead and senior chaplain to the armed forces, and Bishop Taylor-Smith, Chaplain-General to the Armed Forces, 1901–25. As Bishop of London, however, Winnington-Ingram was a prominent figure, and his jingoistic sermon style drew criticism from Prime Minister Asquith as well as from members of the higher clergy. Some clergymen, dismayed at the prospect of a war between Christian nations, blamed the conflict on capitalism, or imperialist arrogance, and warned against jingoism. In a sermon preached at Westminster Abbey on 2 August 1914, the Archbishop of Canterbury, Randall Thomas Davidson, advocated diplomacy, and advised his congregation that the 'resolute and unshakeable disbelief' in the necessity of war was gaining ground.[22] Despite initial reservations, however, most of the higher Anglican clergy adopted the popular view of the war as a battle between the forces of 'good' and 'evil'. By 1915, Archbishop Davidson had exchanged pacifism for righteous belligerence, stating in a sermon at St Paul's Cathedral that the British were fighting for 'a cause which we can, with clear conscience, commend to God', that of 'resistance to the ruthless dominance of force, and force alone'.[23] The Bishop of London was more explicit. In June 1915 he gave fellow clergymen his view of the role of the Church in wartime:

> I think the Church can best help the nation first of all by making it realise that it is engaged in a Holy War, and not be afraid of saying so. Christ died on Good Friday for Freedom, Honour, and Chivalry, and our boys are dying for the same things... You ask for my advice in a sentence as to what the Church is to do. I answer MOBILIZE THE NATION FOR A HOLY WAR.[24]

This statement was published in the *Church Guardian*, and provoked a certain amount of controversy. As one correspondent reminded the Bishop,

> No one was more certain than St Bernard that the last Crusade was a Holy War and was fought against the devil and for God, and when it ended in utter failure the falsification of his predictions did infinite harm to the Church and religion.[25]

Nor could the idea of Britain as a devoutly Christian country withstand much scrutiny. As one commentator observed, 'The English people will always shrink from blasphemy and try to keep respectable, but it cannot be said that there is a Christian England in the sense that there is a Christian Russia, or a Christian Ireland.'[26] Nevertheless, Winnington-Ingram continued to preach the doctrine of 'holy war' throughout the conflict, and in December 1915 informed the congregation at Westminster Abbey that they were

> banded in a great crusade – we cannot deny it – to kill Germans: to kill them, not for the sake of killing, but to save the world... and to kill them lest the civilisation of the world should itself be destroyed.[27]

The Reverend Basil Bourchier, of St Jude's, Hampstead, held similar views, informing soldiers that 'Not only is this a holy war, it is the holiest war that ever has been waged', and one in which 'Odin is ranged against Christ, and Berlin is seeking to prove its supremacy over Bethlehem'. To die for England, he told them, was 'to taste the sweetest vintage of death that can be offered to English lips...and to pass to that which is to come in a veritable ecstasy'.[28]

Such rhetoric may have inspired some, but it drew criticism from others, on the grounds that the clergy were preaching a crusade in which, being exempt from enlistment, they were not prepared to participate. One writer, under the pseudonym 'Junius Redivivus', published a parody of John Bunyan's *The Holy War* (1682), in which he attacked clerical exemption and urged priests to 'Take up the Cross presented to them', while ordinands were exhorted to 'Unfrock – Enlist'.[29] The 1918 Conscription Bill raised the enlistment age to 50, and made the clergy eligible, but this part of the Bill was retracted a few days later, owing to concerns about the political effects of conscripting the Catholic clergy in Ireland, particularly after the Sinn Fein revolt of 1916.[30] Most of the eligible clergy in England were already involved in war-related work by this time, whether as army chaplains, or in the war industries.

The authority of the Church declined throughout the war. Clerical exemption from enlistment – despite the fact that many clergymen lost sons, and army chaplains ran similar risks to the enlisted men – along with the rhetorical excesses described, may have contributed to this. Winnington-Ingram's assertion that 'Moses holding up his hand above the battle swayed it as well as Joshua fighting in the thick of it'[31] lacked persuasion. The Church continued to face criticism, not only over the conscription issue, but also through its perceived inadequacy in addressing the spiritual needs of the nation. Prior to the war, Church leaders were aware that congregations were dwindling, and that Christianity was failing to attract the working classes in significant numbers. When war broke out, some regarded it as an opportunity to re-establish Christianity at the centre of national life, with the Church providing spiritual guidance for the nation, and thereby securing its place in post-war reconstruction. At the start of the conflict, the churches were suddenly and briefly full, and there was talk of a religious revival, but this was short-lived.[32] Yet in some respects the Church remained a powerful force in Britain during the war. Politicians approached Archbishop Davidson, seeking his support for various proposals. In November 1915 Lord Derby requested that the pulpit be used to promote recruitment, which Davidson refused, but in

1917, in response to the threat of a food shortage, he gave Bonar Law, then Chancellor of the Exchequer, his approval for agricultural work to be undertaken on Sundays.[33]

Despite wielding a certain amount of power, in some respects the Church appeared inadequate, preaching a doctrine of ever-lasting life for which it could produce no evidence. Spiritualism, which became popular during the war, claimed to be able to provide this, and while the Anglican Church declined in influence, the spiritualist movement grew. This occurred in spite of adverse publicity from several cases of the prosecution of fraudulent mediums under the archaic Witchcraft and Vagrancy Acts.[34] The growth of spiritualism both during and after the war was assisted by the conversion of a number of prominent people. In 1916 the eminent physicist Sir Oliver Lodge published *Raymond*, in which he claimed to have received messages, through a medium, from his son who had been killed in action.[35] In 1917 the writer Arthur Conan Doyle joined the spiritualist movement and in March 1918 published *New Revelation*, in which he professed his belief in life after death.[36] Spiritualism came under regular attack from both the press and the clergy, but nevertheless remained popular, and by 1919, 309 spiritualist societies were affiliated to the Spiritualists' National Union, compared with 145 in 1914.[37]

Another problem for the Church was that many regarded the militarism of clergymen like Winnington-Ingram and Basil Bourchier as incompatible with the principles of brotherly love and forgiveness associated with the teachings of Jesus. But while Winnington-Ingram's rhetoric of Christian patriotism may have damaged the spiritual authority of the Church, it was apparently effective in recruiting for the army. Initially, at least, some soldiers clearly identified with the notion of self-sacrifice in the name of Christianity, and in the early months of the war, an entire brigade of the London Territorial Rifles reputedly volunteered for the Front after hearing one of his sermons.[38] Harry Sackville Lawson, previously headmaster of Buxton College and serving as a lieutenant in the Royal Field Artillery, regarded the war as the latest in a long line of righteous conflicts, and wrote to his former pupils from the Front, saying

> I've got one thing in particular to say to you all...It's a Christian thing, and it's a British thing. It's what the Bible teaches – it's what the Christian martyrs suffered in

persecution for ... It's the story of the Crusaders, of the
Reformation, of the downfall of the power of Spain, of our
colonization, of the destruction of Napoleon's might, of the
abolition of slavery, and of the coming awakening of
Germany. The thing is this: Playing the game for the game's
sake.[39]

This statement exemplifies the upper-class chivalric tradition that
Mark Girouard has discussed in detail and which was largely
disseminated through institutions such as that at which Lawson
had taught. The idea of 'playing the game' – originally related to the
public school view of the moral value of sport – became transferred
onto the war, and young upper-class men who had been imbued,
through education and juvenile fiction, with the 'knightly' values of
honour, devotion to duty and protection of the weak, responded to
the call to fight. Patriotic and Christian notions of chivalry had also
been relayed to the working classes through the boys' clubs
established by the churches and charities in poorer districts, and
recruits from all classes were encouraged, by the clergy in
particular, to regard themselves as participating in a moral and
spiritual conflict. As Mark Girouard notes, however, upper-class
soldiers were more likely to be portrayed as 'knightly'.[40] But this
was not a war fought solely by noblemen, and 'chivalry' was at
odds both with modern warfare and, with its feudal echoes, a
society that was progressing towards mass democratisation. In
addition, 'crusade' was an inappropriate metaphor for the war
itself; the idea of the soldier as 'knight' relying upon comparisons
with the cavalry, which were hardly used during a war that was
largely fought from trenches. Yet the imagery of 'crusade' took
hold, and was also found in popular songs generated by the war. A
selection of these, entitled *Songs of the Last Crusade*, was published
in 1917.[41] The titular song, dated January 1915, is attributed to the
Australian Army Medical Corps (AAMC), and portrays the army
doctor as a 'knight', whose insignia is the red cross. The song ends
with the line 'God bless the Last Crusade!'[42] An appeal for funds on
behalf of the St John Ambulance Association also drew an analogy
between the medical auxiliary and the medieval crusader, in an
advertisement that appeared in *Punch* in October 1914.[43] This shows
a male medic and a female nurse attending to a wounded soldier,
and being watched by a shadowy knight who holds his sword over
them to make the sign of the cross. The significance of the ghostly

crusader is complex: he evokes the Christian 'martyrs' of a much earlier 'holy war', and in holding the cross over the scene, seems to be both a priestly figure and a conduit for divine protection. He also represents the longevity of the St John Ambulance Association, and the text reminds readers that the group's name derives from the Knights Hospitallers, the Order of St John in Jerusalem, which was founded during the crusades.

Despite criticism from some quarters, the idea of the war as a battle for the future of Christendom took hold, particularly among the civilian population. But this did not necessarily amount to a religious revival. One need not have been a regular churchgoer to respond to the idea that the British were united in a morally justified struggle against Prussian expansionism. Not only was the Christian rhetoric dramatic and emotive, it also suggested Britain's moral superiority in the conflict and offered a basis for the expression of a sense of national unity in a time of crisis. In pamphlets, sermons and the popular press, Germany was depicted as having renounced Christianity, and 'evidence' was produced in support of this. In September 1914 *Punch* reprinted a cartoon that had originally appeared in October 1898, in response to the Kaiser's visit to Damascus during that year. In 1898, Britain and Germany were negotiating a possible alliance, aimed at relieving tensions between the two countries caused by the building up of German naval power. The Kaiser's Damascus speech, in which he had pledged German support for the Muslim nations, aroused suspicion over his sincerity in the discussions with Britain, particularly as Germany had economic interests in the Near East, in the construction of the Berlin–Baghdad railway. The cartoon portrays the Kaiser as a false crusader, in the guise of a Christian, but actually seeking an alliance with Turkey. By 1914 Germany and Turkey were allies, and the cartoon was reprinted in 1914 and presented as 'prophetic'.[44]

In the context of a 'holy war', in which divine sanction was being invoked even as huge numbers of people were dying, it is not surprising that there was a strong desire for 'proof' of the existence of an interventionist God. This is apparent in the stories of 'miracles' that emerged in relation to the war, of which the account of 'the Angels at Mons' is an example. The origin of the story was a piece of fictional writing by Arthur Machen entitled 'The Bowmen', published in the London *Evening News* on 29 September 1914. The story tells of the ghostly appearance of the English archers of the

Battle of Agincourt, who provided covering fire for the British forces retreating from Mons. This fantasy of divine intervention on behalf of the Allies, demonstrated by the 'resurrection' of the dead from an earlier war, took hold. Postcards were produced depicting the scene, the Nonconformist minister Dr R. F. Horton referred to the tale as 'truth' in a sermon of 1915, and Bishop Moule of Durham expressed his belief in the story. The government exploited the story's propaganda potential, and gave the Reverend A. A. Boddy permission to publish *The Real Angels of Mons* (1915), a collection of purportedly 'eyewitness accounts' of the event.[45] Such stories, combined with pseudo-academic discussions of German history and philosophy and the denunciation of Germany as 'godless' by both clergy and politicians, served to justify Britain's involvement in the war and to glorify its purpose. The idea of a 'holy war' rendered Christianity and warfare compatible, and allowed British participation in the conflict to be portrayed as a matter of chivalry, piety, and service to God, rather than the result of imperial rivalry. It also, perhaps, partly served to assuage civilian guilt at the scale of the slaughter. Most soldiers, however, quickly became disillusioned by their experience of war, and the rhetoric of 'crusade' found in Lawson's letter and in the AAMC song became less common. Modern warfare was far from glorious, chivalrous, or 'playing the game'. As an officer at the Somme in 1916 put it: 'I shall never look on warfare either as fine or sporting again. It reduces men to shivering beasts.'[46] Many lost their faith as a result of their experiences. One officer wrote to his wife concerning the religious education of their 3-year-old son, saying

> Don't encourage Vallie to talk about God...tell him all the fairy tales or nonsense stories you please but about God and religious subjects only tell him what you yourself unfeignedly believe to be true: if nothing, tell him nothing.[47]

While the 'crusade' trope was mobilised in an effort to promote Christian unity and a sense of collective mission during wartime, ironically the experience of modern 'holy war' resulted, for some, in a loss of religious faith and disillusionment with the chivalric ideal. The image of the soldier as a Christian 'knight' continued to circulate in civilian discourse, and the notion of 'Christian warfare' contributed to the collective hostility and xenophobia that was generated by the conditions of war. The widespread representation of the conflict as a defence of Christianity against the 'pagan' forces of Germany provoked what might be termed a 'Christian anti-Germanism', which in some cases found a target in Britain's Jewish population.

'YOU CAN'T MAKE A FELLOW GERMAN BY SAYING HE IS'

The construction and promotion of an embattled Christian national identity during the war inevitably aroused hostility towards both foreign nationals and non-Christians, and Jews in Britain became subject to suspicion. The non-Christian status ascribed to Germany and the fact that many Jews had German-sounding names meant that some of the anti-German feeling generated by the war became directed towards them. An article published in *The Times*, shortly after the sinking of the *Lusitania* in 1915, referred to 'the unbridled joy of Hamburg, and of the Jewish financial Press generally' at the news.[48] The *Jewish Chronicle* criticised the article, expressing concern over the popular conflation of 'Jew' and 'German', and asked whether 'people should be taught, day by day, to identify Jew with German'.[49] The *Chronicle* published the names of Jews who had died in the sinking, as well as those who had survived.[50] Some Jews anglicised their names during the war, to distract attention from their German connections, and even George V felt compelled to change the royal name from Saxe-Coburg Gotha to Windsor in 1917. Because of their real or perceived German connections, Jews could be portrayed as disloyal to Britain, and cast as potential traitors or pacifists. Any grounds for such accusations, usually slim, became greatly exaggerated as a result of the Christian nationalism engendered by the conflict. In June 1914, for example, the Jewish Peace Society had met at the Jews' College in London to discuss the prospect of a European conflict. A short report on the meeting was published in *The Times*. At the time, members of the Jewish Peace Society considered pacifism to be consistent with their religious duty and an important part of Jewry's participation in British current affairs. Rabbi Dr Hertz, who had presided over the meeting, admitted that Jewish financial interests in Britain and Germany were also a consideration, but aside from this, he argued that Jews should 'have a corporate profession of their protest against war ... as other religions had'.[51] The existence of this group and its acknowledgement of international financial links between Jews helped fuel later suspicions regarding Jews' loyalty to Britain.

Another fear associated with Jews in Britain was that they acted as spies for Germany.[52] In 1914 Isaac Rosenberg and David Bomberg were arrested on suspicion of espionage while on holiday at Sandown on the Isle of Wight. The two men were students at the Slade School of Art and had been sketching fortifications near their lodgings. They were not released until their landlady verified their identities.[53] Under rather more suspicious circumstances, Princess Lowenstein-Wertheim, a naturalised German by marriage, was arrested in 1917 under the 'Five Mile Act' for exceeding this distance from her registered address without a permit. Prior to her wedding in 1897 she had been known as Lady Anne Savile, daughter of the Earl of Mexborough. Her husband had died in 1899. She had gone to Manchester to enquire about the progress of an aeroplane she was having built, which she wanted finished as soon as possible. The urgency of the matter and the fact that she refused to give a name or address aroused suspicion, but despite this, a combination of class factors and her English parentage secured her release with a fine.[54]

Others with German connections, real or perceived, were not so lucky. In 1915 – a year which brought zeppelin raids; the use of poison gas by the German army; the Bryce report on alleged German atrocities, the sinking of the *Lusitania*, and the execution of nurse Edith Cavell – anti-German riots took place in Leeds and London, and the shops and homes of Jews were attacked. Such incidents found their way into fiction: the Anglo-Jewish writer Gladys Bronwyn Stern's novel *Children of No Man's Land* (1919) explores the complexities of national, religious, and ethnic identification for Jews living in Britain during the war, and describes the effects of anti-Germanism on the Anglo-Jewish community.[55] Gladys Bronwyn Stern (1890–1973) was born in London to a middle-class Jewish family. She had no strict religious upbringing and considered her orthodox cousin 'a strange animal indeed',[56] but she was familiar with the work of Anglo-Jewish novelists, and read Grace Aguilar's books as a child.[57] Stern knew the Anglo-Jewish writer W. L. George, but as she noted in her memoir, almost all of her friends were gentiles.[58] Stern wrote a number of novels, the most well known being the series on the Rakonitz family, which included *Tents of Israel* (1924, reissued as *The Matriarch* in 1948), *A Deputy was King* (1926), *Mosaic* (1930), *Shining and Free* (1935) and *The Young Matriarch* (1942). Her early novels engage with the question of assimilation, particularly with regard to Jewish women, and *Pantomime. A Novel* (1914) and *Twos and Threes* (1916) are discussed in Chapter 4.

Stern seems to have been ambivalent with regard to becoming a writer of 'Jewish' fiction, and attempted to balance the particular and the universal in her work. Her early novels at times draw on the Victorian 'apologist' tradition of Anglo-Jewish literature – her characters are preoccupied with transcending a seemingly problematic 'Jewishness' in order to assimilate – but she also engages with the persistence of 'racial' and gender stereotypes in liberal culture.[59] *Children of No Man's Land* (1919) describes the war experience of the Marcuses, an Anglo-Jewish family of German descent, and seems to have been aimed at a general rather than a specifically Jewish readership. Ferdinand Marcus was born in England to German-Jewish parents and has his certificate of naturalisation. At Christmas 1914 he is forced to resign from his job at the Stock Exchange, accused of spying and treason, and the family move to a boarding house for the duration of the war. His son Richard wants to enlist, but is too young. Walking through the East End in 1915, shortly after the sinking of the *Lusitania*, Richard becomes involved in an anti-German riot, in which a baker's shop, with the name 'Gottlieb Schnabel' painted on the window, is attacked. To Richard, the riot represents an opportunity for vicarious involvement in the war: 'this was action; this was war; he was in direct contact with it at last' (p.73), and he pushes to the front of the mob as they enter the building. He finds the Schnabel family cowering in the bakehouse, and, seeing with a shock that they do not resemble the caricature of 'the Hun', he diverts the crowd away. Arriving home, he announces his determination to enlist, only to be informed by his father that he has not been naturalised, and is therefore regarded as German. Moreover, since he is nearing military age, he is likely to be interned. Richard protests that 'You can't make a fellow German by saying he is', but it is no use (p.79).

From the soldier's perspective, no man's land was a dangerous territory, a place where the wounded became stranded and alienated from their group, caught in the space between the lines of national demarcation on the battlefield. In Stern's novel this territory becomes a metaphor for the experience of Jews in wartime Britain, who inhabit a space between opposing national identities, and are perceived as a threat in a war that was widely portrayed as waged in defence of Christianity. The Marcuses and other Jewish families live a nomadic existence during the war, moving between boarding houses, 'the half-and-half-people' who regard themselves as English but are perceived as German (p. 85). At the end of the novel Richard, having endured hostility from people who were formerly his friends, prepares for internment, a fate that he accepts as inevitable, if unfair. In *Children of No Man's Land*, Stern attempted to portray the complex views and identifications of Jews living in Britain during the war, and the diversity of opinion among British Jews with regard to issues such as religion, politics, Jewish nationalism and feminism. Her characters debate these, and frequently disagree with one another, yet one thing they have in common is that they all suffer as a result of prejudice, and their participation in the wider society is constrained by gentile perceptions of the nature of Jewish identity. Some of the novel's minor characters become active in Jewish nationalism, but ultimately her main characters' strongest identification is with Britain. The Marcuses regard themselves as British, and consider Britain their home. The narrative asserts the existence and validity of a British-Jewish identity, based on Jewish cultural practices and British nationality, an identity that becomes fragile in a climate of belligerent nationalism such as that engendered by war. *Children of No Man's Land* makes explicit the fact that this situation became worse during the First World War, in which anti-alien feeling, backed up by punitive legislation, increased.

Anti-alienism was already prevalent before the war, and David Cesarani has argued that representations of the 'alien' in the press and popular discourse covered all immigrant groups, not just Jews. Yet, as he points out, there were 'significant inflections in particular cases'.[60] Anti-German feeling found expression in the spy novels of the Edwardian period, which portrayed expatriate Germans as secretly engaged in spying for their country of origin, while anti-Jewish sentiment fed on the mass migration of Jews from eastern Europe. In direct response to public opinion, fanned by the press, anti-alien legislation in Britain was increased. In 1904 the Conservative government introduced a bill that would enable immigration officials to refuse entry to anyone considered 'undesirable'. Despite Liberal opposition, the Bill passed into law as the 1905 Aliens Act.[61] Anti-alien law was strengthened further under the conditions of war. On 5 August 1914 the Aliens Restriction Act was presented to Parliament, and quickly became law. Germans and Austrians of military age were arrested and detained, and women, children and men who were not of military age were repatriated. The number of internees rose throughout the war, reaching up to 30,000.[62] Internees were housed in a variety of places, including former factories and workhouses, and, up to late 1915, enemy aliens were kept on liners anchored off the south coast. Large numbers of internees were held at a former holiday camp at Douglas, on the Isle of Man, where accommodation was divided into the privilege camp the Jewish camp, and the ordinary camp. Another camp was set up on a nearby farm. Conditions were generally adequate, and where they were not, internees complained, but the isolation and uncertainty of their position caused suffering to many.[63] In 1918 the Aliens Act was amended, to allow the removal of citizenship and the deportation of naturalised Germans, and was further amended in 1919, to increase restrictions against all aliens, not just Jews and Germans. Under the new legislation, former enemy aliens who had been naturalised could be deported and refused entry for five years. By 1920 aliens resident in Britain had to register with the police, who had the power to detain individuals without a warrant.[64]

There were some attempts to stem the tide of anti-alienism that swept through Britain during the war, but most of these were ineffectual and failed to address the experience of Jews, whether British- or foreign-born. In a pamphlet entitled *Christian Conduct in War Time*, W. H. Moberly reminded readers of the Christian duty to love one's enemies, stating that 'for private individuals to treat all Germans as pariahs and to boycott them socially is... cruel as well as unnecessary'. Such attitudes were not 'Christi an', and to regard the Germans as 'unclean' was to share the snobbish and segregationist views held by 'Jews ... of Gentiles, aristocrats of the multitude, white men of coloured men'.[65] As the war progressed, however, the idea of the 'Unseen Hand' – the notion that German influences were undermining the war effort from within Britain – gathered strength. In March 1917 the Women's Imperial Defence Council passed a resolution demanding a Royal Commission to investigate 'that treacherous influence in our midst known as the Unseen Hand'.[66] The meeting was presided over by Mrs Parker, sister of the late Lord Kitchener, and addressed by, among others, the antisemitic alarmists Arnold White and Henry Beamish.[67] But while the 'Unseen Hand' prompted alarm in some quarters, it caused amusement in others. In July 1916 a contributor to *Punch* wrote 'I LIKE the *Unseen Hand*. It makes excellent copy ... And you are not under the disagreeable necessity of proving your facts.'[68] The writer attributed the origins and popularity of the idea to the press, particularly the *Daily News* and the *Daily Mail*, and satirised the hysteria over 'enemy aliens' as follows:

> Who is it that protects Government officials possessing wives with German uncles? The Unseen Hand ... Who lets the alien enemy in our midst go uninterned? Why, an Unseen Hand slams the prison gates in their very faces.[69]

The notion of the 'Unseen Hand' informed suspicion of Jewish soldiers at the Front, and even Jewish chaplains came under scrutiny. Michael Adler, senior Jewish chaplain to the armed forces, was almost arrested as a German spy by an officer who did not recognise his *Magen David* badge, which was worn by Jewish chaplains and members of the Jewish Legion, as the Jewish brigades of the Royal Fusiliers were known. Whenever possible Adler organised services for Jewish soldiers, and often held them in cinemas, which he referred to as 'cinema-gogues'.[70] To assist him in his arrangements he was given access to the battle plans, which he copied down in Hebrew. This aroused the interest of Staff officers, who, as Adler put it, 'joked' that the information might fall into enemy hands.[71] Anxious to portray an atmosphere of 'racial' and religious harmony at the Front, Adler described incidents in which Jewish soldiers would attempt to undermine enemy morale by shouting insults in Yiddish, which the Germans could understand.[72] For this, he suggests, they earned the praise and admiration of their fellow-combatants. Private Frank Richards of the Royal Welch Fusiliers gave a different view, and describes the soldiers' hostility towards a German-speaking platoon officer, who would get drunk and roam about no man's land, shouting abuse at the enemy. The men suspected him of giving away secrets, and a sergeant was detailed to watch him.[73]

Adler's account of his experiences suggests that there was mutual respect among Jewish and gentile soldiers, and that the war provided an opportunity for Jews to educate Christians about the tenets of Judaism. The letters of Isaac Rosenberg, who enlisted as a private in 1915, reveal a different experience.[74] Rosenberg (1890–1918) was born in Bristol to Lithuanian-Jewish parents. His father had fled Russia to escape conscription into the tsarist army. In 1897 the family moved to the East End of London, and Isaac attended Baker Street School, a State school that sought to anglicise the children of Jewish immigrants and to provide a secular alternative to the Jews' Free Schools. Rosenberg was a talented poet and painter and was supported by, among others, Edward Marsh, patron of the arts and private secretary to Churchill during the Dardanelles campaign. He also received support from the Anglo-Jewish community, and in 1911 entered the Slade School of Art, his fees paid by Mrs Herbert Cohen, Mrs E. D. Lowy, and Lily Delissa Joseph. During his studies he met a number of other Jewish artists and writers, including David Bomberg, Mark Gertler, Simon Weinstein (later Stephen Winsten), Joseph Leftwich, John Rodker and Lazarus Aaronson. Rosenberg enlisted in October 1915, partly to alleviate his family's poverty, since the families of soldiers received a small payment from the government. At the Front, he encountered antisemitism from both the ranks and officers,[75] and wrote the poem 'The Jew':

> Moses, from whose loins I sprung,
> Lit by a lamp in his blood
> Ten immutable rules, a moon
> For mutable lampless men.
> The blonde, the bronze, the ruddy,
> With the same heaving blood,
> Keep tide to the moon of Moses.
> Then why do they sneer at me?[76]

The reference to the Ten Commandments in this poem reminds Christians that they, too, 'Keep tide to the moon of Moses', yet as the final line makes clear, Christian respect for Moses the lawgiver did not extend to the Jews of the modern period. The hostility he encountered, combined with the effects of trench conditions upon his health, prompted Rosenberg to seek alternatives to active service. In 1916 he expressed an interest in joining the camouflage corps led by the Jewish artist Solomon J. Solomon, and a year later was considering a return to civilian life, working as a draughtsman, or in munitions.[77] In early 1918 Rosenberg applied for a transfer to the recently formed Jewish Legion and told Edward Marsh, one of his patrons, that he wanted to write a battle song for the Jewish troops.[78] His application for transfer was never answered, and he was killed on 1 April 1918.

Jewish officers also encountered hostility at the Front, as the case of Gilbert Frankau demonstrates. Born in London to Jewish parents,

Gilbert Frankau (1884–1952) was the eldest son of Julia Davis and Arthur Frankau. His grandfather Joseph Frankau had emigrated to Britain from Bavaria in 1837, and set up a cigar import business in London. His mother Julia used the pen name 'Frank Danby', and was the author of the novel *Dr Phillips: A Maida Vale Idyll* (1887), a sharply critical satire of the preoccupations and aspirations of London's middle-class Jews. The Frankaus discouraged all of their five children from identifying with Judaism, and at the age of 13 Gilbert was baptised into the Anglican Church in 1897. Educated at Eton, he was expected to go to Oxford, but joined the family cigar business instead. Gilbert Frankau enlisted at the start of the war, serving with the Royal Field Artillery, the 9th East Surrey Regiment and the Royal Field Artillery, but resigned his commission in 1917, suffering from war neurosis.

Prior to the war Frankau had published some fiction and poetry, and he continued to write while at the Front, both for civilian readers and for the trench journals, to which he was a regular contributor. These journals, the *Wipers Times*, the *B.E.F. Times* and the *New Church Times*, were unofficial satirical publications, and Frankau's jingoistic poetry, which was strongly influenced by Kipling, was at odds with their style. Nevertheless, almost every issue included one of Frankau's poems. Eventually the editor of the *Wipers Times* received complaints that the journal was dominated by poetry, and Frankau came under attack. A feature entitled 'Aunt Annie's Corner' included a poem that seems to allude to Frankau, suggesting that he was less than a full participant in the war:

> There was a little man,
> He had a little gun,
> He shoots it when he can,
> But has never hit a Hun.[79]

While there is no direct reference to Frankau in this poem or the surrounding material, its author's use of verse to criticise its subject, and the complaints regarding the prominence given to Frankau's poems in the journal, do suggest him as a possible target. This view is supported by subsequent, direct references to Frankau in the trench journals. In August 1916, Frankau had a breakdown, precipitated by his experience at the Somme, and was transferred to Italy on propaganda work. Following this, the *B.E.F. Times* published a poem that referred to Frankau directly as 'valiant with his motto "Write is Might"' and suggested that his literary ambitions had detracted from his military performance. Not only did the play on Germany's perceived motto of 'Might is Right' insinuate a German connection, based on Frankau's name and his alleged lack of commitment to the war effort, but the final line of the poem suggested that he was both a bad soldier and a bad poet, in the assertion that

FRANKAU WOULD NEED A KEATS IF HE WERE SHOOTING!![80]

The tension between Frankau and his fellow soldiers, which seems apparent from the trench journals, may have been partly owing to his continuing pursuit of literary success whilst serving his commission. During his time at the Front, he published two collections of war verse, entitled *The Guns* (1915)[81] and *The City of Fear* (1917), which were well received by civilian readers.[82] This, in combination with his German name, seems to have prompted suspicions that he was not fully committed to the war, an accusation that was made against other soldiers with real or perceived German connections.

Despite the fact that British Jews and gentiles fought and died alongside one another in the First World War, Jewish civilians faced ostracism and attack, and Jewish soldiers encountered hostility from their fellow-combatants. Sometimes this was based on soldiers' envy of the extra leave that Jews were occasionally granted for religious holidays. George Coppard, an infantryman in the Queen's Royal West Surrey regiment and later a gunner in the Machine Gun Corps, recalls a Jewish man named Levinsky, who joined his company and after a month's service, was given a week's leave for Passover.[83] Resentment and suspicion were also generated by the exemption of Russian Jewish immigrants from the 1916 Conscription Act. The Anglo-Jewish Home Secretary Herbert Samuel had allowed the principle of voluntarism to remain open to them, in recognition of their status as refugees from tsarist Russia, and in acknowledgement of their understandable reluctance to fight on the same side as the regime that had oppressed them. After the abdication of Tsar Nicholas II in March 1917, however, politicians and newspapers in the East End launched a 'conscription or deportation' campaign, which spread to the national press, and in July 1917 the Conscription Act was extended to include Russian

Jews.[84] Some of these men served with the Jewish Legion in Palestine, and their experiences are discussed in Chapter 5. The Balfour Declaration, issued in November 1917, pledged British support for a Jewish homeland in Palestine, and the deployment of Jewish battalions in Palestine prompted sections of the press to draw comparisons with the Exodus story. This aspect of the Palestine campaign was obscured, however, by its more widespread representation as the last Christian crusade.

THE 'LAST CRUSADE'

Palestinian Jews also suffered as a result of the outbreak of war. Alexander Aaronsohn was born in the Jewish settlement of Zicron-Jacob. In his memoir *With the Turks in Palestine* (1917), Aaronsohn notes that as citizens of the Turkish empire, both Jews and Christians were called up under the Young Turk Constitution of 1909.[85] Initially, there was broad support among Palestinian Jews for the Turkish side, since they were aware that historically, Turkey had sheltered Jews fleeing the Spanish Inquisition.[86] Following the alliance with Germany, however, Aaronsohn wrote that Jewish and Christian conscripts were discriminated against, and made to serve in labour battalions under Arab supervision, which, he suggested, had the effect of arousing their support for the Allies.[87] Eventually Alexander, along with his older brother Aaron[88] and his sister Sarah, became spies for the British in Palestine, and the information they supplied was used in planning the British invasion led by General Allenby in 1917.

The British plans to invade Palestine meant that, for those inclined to draw historical parallels, the idea of the war as a 'crusade' took on a more literal meaning. As in the medieval period, Palestine was occupied by a Muslim power and a 'Christian' army proposed to recapture it from Turkey and return Jerusalem to Christian control. The notion of historical repetition, the idea that 'Christian' soldiers of the twentieth century were retracing the steps of the medieval crusaders, appealed to many, including King George V, who referred to the Palestine campaign as the 'final crusade'.[89] Nor was this view confined to civilians: Donald Maxwell, who was sent to Palestine by the Admiralty for the Imperial War Museum during the war, described his realisation when writing his diary of that period, that he was 'unconsciously piecing together a story, the story of the Last Crusade'.[90] His memoir, entitled *The Last Crusade*, expresses his excitement at following in the path of his medieval predecessors, and with regard to the location of the British Headquarters, situated between Ramleh and Ludd, he wrote

> History repeats itself, for here was General Headquarters and from here the attack on Jerusalem was planned, as here in the days of the First Crusade the march on Jerusalem was begun eight hundred and eighteen years before.[91]

Similarly, Raymond Savage, a British officer who served under General Allenby in Palestine, described his sense of historical repetition when looking out over the Plain of Sharon, prior to the final battle with the Turkish army:

> I thrilled until I literally shuddered, for I realized that along this identical sea-road, centuries before, had ridden Coeur-de-Lion and his Knights to fight for an ideal, a quest not so vastly different from that upon which these soldiers of the Empire had set out this morning in September 1917.[92]

Savage did not specify what that 'ideal' was, but his account suggests that British officers in Palestine did not regard the campaign as a moral or Christian 'crusade' in the way that some clergymen and politicians in Britain did: their interest was grounded in military history and imperial expansion. There was, however, for both soldiers and civilians a strong romantic appeal in this fantasy of the repetition of history, which this time would end in success for the British 'crusaders'. Led by General Allenby, the British captured Jerusalem from the Turkish army on 9 December 1917 and made a triumphal entry into the city two days later. Allenby's biographer, Brian Gardner, notes that although he was not a religious man, the event generated stories of the piety of the 'Victor of Jerusalem'. In one version of the story Allenby entered Jerusalem with a crucifix in his right hand and a Bible in his left, and in another, fell to his knees in prayer upon entering the city.[93] *Punch* celebrated the victory with a cartoon, dated 19 December 1917, entitled *The Last Crusade*, which showed a ghostly Richard Lionheart wearing chain mail and gazing with satisfaction on the newly captured city of Jerusalem, with the caption 'My dream comes true!'. By this means, Britain's imperial expansion in the Middle East was romanticised, and the capture of Palestine in 1917 portrayed as the realisation of an ancient British dream. Allenby's success, the cartoon suggests, had concluded a venture begun centuries before, and now the dead king could rest in peace, assured that Jerusalem was finally under British control. Allenby's eventual return to Britain was celebrated in another cartoon published in *Punch* in September 1919, entitled *The Return from the Crusade*. This depicted him as a victorious crusader being welcomed home by Britannia. He is riding on horseback and wearing chain mail and a tabard with a cross on the front. In this image Allenby is a chivalric figure, the handsome 'knight' who returns to his 'Lady-love' Britannia bearing the gift of Palestine. Allenby's 'crusader' status had been made 'official' shortly after the capture of Jerusalem, when the Duke of Connaught awarded him the Knighthood of the Order of St John at a ceremony in the city.[94]

It was through the Palestine campaign and the British entry into Jerusalem that the popular view of the war as a Christian 'crusade' was consolidated and found its strongest imaginative appeal. But the Palestine campaign, because of its location and the fact that Jewish battalions took part, also prompted a recourse to Old Testament imagery in rhetoric concerning the war. Just as the narrative of 'crusade' and the idea of the repetition of history were being imposed on the Palestine context, so, too the history of the Jews in Palestine was being asserted, in rhetoric concerning the Jewish Legion and its deployment in that country. As Karen Armstrong has observed, the Christian concept of 'holy war' has a precedent in the Old Testament. The themes of pilgrimage, invasion and conquest that are combined in the idea of 'crusade' are also found in the Exodus story, in the long journey through the desert and the battles between the Israelites and the Canaanites over settlement of the land.[95] In representations of the significance and purpose of the Palestine campaign in the British national press, 'Exodus' was briefly in competition with 'crusade' as a rhetorical theme. 'Exodus' was used specifically with regard to plans for a Jewish Legion which were announced in mid-1917, and also the Balfour Declaration, issued in November that year, the anticipated return of the Jews to Palestine being trumpeted as a re-enactment of the biblical narrative, led by the British. These portrayals of the Palestine campaign will be discussed in detail in Chapter 5.

In conclusion, prior to August 1914, Church leaders in Germany and Britain had been closely involved, through the missionary project and their efforts to promote ecumenism. After 4 August 1914, various means were used to overcome the fact that Britain was at war with another Christian nation, and one of these was the portrayal of Germany as a religious enemy. Academics lent authority to representations of Germany as anti-Christian, through pseudo-intellectual discussions of German philosophy and history, which, it was argued, had produced the doctrine of the supremacy of the German state. These ideas were popularised in pamphlets, political speeches, sermons and the press. There were also rumours, based on the alliance between Germany and Turkey, that the Kaiser had converted to Islam and was claiming that Germans were descended from the prophet Mohammed.[96] Alternatively, the Kaiser appeared in the guise of Herod, an analogy in which the war became the massacre of the innocents ordered by the king in an attempt to prevent the birth of Jesus, and consequently, the Christian faith. Germany, therefore, was portrayed not only as non-Christian, but as actively hostile towards Christianity.[97] The construction of Germany as a 'pagan' power provided moral justification for Britain's entry into the war, and perpetuated the notion, particularly among civilians, that this was a 'holy war', waged in defence of Christianity itself. In this respect, the Church had an opportunity to regain some of the authority it had lost through its failure to keep pace with the political and social changes of the pre-war years. The patriotism expressed by many leading clergymen and their efforts to mediate in wartime industrial disputes indicates concerns regarding the effect of the war upon Christianity in Britain, and a desire to ensure that the Church had a role in post-war reconstruction.

The Christian imagery with which Britain waged its propaganda war aroused hostility, which, although initially applied to the Germans as a 'pagan' people, also became directed towards an older and closer target, the 'Jews'. As the war progressed, Jews living in Britain became conflated with Germans in the popular imagination, whether out of ignorance or racist opportunism, and came under attack. The effect of this confusion between Jews and Germans was the subject of Stern's novel *Children of No Man's Land* (1919), in which Jewish characters go into hiding in boarding houses during the war, or change their names in an attempt to conceal their origins. The pressure to efface a problematic 'Jewishness' in pursuit of 'Englishness' is a frequent theme in early twentieth-century Anglo-Jewish literature, but it was not only Jews that were engaged in a struggle with origins in wartime Britain. In its efforts to assert a hegemonic Protestant national identity (that was itself retrograde and deeply nostalgic), the Anglican Church came into conflict with its Catholic origins.

NOTES

1   See Girouard, *The Return to Camelot*, p. vi for a full discussion of this subject.
2   See Preface, Girouard, *The Return to Camelot*.
3   The phrase 'Huns of Satan' is taken from Junius Redivivus (pseud.), 'Diabolus', in *The Holy War/Diabolus/Extremes: Generosity and Avarice* (London: John Bale, Sons & Danielsson, 1915).
4   See Irene Cooper Willis, *England's Holy War: A Study of English Liberal Idealism During the Great War* (New York: Alfred Knopf, 1928).
5   Announcement by the Neutrality League published in *Daily News*, 5 August 1914, p. 7.
6   G. Lowes Dickinson, 'The holy war', in *The Nation*, 8 August 1914, p. 692.
7   See, for example, H. G. Wells, 'The War That Will End War', *Daily News*, 14 August 1914, p. 4; 'The war of the mind', *The Nation*, 29 August 1914, pp. 788–90; 'Opportunity', *The Nation*, 15 August 1914, pp. 732–4, and 'The Sword of Peace', *Daily Chronicle*, 7 August 1914, p .4.
8   Wells, 'The war of the mind', pp. 788, 789.
9   H. H. Asquith, speech delivered at the Guildhall, London, 4 September 1914, in *The War: Its Causes and its Message: Speeches Delivered by the Prime Minister, August–October 1914* (London: Methuen, 1914), p. 15.
10 H. H. Asquith, speech made at Cardiff, 2 October 1914, in *The War: Its Causes and its Message*, p. 35.
11 'Honour and Dishonour', a speech by the Rt. Hon. D. Lloyd George, at Queen's Hall, London, 19th September, 1914, in *Pamphlets of the German War* (London: Methuen, 1914), p. 9.
12 See, for example, C. S. Burne, *Might Gives Right: The New Gospel of Germany*, Papers for the People Series, No. 2 (London: Central Committee of Patriotic Organizations, 1914); W. E. Orchard, *The Real War*, Papers for War Time Series, No. 10 (London: Oxford University Press, 1914), and E Barker, *Nietzsche and Treitksche: the Worship of Power in Modern Germany*, Oxford Pamphlets Series (London: Oxford University Press, 1914).
13 See, for example, M. E. Sadler, Vice-Chancellor of the University of Leeds, *Modern Germany and the Modern World*, Pamphlets on the European Crisis Series (London: Macmillan, 1914), and Viscount Bryce, *Neutral Nations and the War*, Pamphlets on the European Crisis Series (London: Macmillan, 1914).
14 Heinrich von Trietksche (1834–96) was an eminent German professor of political science. His *Politik* (1899) argued that war was vital to the establishment and continuity of the State, was cited as one of the origins of Germany's new 'paganism'. General Friedrich von Bernhardi's *Deutschland und der nächste Krieg* (1911), based on Treitksche's writings, was regarded as a statement of German imperial policy, and, in effect, a warning unheeded.
15 Barker, *Nietzsche and Treitschke*.
16 First published in the *Westminster Gazette* on 9 September 1914, the *Address of the German Theologians to the Evangelical Christians Abroad* was reprinted with a reply, in a pamphlet entitled *To the Christian Scholars of Europe and America: A Reply from Oxford to the German Address to Evangelical Christians* (London: Oxford University Press, 1914). References apply to this text.
17 *Address of the German Theologians*, pp. 19–21.

18 *Address of the German Theologians*, p. 21.

19 *To the Christian Scholars of Europe and America*, p. 13.

20 See Wilkinson, *The Church of England*, p. 23.

21 Winnington-Ingram, 'The national faith', in *The Church in Time of War: Sermons and Addresses, 1914–15* (London: Wells Gardner, Darton, 1915), p. 39.

22 Randall Thomas Davidson, 'The Eve of a Great War', in *The Testing of a Nation* (London: Macmillan, 1919), p. 7.

23 Davidson, 'The eve of a great war', p. 30.

24 Statement by Bishop Winnington-Ingram, published in *Church Guardian*, 10 June 1915, p. 539.

25 Bernard Holland, letter to the editor, *Church Guardian*, 1 July 1915, p. 606.

26 Shane Leslie, *The End of a Chapter* (London: Constable, 1916), p. 106.

27 Winnington-Ingram, 'The potter and the clay', sermon preached in Westminster Abbey, December 1915. Quoted in Wilkinson, *The Church of England* (1978), p. 217.

28 B. Bourchier, *For All We Have and Are* (London: Skeffington & Son, 1915), pp. 2–3, 48–9.

29 Redivivus,'The Holy War', p. 40.

30 Wilkinson, *The Church of England* (1978), p. 40.

31 Winnington-Ingram, 'Drinking the cup', a sermon preached in St Paul's Cathedral, 9 August 1914, and published in *Kaiser or Christ?: The War and its Issues* (London: James Clarke, 1914), p. 8.

32 See Wilkinson, *The Church of England*, pp. 71–2.

33 Wilkinson, *The Church of England*, pp. 32, 107.

34 See G. K. Nelson, *Spiritualism and Society* (London: Routledge & Kegan Paul, 1969), p. 156.

35 Sir Oliver Lodge, *Raymond, or, Life and Death with Examples of the Evidence for Survival of Memory and Affection after Death* (London: Methuen, 1916).

36 Nelson, *Spiritualism*, p. 157. In 1925, Hannen Swaffer, the well-known journalist and editor of *The People*, announced his conversion to spiritualism (p. 159).

37 Nelson, *Spiritualism*, p. 157.

38 Wilkinson, *The Church of England*, p. 35.

39 Harry Sackville Lawson, letter from France dated 3 July 1917. In John Laffin (ed.), *Letters from the Front, 1914–1918* (London: J. M. Dent & Sons, 1973), p. 83.

40 Girouard, *The Return to Camelot*, p. 287.

41 Ella McFadyen, *Songs of the Last Crusade: Verses of the Great War* (North Sydney: Winn, 1917).

42 See 'The last crusade', attributed to the Australian Army Medical Corps, in Ella McFadyen, *Songs of the Last Crusade*, p. 5.

43 Advertisement for St John Ambulance, in *Punch*, 21 October 1914, p. 334.

44 See the cartoon 'Cook's Crusader', in *Punch*, 16 September 1914, p. 8

45 Wilkinson, *The Church of England*, pp. 194–5.

46 Letter from Graham Greenwell, Light Infantry officer, from the Somme, 17 August 1916. In Laffin (ed.) *Letters*, pp. 54–5.

47 Letter from the actor and playwright Harold Chapin to his wife, 1 September 1915, in Laffin (ed.) *Letters*, pp. 32–3.

48 *The Times*, 12 May 1915, p. 10.

49 *Jewish Chronicle*, 14 May 1915, p. 7.

50 *Jewish Chronicle*, 14 May 1915, p. 8.

51 Meeting of the Jewish Peace Society, June 1914, reported in *The Times*, 8 June 1914, p. 54.

52 In fact, 30 German spies were arrested in Britain during the war, of whom 12 were executed, 1 committed suicide and the rest were imprisoned. See Phillip Knightley, *The Second Oldest Profession: The Spy as Bureaucrat, Patriot, Fantasist and Whore* (London: André Deutsch, 1986), p. 39.

53 Joseph Cohen, *Journey to the Trenches: The Life of Isaac Rosenberg 1890–1918* (London: Robson Books, 1975), p. 93.

54 *Daily Graphic*, 6 October 1917, p. 8.

55 Gladys Bronwyn Stern, *Children of No Man's Land* (London: Duckworth, 1919). All other references to this novel will be made within the text.

56 Gladys Bronwyn Stern, *Monogram* (London: Chapman & Hall, 1936), pp. 286–7.

57 Stern, *Monogram* (1936), p.38.

58 Stern, *Monogram* (1936), pp. 286–7. Stern converted to Catholicism in 1947.

59 For an analysis of these issues in Anglo-Jewish writing, see Bryan Cheyette, 'The other self: Anglo-Jewish fiction and the representation of Jews in England, 1875–1905', in David Cesarani (ed.), *The Making of Modern Anglo-Jewry* (Oxford: Basil Blackwell, 1990), pp. 97–111.

60 David Cesarani, 'An alien concept? The continuity of anti-alienism in British society before 1940', in David Cesarani and Tony Kushner, (eds), *The Internment of Aliens in Twentieth-Century Britain* (London: Frank Cass, 1993), pp. 25–52.

61 Cesarani, 'An alien concept?', pp. 30–2.

62 Figure cited in the Introduction to Cesarani and Kushner (eds), *The Internment of Aliens*, p. 3.

63 See Panikos Panayi, 'An intolerant act by an intolerant society: the internment of Germans in Britain during the First World War', in Cesarani and Kushner (eds), *The Internment of Aliens*, pp. 63–4.

64 Cesarani, 'An alien concept?', pp. 36–9.

65 W. H. Moberly, *Christian Conduct in War Time*, Papers for War Time Series No. 8 (London: Oxford University Press, 1914), pp. 14, 15.

66 Meeting of the Women's Imperial Defence Council, reported in *The Times*, 5 March 1917, p. 5.

67 Arnold White was a founder member of the ultra-nationalist British Brothers League, formed in 1901, and Henry Beamish became a member of the Britons' Society, founded in 1919.

68 N. R. Martin, 'The unseen hand', in *Punch*, 12 July 1916, p. 42.

69 Martin, 'The unseen hand'.

70 Michael Adler, *A Jewish Chaplain on the Western Front 1914–1918*. (Reprinted from *The Jewish Guardian*, Lewes: n. 1920), pp. 24, 22.

71 Adler, *A Jewish Chaplain*, p. 9.

72 Adler, *A Jewish Chaplain*, p. 13.

73 Frank Richards, *Old Soldiers Never Die* (London: Faber & Faber, 1933, reprinted 1964), pp. 159–60.

74 See Cohen, *Journey to the Trenches*, p. 64.

75 Cohen, *Journey to the Trenches*, p. 127.

76 Isaac Rosenberg, 'The Jew', undated, but written while he was in France as a soldier. In Ian Parsons (ed.), *The Collected Works of Isaac Rosenberg* (London: Chatto & Windus, 1979), p. 101.

77 See Rosenberg's letters to Edward Marsh, the first dated August 1916 and the second postmarked 18 January 1917. In Parsons (ed.), *Collected Works of Isaac Rosenberg*, pp. 242–3 and 251 respectively.

78 Letter from Isaac Rosenberg to Edward Marsh, France, 28 March 1918. In Parsons (ed.), *Collected Works of Isaac Rosenberg*, p. 272.

79 'Aunt Annie's corner: tender talks to tiny tots', *New Church Times*, 26 May 1916.

80 'Apologia Pro Vitus-Ejus', by 'Bees Even', *B.E.F. Times*, 5 March 1917.

81 The collection of war verse entitled *The Guns* is incorporated into Gilbert Frankau, *The City of Fear and Other Poems* (London: Chatto & Windus, 1918). *The Guns* is dated September 1915.

82 Frankau, *The City of Fear*.

83 George Coppard, *With a Machine Gun to Cambrai: The Tale of a Young Tommy in Kitchener's Army 1914–1918* (London: HMSO, 1969), p. 73.

84 Sharman Kadish, *Bolsheviks and British Jews: The Anglo-Jewish Community, Britain and the Russian Revolution* (London: Frank Cass, 1992), pp. 46, 47. Newspapers covering the 'conscription or deportation' campaign included the London *Evening Standard*, the *Evening News*, the *Morning Post* and the *Daily Mail*.

85 Alexander Aaronsohn, *With the Turks in Palestine* (London: Constable, 1917). See also Anthony Verrier (ed.), *Agents of Empire: Anglo-Zionist Intelligence Operations 1915–1919. Brigadier Walter Gribbon, Aaron Aaronsohn and the NILI Ring* (London and Washington: Brassey's (UK), 1995), p. 226. NILI stands for the Hebrew motto 'Nezah Israel Lo Ieshaker' ('Jewish Eternity shall not lie').

86   Aaronsohn, *With the Turks*, p. 14.

87   Aaronsohn, *With the Turks*, p. 39.

88   Aaron Aaronsohn kept a diary while working for British military intelligence from 1915 to 1919. In it he recorded the frustration of working with the British, and noted that typically, he 'encountered nothing but distrust and reticence, smallness and pettiness', see Verrier (ed.), *Agents of Empire*, p .226.

89   See R. Meinertzhagen, *Middle East Diary 1917 to 1956* (London: Cressnet Press, 1959), p. 11. Meinertzhagen was Chief Intelligence Officer to the British forces in Palestine during the war. His diary records the hostility among the British forces in the Middle East to the Balfour Declaration and the Jewish soldiers.

90   Donald Maxwell, *The Last Crusade* (London: John Lane, 1920), p. ix.

91   Maxwell, *The Last Crusade*, p. 104.

92   Raymond Savage, *Allenby of Armageddon: A Record of the Career and Campaigns of Field-Marshal Viscount Allenby, GCB, GCMG* (London: Hodder & Stoughton, 1925), p. 257.

93   Brian Gardner, *Allenby* (London: Cassell, 1965), p. 257.

94   Savage, *Allenby of Armageddon*, p. 246.

95   Armstrong, *Holy War*, p. 5.

96   See, for example, Aaronsohn, *With the Turks in Palestine*, pp. 36–7.

97   See 'Herod!', in McFadyen, *Songs of the Last Crusade*, and C. L. Graves, 'The imperial infanticide', in *Punch*, 30 December 1914, p. 537.

4

Conversion, Assimilation and National Identity

In the following poem, written in 1917, the Anglo-Jewish writer Joseph Leftwich reminded Christians of the origins of their faith:

The Jew (II)

All I have been, you are.
All that you are, I am,
How looks your arc-light there,
Against that dim-eyed star?

I see the East aflame.
Our Temple burns there still.
And these are but the sparks,
The great lights that you claim.

You have lain with me, and these
Your children are mine too.
Instead of conquering me,
You have my blood in you.[1]

Leftwich's poem raises a number of issues: not only does it challenge the notion of separate 'racial' identities, it also asserts the antiquity of Judaism and the Jews' claim to Palestine, and emphasises the relative youth of Christianity and the futility of its struggle with its origins as a Jewish sect. It is this struggle with origins, however, that underlies Christian proselytising towards Jews. Another factor is Christian apocalyptic, and the belief in the second coming of Christ, for which the conversion of the Jews is considered a prerequisite. This, according to the Book of Revelation, will be followed by the final battle between the forces of 'good' and 'evil', after which the kingdom of God will be established on earth. At times of religious tension and political change, the Revelation narrative has entered into the foreground of Christian thinking, prompting renewed conversion activity, as in the English Civil War and the period following the French Revolution.[2] Millennialism, with its narrative of cataclysm followed by utopia has, as Mel Scult points out, offered Protestants an explanation for crisis and upheaval and the promise of a better future.[3] That future, however, is dependent not only upon the conversion of 'unbelievers', but also upon demonstrable Christian piety, in order to set the conditions for the second coming. Linked to the conversion of the Jews, then, is the salvation of Christians, and consequently, conversion activity has frequently coincided with evangelical revivals, in a dual process of proselytising and evangelising that has sought to establish a stable national identity through religious homogeneity.

Evangelical activity reflects another struggle with origins: that of Protestantism in relation to Catholicism as an older form of Christianity. Until the middle of the nineteenth century the authority of the Established Church was reinforced by political disabilities against Catholics and Jews, which were removed in 1829 and 1858 respectively. Reflected in the nineteenth-century emancipation debates was a struggle over ideas of 'Englishness', since with legal rights no longer dependent upon Protestant affiliation, the notion of a Protestant national identity was destabilised. A similar struggle over religious constructions of 'Englishness' took place during the First World War, when the Anglican Church attempted to claim the national tradition as Protestant. The Anglo-Catholic revival that occurred during the war represented the resurgence of an older, more ritualised form of worship, which was perceived by some as more appropriate to their needs. Nevertheless, it was seen as a threat and suppressed. Many of the clergy saw the war as an opportunity for Protestantism to regain its place at the centre of national life, and the Anglo-Catholic revival threatened this by revealing internal divisions at a time when the Church was seeking to strengthen its position. At the same time, the Church launched a drive to 'convert' the nation to temperance and piety, through an evangelical mission aimed at civilians, and some clergymen claimed that through the experience of war, soldiers were rediscovering their faith and undergoing a form of 'conversion' through combat. Soldiers, on the other hand, used conversion as a metaphor for what they felt was the necessary suspension of religious belief under the conditions of war.

AN 'EXODUS ROMEWARDS': CONVERSION ANXIETY AND
NATIONAL IDENTITY

During the Middle Ages, the Catholic Church claimed the position of sole Christian authority in Europe, its hegemony challenged only by Judaism and Islam. The Church launched campaigns against both Jews and Muslims, in the Crusades (1096–1215), and the Inquisitions of the twelfth and fifteenth centuries. The sixteenth-century Reformation, however, brought Christians into internecine conflict, over different approaches to worship.[4] In Britain, the split with Rome occurred in the 1530s, when Henry VIII (1509–47) declared himself Head of the Church in England and confiscated Catholic property to raise funds for the treasury. When the devoutly Catholic Mary Tudor (1553–58) attempted to reinstate papal authority in English religious life, large numbers of Protestants were killed for their beliefs, while the reign of Elizabeth I (1558–1603) which saw the consolidation of the Church of England, brought a return of anti-Catholic feeling. Judaism was not considered a threat to Protestant hegemony at this time, as most Jews had been expelled from Britain in 1290. A few Marranos (Jews of Spanish and Portugese origin, whose ancestors had been forced to convert) remained in London during the expulsion, and some Jewish merchants and physicians temporarily entered the country, but their numbers were too low to constitute any real threat to Protestantism.[5]

Those who were not communicants in the Church of England were subject to political disabilities, which were not removed until the nineteenth century. Opposition arguments focused on the idea that membership of the Established Church was an essential component of patriotism and national consciousness. Some felt that the legal recognition of different faiths would compromise Protestant national identity, while others feared eventual domination by the previously excluded groups. In the case of Catholics, this was expressed as the threat of the possible conversion of English national identity, and stories of the horrors of the Inquisition were cited as a warning of the effects of unrestricted Catholicism upon national character.[6] The irony was, as Michael Ragussis points out in *Figures of Conversion* (1995), that this fear of Catholic proselytising was expressed at a time when Protestant missionary activity throughout the British Empire was at its height.[7] Protestant *conversion activity* in the imperial dominions, therefore, was matched by *conversion anxiety* at home, over the possible effects of religious heterogeneity on the authority of the Established Church.

A similar irony is found in Britain during the First World War, when a combination of Protestant self-assertion and insecurity developed with regard to the Church's role in national life. As in the nineteenth century, conversion discourse had a dual focus. In the context of war, the idea of national 'conversion' provided an imagined cause or rationale for German belligerence, and Germany was widely portrayed as an apostate nation, having replaced Christianity with militarism as its new 'creed'. The proposed remedy for German 'apostasy' was its symbolic conversion back to Christianity through military defeat, and religious and secular commentators alike spoke of the 'awakening' of Germany and the restoration of its people to the worship of God rather than the deification of the state. In rhetorical terms, then, the war became a battle to save the 'soul' of Germany. This notion of Britain's missionary function within the conflict, however, was reliant upon a construction of Britain as a devoutly Christian nation. Aware that this was not the case, the Church launched the National Mission of Repentance and Hope in 1916, with the aim of promoting national unity by strengthening the Protestant faith. As chairman of the mission, Bishop Winnington-Ingram urged repentance for national sins, which he identified as drunkenness, a love of entertainment and luxury, and the failure to raise the age of consent in 1912.[8] Despite his best efforts and those of other leading clergymen, however, the anticipated religious revival did not take place. Rather than increasing the authority and influence of the Church, the war revealed its internal divisions, and fuelled existing tensions between Evangelicals, Anglo-Catholics and liberal churchmen over how religious worship should be conducted. The apparent growth of Anglo-Catholicism during the war threatened to further undermine the authority of the Church at a time when an image of unity was desirable. In response, some clergymen expressed strong anti-Catholic feeling, and in the later stages of the war, 'Catholic' practices within the Church of England were suppressed. It should be noted, however, that wartime anti-Catholic feeling was mainly directed towards Anglo-Catholicism, as existing internal divisions in the Church of England were exacerbated, and that generally, Roman Catholic and Anglican clergy co-operated, both at home and at the Front.

The origins of the Church's internal conflict over religious worship could be traced back to the Reformation of course, but more recently to 1904, when a Royal Commission was appointed to investigate alleged 'clerical lawlessness', particularly over the question of ritual in church services. The commission's report, published in 1906, identified among the *'Practices of special gravity and significance'* the invocation of or confession to the Virgin Mary or the Saints; observation of the festivals of the Assumption of the Virgin and the Sacred Heart; Corpus Christi processions with the sacrament, and 'The veneration of images and roods'.[9] Any practices, in fact, that could be construed as Roman Catholic. The report concluded that discipline had indeed broken down, but that Anglican law should adapt itself to accommodate the broadness of modern religious life.[10] By 1913 some felt this had gone too far, and Bishop Gore of Oxford threatened resignation over 'modernism' among the clergy, or the view that the miracles described in the New Testament were not to be taken literally. Archbishop Davidson dissuaded him, pointing out that this would cause alarm and possibly an 'exodus Romewards', and Gore withdrew his threat.[11] Eventually a statement was issued which acknowledged that the clergy were entitled to their private views on the interpretation of the Scriptures, but advised them that as representatives of the Church of England they had a public duty to profess orthodoxy.[12] This orthodoxy, however, should remain recognisably distinct from Roman Catholic doctrine.

In effect, then, the issue was never fully resolved, and the tensions between an orthodoxy that some felt was too 'Catholic' and a 'modernism' which to others seemed blasphemous, continued into the war years. Religious hegemony became more important in a 'holy war', and Anglo-Catholicism came under direct attack. In 1915 the Reverend Basil Bourchier, Vicar of St. Jude's, Hampstead, and a senior army chaplain, declared that,

> When men exhibit the fruits of the Spirit, to know them is to love them, but oh! if they come labelled 'strictly orthodox', vaunting themselves as Catholics, with snarls and sneers on their lips, talking Beatitudes, but acting Inquisitions, exalting Churchianity over Christianity and converting Religion into Religionism, I fail to recognise them. They are impostors, frauds, shams.[13]

His words are an extreme example of anti-Catholic feeling in wartime Britain. For the sake of an appearance of unity, most clergymen sought to reconcile the Catholic, Evangelical and liberal elements within the Church, but during 1917 several incidents occurred which necessitated a response from the Church authorities. In October that year the vicar of one London church announced his intention to conduct a Holy Communion service based on that found in the English Prayer Book of 1549.[14] The 1549 Prayer Book contained England's first Protestant Mass, in which prayers were offered for the dead and the saints and martyrs; the prophets and patriarchs were venerated, and the priest was required to wear Mass vestments. In these respects it was more derivative of the Roman Catholic Mass than the service in the more frequently used 1552 Prayer Book. As Bishop of London, Winnington-Ingram granted permission for one such service to be held, which he proposed to attend. The event aroused controversy, however, and was cancelled because it was seen as dividing the Church at a time when it should appear united.[15] In November 1917 the vicar of St Saviour's Church in Hoxton, London, held a service to mark the Corpus Christi festival, which included a procession with the sacrament around the outside of the church. Winnington-Ingram was compelled to respond, and stated that as a result of this deliberate breach of Church law, he and other bishops would be unable to visit St Saviour's in the future. On another occasion, the sale of Roman Catholic literature was forbidden at the Church of St Mary the Virgin in Sloane Square.[16] Finally, Joan of Arc, once the icon of the militant suffragettes, became a somewhat controversial figure in the spring of 1917. It was proposed that a Joan of Arc Day be held in May that year, to raise money for the Three Arts Women's Employment Fund.[17] 'Joan' would ride through the streets of London in a 'Pageant of Fair Women', made up of society women dressed to represent different countries. An article in *The Times* reported 'Widespread disapproval' at the proposal, and noted

> it is felt that the impersonation of the Maid of Orleans, the national heroine of our French Allies and a beatified Saint of the Roman Catholic Church, by a lady riding through the streets of London, or in public masquerade ... would offend many legitimate susceptibilities.[18]

The organisers of the pageant expressed surprise at the idea that a representation of Joan of Arc should cause offence, and justified their choice on the grounds that 'she, above all the women of history, typifies that spirit of devotion and self-sacrifice which animates millions of the women of to-day'.[19] Although *The Times* did not explain why Joan was an inappropriate subject, it seems likely that, in the context of the religious tensions which became apparent during 1917 in particular, some of the objections came from the fact that she was a Catholic saint. There was also, perhaps, the question of guilt over her martyrdom at the hands of the English, now in alliance with the French, and a sense that she would be an unwelcome reminder of (albeit long past) hostility between the two countries. In addition, her function as a suffragette icon before the war could have made the pageant uncomfortably reminiscent of the WSPU processions, many of which were led by a woman in armour and on horseback, in emulation of Joan. Whatever the real nature of the objections, it was eventually announced that there would be no representation of Joan at the Pageant of Fair Women.

Rather than strengthening the Church, then, the war revealed its internal divisions and inability to adapt. The drive to convert the nation through the National Mission of Repentance and Hope was a failure, and the anticipated religious revival did not occur. At the Front, too, Christian faith was in decline, despite the Reverend Basil Bourchier's claim, made in 1915, that 'In the trenches men are quickly learning to probe to the realities of things. Through living the war they are finding God.'[20] In fact, the opposite was occurring, and despite the efforts of the clergy and various Christian organisations,[21] many soldiers lost their faith. Enlisted Christians had to overcome the opposition to violence found in Jesus' teaching, and reconciling Christianity and warfare proved difficult. Some soldiers used conversion as a metaphor for the temporary but necessary rejection of the principles of brotherly love and forgiveness which active service demanded. Lieutenant Robert Callaway was a mission priest in South Africa before the war. He enlisted as a chaplain in 1914 and then became an officer. He described his military experience as a process of transformation, and felt his regiment's bayonet training stood for 'the entire conversion of our whole attitude of mind as a nation. For it was instruction as to how best to *kill'*.[22] Another soldier, who had not formerly been a priest, felt that in going to war the British were obliged to become as belligerent and 'pagan' as their enemy. Writing to his mother in 1917, Captain John Crombie observed that 'the moral situation is damnable – we can only beat Germany by assuming her mentality, by recognising the State as the Supreme God whose behests to military efficiency must be obeyed, whether or no they run counter to Christianity and morality'.[23]

The journalist C. E. Montague, who served in the trenches throughout the war, used conversion as a metaphor for the loss of faith among soldiers, and recalled that 'it was a kind of trench fashion to meet the demoded oaths of a friend with the dogma that "There *is* no – God."'[24] His memoir, entitled *Disenchantment* (1922), describes his view of the conversion to 'Satanism' among combatants, defining Satanism as the rejection of Christian doctrine by the 'plain working-man', owing to bitter experience under 'a world order which has called itself divine but shown itself diabolic'. As a result, the disillusioned Christian turned instead to 'the only other world order supposed to be extant; the one which the former order called diabolic...So the plain man emerges a Satanist.' Montague suggested that 'in several portions of Europe the war made conversions abound', since national and religious loyalties were tested to the limit and the post-war period had brought only further hardship, especially for the poor.[25]

Yet despite the rejection of orthodoxy by many soldiers, a form of folk religion developed which used Christian imagery to express a belief in the supernatural. Stories of 'miraculous' events circulated among troops at the Front, such as that of the preservation of the altar in a bombed-out church, or the story of the 'Angels at Mons', discussed in Chapter 3. Soldiers were fascinated by the statue of the Virgin and Child which hung precariously from the damaged basilica of the church at Albert, and attributed this to divine protection.[26] Army chaplains noted this development, and Neville Talbot, assistant chaplain general to the Armed Forces, observed that 'The soldier has got religion. I am not sure he has got Christianity.'[27] The soldiers were not, he thought, against religion as such, but felt themselves to be 'outside and not in possession' of the Christian faith.[28] The problem, he concluded, was not religion but religiosity: the clergy had failed to articulate the relevance of Christianity in the modern period, and religion had become separated from daily life. Although the war had changed this somewhat, revealing 'the unconscious Christianity in men' in acts of comradeship and selflessness, unless the Church could somehow maintain this spirit of co-operation after the war, its relevance and influence would continue to decline.[29] Talbot called for 'the Twentieth-Century Reformation', a radical restructuring of the

Church in which the clergy would become less aloof from the mass of ordinary people, and possibly even disappear as official religious representatives.

By 1917 the need for Church reform had become clear both at home and at the Front, but the clergy seemed unable to act. The threat represented by Anglo-Catholicism had been suppressed, but this had intensified divisions within the Church and undermined its strength. The war as a project for the conversion of 'pagan' Germany was failing, since the German army remained undefeated. In addition, the drive to promote temperance and piety through the National Mission was proving unsuccessful: the rate of illegitimate births increased during the war, and drunkenness aroused sufficient concern for the king to set an example by declaring he would be teetotal for the remainder of the conflict.[30] At the Front, soldiers became superstitious and religious worship seemed meaningless. There remained one area in which conversion might still be applied, but in which the mainstream Church showed little interest.

'IT IS BUT RIGHT THAT WE SHOULD TRY TO PRESENT CHRIST TO THE JEWS AFRESH'

Efforts have been made to 'present Christ to the Jews'[31] since their return to Britain in 1656. Like many periods of political instability, the English Revolution prompted a growth in millennial speculation, and Cromwell was urged to glorify the new Puritan republic and hasten the fulfilment of prophecy by readmitting the Jews and facilitating their return, after conversion, to the Promised Land.[32] Conversion activity decreased after the restoration of the monarchy in 1660, but the French Revolution prompted a renewal of interest in prophecy, and Protestant proselytising movements were active during the Evangelical Revival of the 1790s, and in the 1820s, in the economic depression after the Napoleonic Wars.

It was during the nineteenth century that the most concerted effort at the mass conversion of the Jews took place. A number of Protestant conversion societies were founded in the early part of the century, the most prominent being the London Society for the Promotion of Christianity among the Jews. Established in 1809, it focused its efforts solely upon Jews in Britain, and included members of Parliament and the nobility among its supporters.[33] The

Society exploited the impoverished condition of Jewish immigrants, and its methods aroused controversy and debate over the desirability of conversion in general. From 1870 to 1914 a number of new missions were established in the East End, in response to the influx of Jewish refugees from Russia and Poland, many of whom were desperately poor, and willing to sit through a Christian service in return for food and clothing.[34]

Prior to and following emancipation in 1858, some Jews in Britain opted for religious conversion, for what Todd Endelman has termed 'pragmatic reasons',[35] while others sought to acculturate without baptism, and to find a balance between integration into the wider society and the preservation of links with the Jewish community. In either case, the price of acceptance was the at least partial effacement of Jewish identity. The pressure upon Jews to transform themselves derives chiefly from gentile anxiety over the nature of 'Jewish' difference, whether constructed in religious, national or cultural terms, and the internalisation of this anxiety by acculturating Jews.[36] The capricious nature of such constructions can be seen in the development of political and 'racial' antisemitism after 1858. These discourses erected new barriers to assimilation to replace the old legal disabilities, and portrayed Jews as a moral, sexual or political threat to the Christian nation. One of their effects was to increase the pressure upon Jews to assimilate, although the concept of 'racial' difference also represented 'Jewishness' as something that could not be transcended. This became intensified in the anti-alien climate of the war years, and the politics of assimilation is a recurrent theme in Anglo-Jewish writing of the period. Some Anglo-Jewish writers attempted to define an English identity which also allowed for the preservation of Jewish traditions, and sought to resolve seemingly conflicting ideas of 'Englishness' and 'Jewishness' in their fictional writing. Jews in Britain were subject to pressure to assimilate, even as the xenophobia exacerbated by the war made this difficult.

Religious conversion remained a marginal Protestant concern during the war, despite the widespread use of millennial rhetoric in relation to the conflict, and the wartime suspicion and hostility towards Jews. Conversion activity continued into the war years, but was not nearly as widespread as it had previously been, being mostly confined to marginal groups or academic theologians. A few cases of proselytising made the papers, however, and in 1915 the Coroner attacked conversionists for their part in the death of Esther Hyams of Bethnal Green, who collapsed and died upon learning that her daughter was training to be a missionary. Giving his verdict, the Coroner remarked that 'it was an unwarrantable impertinence for one person to interfere in the religious affairs of another', and added, 'If people would only lead their own lives according to the teachings of their own religion, they would find their time fully occupied.'[37]

The conversion of 'unbelievers' is, however, part of Christian doctrine, in preparation for the second advent and the millennium. One conversionist strategy has been to portray Judaism as a primitive proto-Christianity rather than acknowledging that Christianity developed from Judaism. This was the favoured approach of the Prophecy Investigation Society (PIS), a marginal Protestant group which was founded in 1842 and met twice a year.[38] At the outbreak of war the PIS were the only premillennialist group in Britain.[39] The war seemed to strengthen the Society's sense of mission, and from 13 December 1914 public meetings were held monthly in London.[40] Membership figures were never high, and even during the crisis of war numbered only around 100 people.[41] The group discussed 'signs' of the second coming and published a series of papers on the perceived unfolding of the Revelation narrative against the backdrop of the war.[42] In May 1916, A. M. Hodgkin, a member of the Women's Branch, gave a paper in which she sought to establish the existence of proto-Christian themes in the Old Testament, and asked:

> Is there no suggestion of the Church through the books of the Old Testament? Is there not a foreshadowing of the Church in the help-meet for Adam formed from his riven side? Or in the Gentile brides of one Israelite after another, each of them a recognised type of our Lord – Joseph, Moses, Salmon, Boaz, Solomon?[43]

Here, Christianity is feminised in relation to Judaism, as Eve represents the Christian Church, made from Judaism's 'riven side'. In this metaphor, Hodgkin seeks to establish Christianity and Judaism as partners at the beginning of monotheism. Yet Hodgkin's analogy between Eve and Christianity, if taken to its logical conclusion for a believer in the Scriptures, actually undermines her argument, since according to Genesis it was Eve who first ate the forbidden fruit and persuaded Adam to follow suit, an act that precipitated the Fall. This, however, was not the purpose of such texts. Conversion writing is preoccupied with Christian self-congratulation and self-assertion rather than any concrete plan of action towards Jews. The nineteenth-century conversionist societies were largely unsuccessful in retaining Jewish converts,[44] and their real function seems to have been to bolster and reproduce the Christian self-image. Hodgkin's concern with finding the roots of Christianity in the Old Testament reveals the uncertainty behind the assertion of Christian authority in her paper. She then argued that the Feast of Weeks was a metaphor for the resurrection of the saints prior to the return of Christ, and suggested that the absence of any sin offering in the instructions for observing the feast represented Christ's sinlessness; thus Christ was the Christians' Firstfruits.[45] In a similar vein, Ada Habershon, president of the Women's Branch of the PIS, gave a paper entitled 'The Day of Atonement in its Prophetic Aspect', in which she read the Passover as a prophecy of the Day of Judgement.[46] Israel, she argued, could not keep the Passover, because according to Jewish law, any Jew who had had contact with a dead body was unclean (Numbers 9: 7–12). It followed, then, that all Jews were 'unclean' as a result of their alleged role in Jesus' death, and therefore only Christians could 'partake of the feast'.[47] Ultimately, the PIS, and particularly the Women's Branch, seem to have been more concerned with the denunciation of the Jews than their conversion.[48] Their attention was focused on contemporary 'signs' of the impending apocalypse, and for many of them, the 'last days' were simply too close to warrant coherent conversionist proposals. It was left to academic theologians to explore ways in which the Jews of the modern period might be brought to Christianity.

When the Reverend A. L. Williams declared in 1916 that 'it is but right that we should try to present Christ to the Jews afresh', he had in mind a detailed plan, which he presented in a series of lectures that were later published as a book.[49] Williams' proposal aimed to construct modern Jewish converts in relation to St Matthew, as Jews practising Jewish customs but professing Christianity. In an attempt to revive the late nineteenth-century 'Hebrew–Christian' movement he suggested the formation of a 'Hebrew–Christian Church', imagined as a specific branch of the Catholic Church, whose congregation would consist solely of converts who were 'Jews except in religion'.[50] The term 'Hebrew' was preferred to 'Jewish', as 'savouring more of nationality than religion',[51] and the proposed Hebrew–Christian Catholic Church would, it was argued, mean that Jews could convert without the sense of national betrayal which had historically accompanied apostasy, and also enable Christianity to retain its Jewish converts. Members of the Church would celebrate the festivals of the Old Testament, but their significance for Jews would be interwoven with Christian themes; for example, at the Passover Hebrew–Christians would be reminded of the death of Jesus, 'the true Passover Lamb'.[52] Prayers would be in Hebrew, adapted from Jewish prayer books, and Jewish nationalism promoted. He also proposed the appointment of a Hebrew-Christian bishop, who would 'act as a shepherd and guide' to the congregation.[53] Williams admitted, however, that in 1916 there was 'very little demand...for such an officer'.[54] These kinds of arguments and interpretations of prophecy were common to Victorian conversion societies, and had survived into the twentieth century only at the margins of religious discourse. Their very limited uptake during the war suggests that conversionism was by this time an old-fashioned idea, and despite the widespread use of religious rhetoric in relation to the conflict, there was no discernible renewal of interest in the religious conversion of the Jews. Like the concept of chivalry discussed in Chapters 2 and 3, although conversionism continued into the twentieth century, it was rapidly undermined by political and social changes, war and modernity.

A more modern approach, perhaps reflecting the development of psychoanalysis, was formulated in 1917 when James Alexander Robertson, of the United Free Church College, Glasgow, attempted to trace the psychological process of conversion, or the route through which Jesus had developed from practising Jew to professing what would become Christianity. He described his book, *The Spiritual Pilgrimage of Jesus*, as an attempt to trace the 'moral and psychological pathways' by which Jesus had gained his sense of vocation.[55] What, Robertson asked, was the process of Jesus' awakening to 'God-consciousness',[56] and how could it be applied in 1917? According to Robertson, the un-making of Jesus as a Jew had begun with the incident with the money-lenders in the Temple, when he was 12 years old. This, it was suggested, was followed by a sense of commission at his baptism and finally by 'the apprehension of the cross' during the last days of his life.[57] Robertson argued that Jesus had been a religious reformer rather than a political figure, and that the Jews had completely misunderstood messianism, and had understandably but regrettably developed an expectation of political deliverance:

Upon the brow of His people there had long flickered the pale light of expectation. But in the mind of the street and the market-place this holy forward-look had suffered the too-frequent fate of spiritual things. It was transmuted into something gross and earthy. And that debasing touch of the spirit of the age was aggravated by the rankling bitterness which is the inevitable result of a corrupt political oppression. The Annointed of God, for whose coming they were taught to look, loomed up in their distorted fancy as a political deliverer.[58]

The distaste for politics apparent in Robertson's 1917 account of the development of Jesus' sense of mission perhaps reflects the rise of revolutionary politics during the late nineteenth and early twentieth centuries, and the threat this represented to the already declining authority of the Church. Marxism promised a better world through the removal of the structures that perpetuated inequality; namely monarchy, class, religion and property relations, whereas Christianity could only promise a better life beyond the grave. Yet the Church was aware that its survival during the war was dependent upon a greater involvement in the political aspects of national life, to which it deliberately addressed itself, mindful of the threat that revolutionary politics represented to its position.[59] In Bolshevism, which will be discussed more fully in Chapter 5, the Church perceived itself as under attack by a politics that was widely regarded as 'Jewish', owing to Marx's Jewish heritage and the perceived prominence of Jews in the ranks of the Bolsheviks.

One Christian writer, Margaret Dorothea Rose Willink, engaged with the threat of Bolshevism directly, and found the 'solution' in a Christian theocracy based on Mosaic Law. By this means, Christianity would become the political creed of post-war Britain and Jews would be forced to convert, according to the rules of their own faith, as laid down in Leviticus. Her apocalyptic fantasy *Utopia According to Moses* (1919) takes the form of a narrative set during the First World War, in which the main character, Michael Davidson, describes his revelation of God's plans for the post-war period.[60] The story opens some time before August 1914, and is constructed around a debate on utopianism between Perceval, a communist, and Michael, an amateur theologian. Various utopian proposals are assessed, including More's *Utopia* and Plato's *Republic*, and all are found wanting because they are either divisive or inegalitarian. What is required is a communitarian model that allows a certain amount of personal freedom but imposes moral and ethical standards and leaves property relations intact. Such a model, argues Michael, can be found in the Old Testament, in the Law as revealed to Moses on Mount Sinai.

Soon afterwards, war breaks out and Michael rejoins his regiment, but returns home some months later after being injured in a shell-blast that he claims catapulted him into a form of religious time-travel, in which he visited a Jewish utopia, somewhere in the pre-Christian era: 'It was after Ezekiel, because it was his temple I saw... But really it was a time that never was, because the Covenant was being properly kept with all the promised results.'[61]

While in 'Zion', Michael uses a Hebraised version of his name, identifying himself as 'Michael ben-David, of the dwellers in the Isles of the Sea'.[62] He finds much to admire, and the Mosaic utopia is repeatedly contrasted with communism. Class divisions, he reports, were avoided through agricultural self-sufficiency, which meant there was very little surplus and consequently no commerce. In addition, the religious prohibition against theft and covetousness led to an 'independence of possessions', which produced 'a temper of dependence on GOD', and this was the secret of the success of 'Zion'.[63] The first utopia had been promised to the Jews, but they had failed to fully observe the conditions of the covenant, and had therefore forfeited God's protection as well as their land and nationhood. Obedience to divine will was vital to the success of any utopian plan. The utopia that did not have God at its centre was destined for failure, which meant that Bolshevism, with its hostility towards religion, presented no real threat. In Michael's view, it was the Jews' reluctance to integrate, and 'become one body with the Gentiles' which had prevented the realisation of the Mosaic utopia.[64] It now fell to Christians to create 'Christ's utopia', through the establishment of a Christian theocracy in post-war Britain, and to ensure that the Jews were absorbed into the gentile body, in accordance with God's will as revealed to Michael during his illness.

Once again, the Old Testament provided a model, in the story of the son of Shelomith (Leviticus 24: 10–16). The story concerns a man of mixed Egyptian and Israelite parentage, who cursed the name of God when visiting his mother in the Israelite camp. For this, it was commanded that he should be stoned. Contrary to popular belief, Michael argues, this is not simply a narrative of punishment for sacrilege, but is 'really a piece of very interesting case-law on the treatment of aliens'.[65] In Britain in 1919, the term 'aliens' would most likely have referred to Jews, as they were the largest immigrant group in the population at that time. According to this interpretation of Levitical law, any 'alien' in the Christian theocracy would be obliged to observe the law of the land, and, like the son of Shelomith, face severe penalties for blasphemy or disrespect towards the deity. The effect of this on Jews in the proposed Christian theocracy would be that they would be obliged to become Christians in practice, if not to actually convert. Willink's elaborate and topical conversion proposal, therefore, appropriated Jewish law in support of an argument for a Christian socialist utopia as an alternative to communist utopianism. A religious utopia based on Jewish foundations but professing Christianity would amount to a state embodiment of the conversionist argument that Christianity was Judaism 'refined' or 'perfected'. Such a state, built upon a synthesis of Judaism and Christianity, would mean the eradication of religious or political heterogeneity, and effect the conversion of any Jews who wished to live in it. At the time Willink was writing, however, 'Jewishness' was being constructed in political, 'racial' and national terms, and religious conversion was no longer considered the route to assimilation. In the next section, I examine how some Anglo-Jewish writers attempted not only to render assimilation un-threatening, but also to explore the limits of assimilation in their fictional writing.

'THE HALF-AND-HALF-PEOPLE'

In the late nineteenth century, religious conversion was one route to assimilation, but the status of the converted Jew was ambiguous and could result in a double alienation, from both Jewish and gentile societies. The preferred route for many was intermarriage, despite the tradition of endogamy, but this, too, had its drawbacks. As Todd Endelman has noted, English 'toleration' was qualified and hostile to ethnic and cultural diversity, especially among the upper classes, and assimilation demanded the effacement of Jewish identity, with no reciprocal adjustment on the part of gentiles.[66]

In her memoir, *Monogram*, the Anglo-Jewish writer Gladys Bronwyn Stern recalls that although her childhood was 'a sanctuary perfectly free from pogroms', and she had numerous gentile friends, she was constantly reminded of the threat of antisemitic attack by the Dreyfus case (1894–1906).[67] The threat of persecution as a Jew was the 'King Charles' Head' which kept returning to haunt her childhood imagination, and it is a theme found in her early novels, whose Jewish characters are keen to integrate, but are repeatedly confronted by their apparently unassimilable 'difference'. Stern's early novels deal with the difficulty of this for Jewish women in particular, who are portrayed as caught between a simultaneous identification with Jewish tradition and the desire to escape it, and are exoticised and trivialised by well-meaning gentiles. This combination renders futile their attempts at integration, and eventually forces them to obey tradition and make a suitable match with a Jewish man. Stern's first novel *Pantomime* (1914) explores the attraction of 'bohemianism' for the middle-class Jewish woman, and the conflict that arises between the desire for freedom and her religious background.[68] Nan Hartmann is bright and rebellious, and wants to be one of the 'Other People' – artists, writers and musicians – rather than a devoted wife and mother. She goes to drama school and becomes involved with Tony Morrice, a Christian, but the relationship quickly founders as a result of interference by her family (after six weeks, Nan's uncle wants to know whether Tony intends to marry his niece). The issue of marriage brings their cultural differences into relief, and the engagement is eventually cancelled. Tony realises of Nan that 'She would never make a Bohemian' (p. 283) and Nan admits this too:

> She had not been armoured or equipped for it. Her dim, early ideal of happiness resolved itself into a country-house, and soft shaved lawns, and two children playing in the sunshine, and – someone – coming home to her at six o'clock every evening. Deep down in her heart this picture still held good. (p. 291)

Her desire to escape convention is frustrated by the force of 'seventeen years' training and whole generations of instinct' (pp. 291–2), and she opts instead for marriage to the wealthy August Goldschmidt. *Pantomime* suggests that intermarriage, at least for Jewish women, is almost impossible because their upbringing militates against the very things that attract them to gentile society, its apparent lack of restrictions and greater personal freedom. This is portrayed as the attraction of the incompatible opposites of tradition and modernity, and, Stern suggests, relationships that try to reconcile these differences will inevitably fail.

This theme is repeated in *Children of No Man's Land* (1919)[69] as, in a metaphor for gentile constructions of Jewish identity, Deb Marcus is portrayed as a blank canvas onto which her gentile friends project their fantasies:

> For Deb's looks were of that mutable type which inspired every fourth-rate art faddist to paint her Holding a Melon; or in a Blue Jacket; or with head flung back against their favourite bit of Chinese drapery; or absorbed in the contents of a dust-bin (symbolic realism); or as a figure on an Egyptian frieze; or as Mary Magdalene; or as a Wood-nymph pursued by Silenus; or as a coster girl dancing to a barrel organ by naptha-lights or merely as 'Deborah, an Impression'. (p. 49)

Anxious not to appear prim, Deb affects sexual knowledge and sophistication when she is with 'the Studio gang', and on one occasion stays overnight with a male friend at a seaside cottage, unchaperoned (p. 134). This incident prompts one of her friends, Antonia Verity, to attempt to 'save' her from further 'sin' and introduces another 'conversion' theme into the narrative besides Deb's attempts at self-transformation into a 'bohemian'. Antonia becomes Deb's self-appointed moral missionary, and with 'the passion of the earnest priestess for a convert in danger', tries to prevent any further 'corruption' of her charge (p. 150). In her attempt at Deb's moral conversion, Antonia enlists Samson Phillips, an Anglo-Jewish army captain who is looking for a wife. Deb, however, finds him overbearing, 'a fanatic, whose gospel was Simple Goodness; but who...would have made martyrs where he could not make converts', and she turns his proposal down flat (pp. 156–7). Eventually, however, she realises that there is no real place for her in gentile society, especially in the anti-alien climate of the war, and accepts him. Her moment of 'conversion' occurs during the marriage ceremony, in which she is reconciled to Judaism, as, standing under the wedding canopy, she felt that 'at last she belonged; that this was her faith, and these her people' (pp. 284–5).

What I have termed the 'conversion theme' in *Pantomime* and *Children of No Man's Land* functions in relation to the novel's portrayal of sexual politics and the force of Jewish tradition. It is concerned with the young Jewish woman's desire for greater personal freedom, which she associates with 'bohemianism' and gentile society; her efforts at self-transformation in order to gain this freedom, and the attempts by both gentiles and Anglo-Jews to control her behaviour in accordance with their own expectations. In seeking to escape the confines of traditional female roles, both Nan and Deb attempt a process of self-transformation based on the values of others: Nan tries to be 'bohemian' because this is Tony's fantasy, while Deb affects sexual knowledge because her friends do so, and out of a felt pressure, as a Jewish woman, to embody the 'oriental' stereotype. In attempting this transformation they are confronted by its impossibility, since 'bohemianism', whether portrayed as romantic poverty or sexual promiscuity, is incompatible not only with their upbringing, but also their desires and values, and ultimately reflects not their own interests but those of the gentile majority. The Anglo-Jewish community responds to the disaffected Jewish woman by locating a suitable and persistent marriage partner and waiting for her (inevitable) return to her origins, having experienced alienation among the gentiles. The eventual endogamous marriage represents the consolidation of a Jewish collective identity that is based not so much on religion or nationality as tradition. The attempt at self-transformation results in a return to origins, as the Jewish women in these novels finally acknowledge a correspondence between the expectations of Anglo-Jewry and their own needs and desires. Both novels suggest, however, that the Jewish woman lacks autonomy in Jewish and gentile societies, and that ultimately, acceptance into either group demands of her a process of transformation in accordance with that group's values, which she may only partly share.

In *Twos and Threes* (1916), Stern explores the dynamic of assimilation through the relationship between two men: a neo-Nietzschean 'master', the gentile Stuart Heron, and his Jewish 'disciple', Sebastien Levi, and frames the pressure upon Jews to transcend their origins in philosophical terms.[70] The novel satirises the efforts made by assimilating Jews to avoid fulfilling antisemitic stereotypes or confirming aspects of popular antisemitic discourse. Stuart, a diamond merchant, is concerned with the practical application of his own brand of nihilism, 'the philosophy of the shears', and fantasises about starting at the bottom of society, without inheritance, and working his way upwards through merit alone. Sebastien is an aspiring poet and heir to the Universal Stores in Holborn. His father is an assimilated Jew who has taken care not to embody any 'racial' stereotypes:

Ned Levi was of that species known as the strictly agnostic Jew. He neither went to Synagogue, nor did he keep the picturesque Jewish holidays. He did not tactlessly allude to himself, in company, as 'the Chosen of the Lord'. He did not wear enormous flashing diamonds in his shirt-front, nor gesticulate over-violently, nor control, spider-fashion, the entire financial affairs of Great Britain. Likewise, he ate ham with relish ... He was a little unostentatious man, with light red hair and moustache grizzling untidily to grey, a quiet taste in clothes, and nothing to stamp him Israelite save a slight lift at the bridge of the nose, a kindly concern for the fortunes of even the most distant of his cousins, and a keen sense of business acumen which had led him from a small grocery shop in the East End, to the massive and celebrated stores in High Holborn. (pp. 247–8)

In fact, Ned Levi embodies Stuart's ideal of the man who starts with nothing and becomes a success. Ned married a Christian girl of humble origins, after he had made his fortune, so could not be accused of marrying his way into society. Sebastien has followed his father's example, and is engaged to Letty Johnson, a costermonger, who wants him to change his name to Lovell upon marriage, to which he agrees. Influenced by Stuart's ideas, Sebastien refuses his father's allowance of £1,500 a year, a decision that Stuart dismisses as 'theatrical', arguing that he has not fully understood his philosophy, which is to cultivate genuine independence from material and physical ties. On Stuart's advice, Sebastien breaks off his engagement to Letty, applying the 'philosophy of the shears' and ending the relationship at its highest point of pleasure, since, according to Stuart's theory, this can only be followed by deterioration. When Sebastien tells the 'master' that he feels he is becoming more like him, Stuart is dismissive:

Nonsense; you can't possibly grow more like me, because I'm not there; not permanently. You can grow like your father, or the Albert Memorial, anything fixed and solid, – but you can't grow like the spot where I stood a minute ago before I began to run. (p. 343)

The dynamic between Sebastien and Stuart, in which the former tries to meet the latter's shifting criteria, may be read as a metaphor for assimilation into a society in which the conditions for belonging are subject to constant revision. Stuart purports to be instructing Sebastien in his philosophy, yet resists and obstructs the latter's success by insisting that he has not understood. His response to Sebastien's efforts is disdain and further differentiation between himself and his 'disciple'. As Sander Gilman has noted, 'as one approaches the norms set by the reference group, the approbation of the group recedes...For the ideal state is never to have been the Other, a state that cannot be achieved'.[71] Nevertheless, Sebastien tries, and his enthusiasm arouses discomfort in Stuart, who reacts with the thought that 'This Jewish boy was too responsive, too enthusiastic, too flexible altogether' (p. 272). As long as Stuart has control of and can change the criteria, Sebastien can never fully meet them. This dynamic suggests a parallel with assimilation and the expectation that Jews should shed most of their heritage and traditions and conform to a homogeneous construction of 'English-ness', which is itself based on changing criteria. Here, Stern appears to attack the notion that there is a fixed and attainable 'English' identity to which Jews should aspire, by showing how readily the construction of that identity can change. Status and confidence in this novel are portrayed as based on a combination of class, wealth, and an 'Englishness' which is not in any way 'Jewish'. Stuart Heron has all of these, and as one of the 'Insiders of Society' (p. 59), enjoys a sense of belonging that Sebastien, despite his wealth and education, does not. There are several non-Jewish characters that lack either money or class advantages, and are therefore insecure, but none of them is as anxious or as willing to change as Sebastien. This extends to the breaking of his engagement to Letty, which he does at Christmas:

> He did not know any more for what strange reasons he had performed this strange act. But since the master knew, that was sufficient; the disciple was content to follow blindly. He would go now and lay his shattered world as a tribute at Stuart's feet...where he had already laid his father's disappointment...his own ambition. (p. 375)

Hearing of this, Stuart experiences sudden remorse: 'His meta-physics dropped away from under his feet, leaving him treading upon a void' (p. 379). He decides that his philosophy is destructive and misguided, and renounces it. Sebastien, however, has given up everything for an illusion constructed by someone who assumed superiority and exploited his insecurity. *Twos and Threes* suggests that gentiles have unrealistic expectations of Jews, wanting them to embody ideals that they do not themselves seriously pursue. Stuart demands that Sebastien renounce his inheritance although he has no intention of doing likewise. Each time Sebastien meets the 'master's' criteria another set of demands is made. The effect of this is that Sebastien rejects his origins and relinquishes his personal autonomy in an effort to live according to the values and beliefs of another. Ultimately, Ned Levi is the character who sees the truth of it all: that behind the neo-Nietzschean rhetoric lies contempt for the self-made man, and by extension, behind the liberal rhetoric of inclusion lies the desire to maintain a hierarchy of 'Englishness', in which assimilating Jews can only be, as Stern puts it, 'the half-and-half people'.[72]

Leonard Woolf's short story 'The Three Jews' (1917) depicts assimilation as a process that is never complete, and explores the construction of a hierarchy among Jews that is based on the perceived extent to which they have effaced their 'Jewishness' in the process of Anglicisation.[73] Leonard Woolf was born in Kensington, London, in 1880, the third of nine children. His father, a barrister, was an orthodox Jew, and Leonard attended synagogue until just before his eighteenth birthday, but then rejected all formal religion. After attending Cambridge University he joined the Civil Service, serving in Ceylon from 1904–11, but later became critical of imperialism and an active socialist. After his marriage to Virginia Stephen in 1912, he decided to make his living as a writer, and published novels, short stories and non-fiction advocating socialism.

In 'The Three Jews', the characters judge one another's assimilatory success according to criteria based on antisemitic stereotypes, and this internalisation of 'racial' antisemitism creates a bond of anxiety between them. Sander Gilman has termed this mechanism 'Jewish self-hatred', and argues that it occurs when the desire for acceptance forces Jews into an acknowledgement of 'Jewish difference' as defined by antisemites. This, he suggests, leads to a fragmentation of identity, as Jews create a new 'other' within Jewry that is often based on the 'Eastern' or 'oriental' stereotype.[74] Woolf's story would seem to bear this out.

The first Jew in the story goes to a café in Kew gardens, and is approached by the second Jew, who asks to share his table. The first Jew, as narrator, identifies his companion as Jewish by his physiognomy:

> I noticed the thickness of his legs above the knee, the arms
> that hung so loosely and limply by his sides...his dark fat
> face and the sensual mouth, the great curve of the upper lip
> and the hanging lower one. A clever face, dark and
> inscrutable, with its large mysterious eyes and the heavy lids
> which went into deep folds at the corners. (p. 7)

His views are confirmed when the man speaks, in 'the slight
thickness of the voice, the over-emphasis, and the little note of
assertiveness in it' (p. 7). A conversation follows, in which each
Jew tries to determine the extent of the other's acculturation. One
of the criteria is a lack of religious observance. It is quickly
established that neither of them goes to synagogue, although the
second Jew attends on Yom Kippur, but only out of 'pure habit' (p.
9). The first Jew then notices his companion's apparent incongruity
with his surroundings, his 'large dark head' framed against a
backdrop of 'delicate apple-blossom and...pale blue sky' (p. 8).
This impression is reinforced when the second Jew suggests that
Zionism has replaced Judaism as the basis of collective Jewish
identity, and observes that 'we belong to Palestine still', a
statement that the first Jew leaves unanswered (p. 9). Presently, the
conversation moves to a third Jew, a cemetery-keeper. The second
Jew describes this man to the first, using the same 'racial' criteria
by which the latter had identified him; thus the cemetery-keeper's
clothes appear ill-fitting, he has 'cunning grey eyes', and 'a nose,
by Jove, Sir, one of the best, ...side-face it was colossal; it stood out
like an elephant's trunk with its florid curves and scrolls' (p. 11).
The second Jew recounts how the cemetery-keeper professes a lack
of religious feeling, and states that 'one can't believe everything in
the Bible', adding that 'now you may think for yourself' (pp.
12–13). He describes 'the old spirit, the old faith' as 'vanishing in
the universal disbelief', which he associates with the decline of the
idea of 'race' among Jews (p. 13). Yet the extent of his son's
estrangement from the 'old spirit' proves too much for the
cemetery-keeper, and when he marries their Christian servant-girl,
the father disowns him. This is not, he says, because of her faith
but because she is his class inferior, although the principle of
endogamy is also a factor, in his remark that 'Our women are as
good, better than Christian women' (p. 18).

Woolf's story suggests that without Judaism or Zionism as the
basis of Jewish collective identity, there remains only the concept of

'race' as a means of defining 'Jewishness', as in the second Jew's reflection that 'We're Jews only externally now, in our black hair and our large noses, in the way we stand and the way we walk' (p. 14). None of the Jews in this story has converted to Christianity, but all have rejected Judaism as the basis of Jewish identity, and replaced it with a negative construction of 'race', which they seek to avoid embodying in any way. Since antisemitic stereotyping is so exhaustive, ranging from religious to national, physical, psychological, vocal, gestural and postural constructions, the avoidance of all these requires considerable effort on the part of the assimilating Jew. As portrayed in this story, the process of assimilation demands a transformation whereby the Jew becomes, in a sense, an antisemite, recognising other Jews on the basis of an internalised and then projected 'racial' antisemitism. As Nathania Rosenfeld has pointed out in *Outsiders Together: Leonard and Virginia* Woolf (2000), it is difficult to tell whether Anglicisation represents success or self-delusion on the characters' part, as each of them recognises one another as Jews, and both first and second Jews feel a sense of both loss and failure in that recognition.

Another Anglo-Jewish writer, Gilbert Frankau, framed assimilation in terms of the fragmented subjectivity of the 'shell-shocked' soldier, in his novel *Peter Jackson, Cigar Merchant* (1919), and portrayed the psychological integration of 'the Jew' as part of the process of recovery and return into civilian society.[75] A number of ex-combatants published novels about their war experiences, and the readership for these was wide. *Peter Jackson* is an unusual example of this genre, however, because it addresses the relation of 'Jewishness' to 'Englishness'. Frankau developed war neurosis after his experiences at the Somme, and was discharged from his commission in 1917. In his autobiography, *Self-Portrait: A Novel of his Own Life*,[76] he claims to have psychoanalysed himself while writing *Peter Jackson*, thereby curing himself. In 'Creative Writers and Day-Dreaming' (1908), Freud noted the tendency among contemporary writers to include fragmented representations of themselves in their work:

> The psychological novel in general no doubt owes its special nature to the inclination of the modern writer to split up his ego, by self-observation, into many part-egos, and, in consequence, to personify the conflicting currents of his own mental life in several heroes.[77]

This seems to have been Frankau's strategy in *Peter Jackson*, and the two central characters, Peter and his cousin Francis, appear to be representations of Frankau himself. Both men are partly Jewish, their fathers having married Sephardic women, who were sisters. Peter, a businessman, is represented as the more 'English' of the two, and Francis, a writer, the more 'Hebraic'. Prior to the outbreak of war, Peter is portrayed as a coherent, integrated subject. As the narrative progresses, his subjectivity becomes fragmented under the stress of war, and separates into multiple 'selves'. The second half of the novel explores the process by which Peter's various 'selves' are re-integrated, through psychotherapy, into a new peacetime identity that safely incorporates 'the Jew'.

The crisis occurs when Peter, like his creator, develops 'shell-shock' and is declared unfit for any form of military service. War neurosis is described as an internal conflict and a crisis of masculinity, 'the battle of the neurasthenic with his own soul... feeling himself lost to all honour, coward and traitor in sight of his own manhood' (pp. 322–3). The symptoms of war neurosis were not always considered genuine, and there was a popular view that the 'neurasthenic' was indeed a coward and a shirker.[78] In *Peter Jackson*, cowardice is associated with non-combatant Jews. The Bramsons, owners of a rival cigar importing business, are represented as profiteers who continue to trade while other men fight and die at the Front. Sam 'Pretty' Bramson, a young man whose effeminacy is implied in his nickname, panics at the outbreak of war, fearing conscription, while Peter enlists. When he is discharged from the army on the grounds of ill health, Peter experiences shame and self-hatred, and in accordance with the novel's representation of cowardice as a 'Jewish' trait, it is as though his 'Hebraic' self has temporarily gained ascendance and rendered him a coward.

Peter's subjective fragmentation under the strain of war has taken several forms. First, there is 'Peter the neurasthenic – a huddled, frightened soul who lived alone in its black caves of gloom, and still prayed occasionally with whining ingratiation for death' (p. 349). This 'soul' is dismissed by his psychoanalyst, as 'Purely physical', created by the experience of war. The second is the 'new soul', emerging through analysis. Peter's 'original soul' views both of these as mere products of the imagination. Then there is 'the soul of "P.J.", sometime a gunner in Kitchener's Army', and finally 'the soul of Peter Jackson, worker by instinct' (p. 349). As

Peter adapts to civilian life, and searches for a new occupation, other 'selves' emerge, demanding to be accommodated. One of these is Jewish:

> Peasant, soldier, Jew and business man met round the boardroom table of Peter's brain. First the land; then the men to work the land. 'Don't pay rent. Buy outright', said business. 'Keep 'em in order', rasped the soldier. 'Crops and stock', said the peasant...'And your markets', whispered the Jew; 'never forget your markets...'...All of which counsels the old Etonian crystallised into the words 'Why not become a gentleman farmer?' (p. 372)

As a result of this decision, Peter's multiple 'souls' are re-integrated and his neurotic symptoms alleviated, and 'the Jew' within, made visible by war neurosis, is assimilated through a professional connection to the land. By this means, the idea alluded to in Woolf's story, that 'the Jew' is an urban creature and alien to the English landscape is overcome, and, in a Disraelian twist, the business acumen associated with Peter's 'Jewish' self becomes an asset.[79] Other anxieties related to 'Jewishness' are also resolved: Peter's analyst assures him that unlike 'Pretty' Bramson he is not a coward; this reassurance means that his sexual potency is restored, and his wife gives birth to a son. Frankau's preoccupation, then, is not the difficulty or impossibility of assimilation, but the necessity of it for psychological health, and the role of gentleman farmer effects the transformation whereby his 'Jewish' difference is contained.

Frankau was British-born, baptised an Anglican, and Eton-educated, and therefore enjoyed certain advantages of class and status that immigrant Jews did not. Moshe Oved came from Poland to Britain shortly before the First World War and set up a jeweller's shop in London. In 1925 he published his autobiography, *Visions and Jewels*, in which he discusses the effect of exile and the First World War on Judaism and Jewish identity.[80] In one anecdote he describes how a watch belonging to the Zionist Nahum Sokolow was brought to him for repairs. The story becomes a metaphor for the condition of Jews in the diaspora:

> I would recognize a Jewish watch miles off, by the groaning of the spring when it is being wound up...and by its two

little 'Mezuzah' hands, one of which drags westwards, whilst the other drags still farther eastwards, and both of which entangle themselves in the second hand which throws itself about on all sides, rubs itself against the dirt of the dial, and cannot crawl out for love or money. (p. 78)

This image captures the feeling of paralysis caused by conflicting identifications, a theme which features in Stern's novels and Woolf's story, and is used here to suggest that Jews in exile are torn between identification with the 'old' and 'new' countries. Oved set to work repairing the watch, which becomes a metaphor for the process of Anglicisation:

I myself took that watch to pieces, made a careful diagnosis, and saw that not only the little glass, but its whole outlook, body and life were in danger. So, I threw away the worn-out over-turned screws...replaced them by the best English screws, cleaned the teeth, and filed down the unnecessary parts. Afterwards, I set the dial on two straight, sound little legs and cleaned and polished every little bit.

But to this day it does not go accurately. It either goes too well or not at all. But it does not go accurately. (pp. 78–9)

Like Stern and Woolf, Oved suggests that Anglicisation can never be complete, and that 'the Jew' will never 'go accurately' in gentile society. Unlike these writers, however, Oved does not appear to have regarded this as a problem, treating it with humour rather than the frustration found in Stern's writing and the anxiety that Woolf's characters display. In Stern's novels the 'two little "Mezuzah" hands' that drag Jews in opposite directions are the force of Jewish tradition and the desire to acculturate, while the 'second hand' in which they become entangled is the impossibility of reconciling the two conflicting identifications and the resulting alienation. Ultimately, the attempt at self-transformation in accordance with gentile values is abandoned, and Stern's female characters retreat into the Jewish community. In *Peter Jackson* there is no Jewish community into which to retreat, and Peter's internal conflict is resolved through a new professional identity in which 'the Jew' is connected to the land, as if to secure his integration by rooting it in the soil. In 'The Three Jews', however, it is the English spring that brings the Jew's incongruity into focus, and enables the first and second Jews to recognise one another as 'outsiders'. Stern's Jews are bonded together by tradition, while Woolf's characters are connected by pejorative notions of 'race' that they anxiously seek to shed. None of these writers engages with religious conversion as a means of integration, however, despite the fact that Stern converted to Catholicism in 1947, and Frankau was baptised an Anglican and later became a Catholic. Woolf, in contrast, rejected Judaism in young adulthood, and adopted and maintained what his biographer terms a 'rather militant atheism'.[81] The excesses of the late nineteenth-century conversionist societies had damaged the credibility of conversionism, and the former emphasis on religious observance was being replaced by 'racial' and national constructions of Jewish identity. It is on these more complex markers of 'difference' that these writers focus.

Although religious conversion activity declined in the early twentieth century, the xenophobia of the war years increased the pressure upon Jews to assimilate, while making it harder for them to do so. Moshe Oved suggests that the effacement of Jewish identity reached such an extent under wartime conditions that by the early 1920s Judaism represented little more than a cuisine, in which 'The original, grandiose conceptions of Judah, from whose seed the nation expected that a Messiah would blossom forth, ultimately resulted in a little liver and goose-fat, chopped up with onions.'[82]

This loss, although mourned, is treated with Oved's characteristic blend of sadness and humour, which is sustained throughout his book. The only occasion on which his writing takes on an angry tone is in relation to gentile embarrassment at the fact that he was Jewish. This occurred when he was invited as guest of honour to a P.E.N. Club dinner in London.[83] The novelist and dramatist John Galsworthy announced his arrival:

> According to custom, he called out the name, branch of art and nationality of each guest of honour.
>
> When it came to my turn he announced: 'Mosheh Oved, a Polish poet.'
>
> It was a smack in the face the finger-marks of which will remain for a long time to come.
>
> The reason why this happened was that John Galsworthy is an aesthetic gentleman, a man who is full of pity for the living and who is a friend of the Jews. It seems that he did not

want to offend me before such a large audience by
announcing that Mosheh Oved was a Jew. (p. 98)

Oved, an immigrant, does not appear to have struggled with
relating 'Jewishness' to 'Englishness' in the way that some of the
British-born Jewish writers of the period did. This was perhaps
because he had Zionist sympathies and defined 'Jewishness' at least
partly in national terms, although he decided to stay in Britain and
became a naturalised British citizen in 1924. His autobiography
suggests he was less concerned with 'passing' than the Anglo-
Jewish writers discussed above, and there is a pride and humour in
his writing about 'Jewishness' that is not found in Stern's or
Frankau's work, much of which is characterised by anxiety and
frustration with regard to finding an English–Jewish identity. Oved
does not idealise Jews in Disraelian fashion, or seek to escape
Judaism or Zionism, and of antisemitism he takes a wry view, as in
his account of the P.E.N. Club dinner:

> After dinner, I ran across an Anti-Semitic woman whose Anti-
> Semitic arguments were very feeble and banal. I have much
> more to say against Jews than she has; but, for the sake of my
> people, I did her no harm and let her live! (p. 98)

In conclusion, there are a number of layers to this discussion of
the theme of 'conversion' or transformation in rhetoric and fiction
relating to the First World War. Most, however, can be linked to a
crisis of relation to constructions of 'Englishness' and the Church's
attempt to claim the national tradition as Protestant during this
period. First, there is the crisis of authority and what I have termed
'conversion anxiety' within the Anglican Church. This was linked to
the Anglo-Catholic revival, in which individual clergymen took the
initiative in providing the ritual elements felt necessary to contain
the experience of war. As a result, earlier conflicts over Protestant
orthodoxy were revived, contributing to the general decline in
authority that had begun before 1914. Although the Anglo-Catholic
revival was never explicitly identified as the threatened conversion
of Protestant orthodoxy to a more Catholic form of worship, the
wartime suppression of ritualism by the higher clergy does suggest
a fear of this. Then there was the attempted 'conversion' of the
nation to Christian piety, through the evangelical National Mission
of Repentance and Hope, in keeping with the rhetoric of 'holy war'

and the construction of the nation as devoutly Protestant. The idea of 'national conversion' was also applied to Germany, portrayed in popular rhetoric as having renounced Christianity for the new creed of militarism, the remedy for which was its symbolic conversion back to Christianity through military defeat. British soldiers, on the other hand, used conversion as a metaphor for their personal transformation through combat, as an image of their brutalisation in war, or to convey a loss of religious faith.

Religious conversionist societes were discredited by the early twentieth century, and the conversion of the Jews was a subject confined to the margins of Protestantism and to academic theologians. Proposals included Margaret Willinks' argument for a Christian theocracy in post-war Britain, Robertson's psychological exploration of the process of conversion, and Williams' call for the revival of Hebrew-Christianity. But although religious conversion activity decreased, Anglo-Jewish fiction of this period suggests that the pressure to assimilate increased, while the anti-alienism of the war years made it harder for Jews to do so. Jewish writers were also struggling with ideas of nationhood during the war, not only with regard to constructions of Protestant 'Englishness', but also to the publicity given to political Zionism at this time. The Anglo-Jewish fiction discussed above indicates the difficulty of asserting an English–Jewish identity and the anxiety and alienation caused by antisemitism. Both Stern and Woolf wrote about the desirability and the futility of the attempted self-transformation of 'the Jew'. Stern portrayed assimilation as a struggle to meet impossible and shifting criteria and as such, a process that could never be complete. Leonard Woolf's 'The Three Jews' explored the internalisation of antisemitism, and its role in the process of assimilation. Without a collective religious or national identity, Jews in this story define themselves in terms of 'race', a discourse dominated by antisemitic constructions of Jewish physiognomy and psychology, which portray 'Jewishness' as something negative that can never be trans-cended. Only Frankau resolves the matter, attempting a Disraelian assertion of the value of 'the Jew' to Britain by incorporating this aspect of Peter's character into a role that is deeply connected to the land, as a financially astute gentleman farmer. In this way, 'the Jew' is safely incorporated into post-war English identity. But the anxiety regarding the nature of 'Jewishness' in his writing is recognisable, in the portrayal of Jewish characters as non-combatants, cowards, profiteers, effeminate, impotent and parasitic.

The notion of unassimilable 'Jewish difference' increased during the war, and the next chapter discusses the development of this, and considers the theme of political 'conversion' in the British government's 'Zionist' mission to the Jews, which began in the summer of 1917. Rather than demanding that Jews should transcend their 'Jewishness', this campaign constructed Jewish identity as national and put Jews in Britain under a new pressure: not to struggle with their origins, as the process of assimilation demanded, but to return to them, in Palestine.

NOTES

1   Joseph Leftwich, 'The Jew II', in *Along the Years, Poems 1911–1937* (London: Robert Anscombe, 1937). See Chapter 2, note 83 for biographical information on this writer. Unlike some of the other British-Jewish writers discussed in this thesis, Leftwich did not convert to Christianity, and wrote a number of poems during and after the war in which he criticised Catholicism in particular as idolatrous, and Christians in general as unsympathetic towards Jews. See 'Rome' (1924), 'In the tube' (1916) and 'They laugh' (1917), in Leftwich, *Along the Years*.

2   For information on conversion discourses in Britain in the seventeenth, the late eighteenth and nineteenth centuries, see Mel Scult, *Millennial Expectations and Jewish Liberties: A Study of the Efforts to Convert the Jews in Britain, up to the Mid Nineteenth Century* (Leiden: E. J. Brill, 1978).

3   Scult, *Millennial Expectations*, p. 17.

4   The German Reformation took place in 1520, and the movement spread to Switzerland in 1523, Prussia in 1525, Denmark in 1536, Netherlands in 1566 and Scotland in 1560. France remained Catholic partly because Francis I was reliant on income from the Church. Hermann Kinder and Werner Hilgemann, *The Anchor Atlas of World History*, Vol. 1 (New York, London, Toronto and Sydney: Anchor Press, 1974), pp. 230–8.

5   Todd M. Endelman, *Radical Assimilation in English History, 1656–1945* (Bloomington and Indianapolis, IN: Indiana University Press, 1990), p. 9.

6   Ragussis, *Figures of Conversion*, pp. 131–2. Ragussis gives John Stockdale's *History of the Inquisitions* (1810) as an example of this. Stockdale suggested that Catholic proselytising during the Inquisition had 'perverted' the Spanish national character, and implied that the emancipation of Catholics in Britain would have a similar effect upon the English national character.

7   Ragussis, *Figures of Conversion*, p. 132.

8   See 'Heaviness and joy', an address given at Islington Parish Church, 1914–1915, in Winnington-Ingram, *The Church in Time of War*, pp. 227–8, and 'In time of War', a sermon preached at St Paul's Cathedral, 9 August 1914, in *Kaiser or Christ?*, p. 6.

9   G. K. A. Bell, *Randall Davidson, Archbishop of Canterbury*, (London, New York and Toronto: Oxford University Press, 2nd edn 1938), pp. 470–1.

10   Bell, *Randall Davidson* (1938), pp. 461–71.

11   Letter from Archbishop Davidson to Bishop Gore, 25 February 1913, quoted in Bell, *Randall Davidson*, p. 673.

12   Bell, *Randall Davidson*, pp. 671–87.

13   Bourchier, *For All We Have and Are*, p. 3.

14   *The Times*, 26 October 1917, p. 9.

15   *The Times*, 26 October 1917, p. 9.

16 *Church Guardian*, 28 June 1917, p. 505.
17 The Three Arts Women's Employment Fund found work for women who had lost their usual employment through the war, and were not suited to munitions work.
18 *The Times*, 25 April 1917, p. 7. Joan of Arc was beatified by the Catholic Church in 1909 and canonised in 1920.
19 Letter from organiser Clara Butt-Rumford to the Editor, *The Times*, 26 April 1917, p. 6.
20 Bourchier, *For All We Have and Are*, p. 37.
21 Seventy-five per cent of British troops were registered as Church of England, and the Church, the Society for the Promotion of Christian Knowledge (SPCK) and the Foreign Bible Mission distributed over 40 million Bibles, prayer books and hymn books to the troops during 1914–16. Wilkinson, *The Church of England* (1978), pp. 126, 153.
22 Lieutenant Robert Furley Callaway, letter dated 2 September 1916. In Laurence Housman (ed.), *War Letters of Fallen Englishmen* (London: Victor Gollancz, 1930), pp. 58–9.
23 Captain John Eugene Crombie, letter dated 2 March 1917. In Housman, (ed.), *War Letters*, p. 80.
24 C. E. Montague, *Disenchantment* (London: Chatto & Windus, 1922), p. 65.
25 Montague, *Disenchantment*, p. 184.
26 See Wilkinson, *The Church of England*, pp. 195–6.
27 Neville S. Talbot, quoted in Wilkinson, *The Church of England*, p. 161.
28 Neville S. Talbot, *Religion Behind the Front and After the War* (London: Macmillan, 1918), pp. 20–1.
29 Talbot, *Religion Behind the Front*, p. 67.
30 The divorce rate in Britain increased threefold, from 596 in 1910, to 1,629 in 1910. See Arthur Marwick, *The Deluge: British Society and the First World War* (London: The Bodley Head, 1965), p. 111. The rate of illegitimate births rose in 1916, and was attributed to economic and social change, and the effect of war on morality (see p. 108). On drunkenness, see pp. 65, 67–8.
31 A. Lukyn Williams, *The Hebrew-Christian Messiah: Or the Presentation of the Messiah to the Jews in the Gospel according to St. Matthew* (London: SPCK, 1916), p. 8. Williams was Honorary Canon of Ely Cathedral and former Tyrwhitt Hebrew Scholar at Cambridge University.
32 See Endelman, *Radical Assimilation*, pp. 145–6 and David S. Katz, *Philo-Semitism and the Readmission of the Jews to England 1603–1655* (Oxford: Clarendon Press, 1982), chs 3 and 5.
33 See Ragussis, *Figures of Conversion*, p. 15.
34 The missions were also the only places where immigrants could obtain free health care, see Endelman, *Radical Assimilation*, pp. 167–8.
35 Endelman, *Radical Assimilation*, p. 7.
36 See Sander L. Gilman, *Jewish Self-Hatred: Anti-Semitism and the Hidden Language of the Jews* (Baltimore, MD, and London: Johns Hopkins University Press, 1986) for an account of the mechanisms of the projection and internalisation of constructions of the Jewish 'other'.
37 *The Times*, 28 September 1915, p. 5.
38 D. W. Bebbington, *Evangelicalism in Modern Britain: A History from the 1730s to the 1980s* (London: Unwin Hyman, 1989), p. 85.
39 Premillennialists believe that Christ will return before the millennium, unlike postmillennialists, who believe that Christians must strive to create the conditions for his return, by spreading the faith.
40 Bebbington, *Evangelicalism*, p. 193.
41 See Bebbington, *Evangelicalism*, pp. 85, 192.
42 These papers were published as individual pamphlets, as part of *The Dispensational Series. Papers read at the Women's Branch of the Prophecy Investigation Society* (London: Alfred Holness, 1913) and *Various Tracts on British Israelism and Modern Apocalyptic. Papers read to the Prophecy*

Investigation Society, 1912–1921 (London: Covenant Publishing, 1921).

43   A. M. Hodgkin, 'The firstfruits', a paper read to the Women's Branch of the Prophecy Investigation Society, 11 May 1916, *The Dispensational Series*, No. 10, p. 9. The reference to 'Salmon' was not an error on Hodgkin's part. He was the father of Boaz, who married Ruth, the great-grandmother of King David. See Ruth 4:20.

44   It is difficult to establish accurate figures, since the records kept by conversionist societies were generally somewhat inflated. See Endelman, *Radical Assimilation*, p. 161, and Scult, *Millennial Expectations*, pp. 115–23.

45   Hodgkin, 'The firstfruits', p. 11.

46   Ada R. Habershon, 'The Day of Atonement in its Prophetic Aspect', a paper read to Women's Branch of the Prophecy Investigation Society, 11 May 1916. Published in pamphlet form as No. 11 in *The Dispensational Series*, pp. 7–8.

47   Habershon, 'The Day of Atonement in its Prophetic Aspect', p. 7.

48   E. A. Bland's paper 'The Church and the tribulation', read to the Women's Branch of the Prophecy Investigation Society on 18 November 1915, is a typical example of the denunciatory approach. The paper is an incoherent and confusing rant about the necessity of the Jews' acceptance of Jesus as the Messiah and their conversion to Christianity. See E. A. Bland, 'The Church and the Tribulation', pamphlet No. 8 in *The Dispensational Series*.

49   Williams, *The Hebrew-Christian Messiah*, p. 8.

50   'Hebrew-Christianity' segregated converts from other Christians, ostensibly as a reminder to both Jews and Christians of the redemptive role ascribed to the converted Jew in the New Testament. See Endelman, *Radical Assimilation*, pp. 160–2.

51   Williams, *The Hebrew-Christian Messiah*, p. 205.

52   Williams, *The Hebrew-Christian Messiah*, p. 208.

53   Williams, *The Hebrew-Christian Messiah*, p. 206.

54   Williams, *The Hebrew-Christian Messiah*, p. 206.

55   J. A. Robertson, *The Spiritual Pilgrimage of Jesus, the Bruce Lectures, 1917* (London: James Clarke, 5th edn 1922), p. 121.

56   Robertson, *The Spiritual Pilgrimage*, p. 23.

57   Robertson, *The Spiritual Pilgrimage*, p. 41.

58   Robertson, *The Spiritual Pilgrimage*, p. 138.

59   See the 'Woolwich crusade' of September 1917, discussed in Chapter 2, as an example of the deliberate involvement of the Church in wartime politics.

60   Margaret Dorothea Rose Willink, *Utopia According to Moses: A Study in the Social Teaching of the Old Testament* (London: SPCK, 1919).

61   Willink, *Utopia*, p. 20.

62   Willink, *Utopia*, p. 24.

63   Willink, *Utopia*, pp. 53, 58.

64   Willink, *Utopia*, p. 69.

65   Willink, *Utopia*, p. 74.

66   Endelman, *Radical Assimilation*, p. 209.

67   Stern, *Monogram*, p. 286.

68   Stern, *Pantomime*. All other page references will appear in the text.

69   Stern, *Children of No Man's Land*. Further page references will be made in the text.

70   G. B. Stern, *Twos and Threes* (London: Nisbet, 1916). Subsequent page references will be made in the text.

71   Gilman, *Jewish Self-Hatred*, p. 3.

72   Stern, *Children of No Man's Land*, p. 85.

73   Leonard Woolf's story 'The three Jews' was published with a story by Virginia Woolf entitled 'The mark on the wall', in Leonard S. Woolf and Virginia Woolf, *Two Stories* (Richmond: Hogarth, 1917). All subsequent page references will be given in the text.

74   See Gilman, *Jewish Self-Hatred*, for a full discussion of this theory.
75   Gilbert Frankau, *Peter Jackson, Cigar Merchant. A Romance of Married Life* (London: MacDonald, 1919). Subsequent page references will be included in the text.
76   Gilbert Frankau, *Self-Portrait: A Novel of his Own Life* (London: The Book Club, 1941), p. 160.
77   Sigmund Freud, 'Creative writers and day-dreaming' (1908), *Standard Edition of the Complete Psychological Works of Sigmund Freud*, trans. James Strachey in collaboration with Anna Freud (London: Hogarth, 1959), p. 150.
78   On attitudes to war neurosis see Anthony Babington, *Shell-shock: A History of the Changing Attitudes to War Neurosis* (London: Leo Cooper, 1997).
79   Disraeli's novels portray the Jews as a 'racial' aristocracy and argue for a continuity between 'Hebraic' and English culture that is beneficial to British imperialism. See Ragussis, *Figures of Conversion*, and Cheyette, *Constructions*, chapter 3, on the subsequent uptake of these ideas by gentile writers including John Buchan and Rudyard Kipling.
80   Moshe Oved, *Visions and Jewels: Autobiographic in Three Parts* (1925, London: Faber & Faber, 1952). Subsequent page references will appear in the text.
81   Duncan Wilson, *Leonard Woolf: A Political Biography* (London: Hogarth, 1978), pp. 12–13.
82   Oved, *Visions and Jewels*, p. 87.
83   The P.E.N. Club was an international association of writers founded in 1921 by Mrs Dawson-Scott. The lawyer and writer John Galsworthy (1867–1933), who received the Nobel Prize for Literature in 1932, was president.

5

The Political 'Conversion' of the Jews

One of the characteristics of antisemitic discourse is its ability to adapt in response to changing political and social circumstances, and its efforts to make Jews embody whatever is perceived as threatening the nominally Christian state and society at any time. The conspiracy theories that antisemitism generates focus on the fact that the Jews have been a people in dispersion, and this has given rise to various constructions of the 'international Jew' as actively hostile to the Christian nation-state. An extreme example of this was the fear of the 'world Jewish conspiracy' that was expressed in the forged *Protocols of the Learned Elders of Zion*, published in Russia in 1905 and in England in 1920.[1] In the mid to late nineteenth century the sexual and moral threat that international prostitution was perceived as representing to British society was projected onto Jewish immigrants, giving rise to the idea, discussed in Chapter 2, that the 'white slave traffic' was run by a network of Jewish immigrant procurers. In the early twentieth century Jews were made to embody the political threat represented by anarchism, socialism and especially communism, all of which were popularly portrayed as 'Jewish' ideologies. In response to the emergence of these political movements new conspiracy theories regarding Jews developed, fuelled in Britain, like the 'white slavery' scare, by the sharp increase in immigration from the 1880s onwards of Russian and Polish Jews fleeing tsarist antisemitism. Many of the young people among the refugees were politically disaffected, and some became involved in radical politics. It was from this small basis in fact, as with all 'Jewish' stereotypes, that the image of the international 'political Jew' developed and became the focus of gentile fears regarding national stability and political change. In Britain this tendency began with anarchism, as both Jewish immigrants and anarchists were concentrated in the East

End of London. A popular association between the two developed, assisted by the national press, and it was this association that laid the foundations for fears regarding the spread of 'Jewish Bolshevism' that accompanied the rise of the Bolshevik party in Russia in 1917.

This chapter explores the popular notion that there was an inherent connection between Judaism and revolutionary politics. The first section traces the development of political antisemitism in Britain from the 1880s into the First World War, placing particular emphasis on the confusion between religion and politics that characterised this discourse, in which the fear of the political 'conversion' of the nation by 'Jews' can be detected. This confusion between religion and politics arises partly because of wartime representations of the nation as devoutly Christian, and partly because, in effect, political antisemitism attempted to reconstruct the barriers to Jews' participation in national life that had been removed by emancipation in 1858. The old argument that membership of the Established Church was intrinsic to national consciousness and loyalty was replaced by the view that it was the Jews' political rather than religious affiliations that threatened the state. Later in this chapter I draw on Michael Ragussis' view of the 'double ideology' of tolerance and conversion with regard to Protestant attitudes towards Jews,[2] and argues that in response to the threat of 'Jewish Bolshevism' the British government mobilised another construction of Jewish political identity, namely Zionism, and used the Balfour Declaration and the Jewish Legion to attempt a political 'conversion' of the Jews.[3] By this means the Jews would be transformed from an international to a national group, from potential Bolsheviks to Jewish nationalists.

'THE MESSIAH WILL BE A SOCIALIST'

The idea that there is a link between Marxism and Judaism stems from, as Robert Wistrich has argued, a theological perspective on Marxism, which distorts both the Marxist view of religion and Jewish messianism.[4] Although a number of Jews were active in late nineteenth- and early twentieth-century European radical politics, utopian socialism was dominated by gentiles, a fact frequently overlooked by those who wanted to racialise revolutionary political movements.[5] However, representations of 'the Jew' are frequently dual and contradictory in nature, and this figure could also embody the evils of capitalism.[6] Marx himself equated Judaism with capitalism in his 1843 essay 'On the Jewish Question', and suggested that Jews had 'converted' Christians to the 'worship' of money:

> The Jew has emancipated himself in a Jewish manner, not only annexing the power of money, but also because through him and also apart from him money has become a world power and the practical spirit of the Jew has become the practical spirit of the Christian people. The Jews have emancipated themselves in so far as the Christians have become Jews.[7]

In contrast with Aaron Lieberman, who found socialist principles in Mosaic Law, Marx saw capital as the secular face of Judaism, and stated that 'an emancipation from haggling and money, from practical, real Judaism would be the self-emancipation of our age'.[8] Lieberman, on the other hand, saw the Jews as the inheritors of a radical social tradition that had its roots in the Pentateuch, and wrote:

> The community has always been the basis of our whole existence... The community was the basis of our legislation, which in unmistakeable words forbade the sale of the land, and in the sense of equality and brotherhood which required a redistribution of the soil every seven years. Our most ancient social system is anarchy; our true federation over the entire earth – the International.[9]

Aaron Lieberman (1849–80) founded the Hebrew Socialist Union in Whitechapel in May 1876. This passage from the Russian anarchist journal *Vpered!* (*Forward*) was quoted in translation by Rudolf Rocker, one of the gentile leaders of Jewish immigrants in the East End from 1898 to 1914, in his memoir, *The London Years* (1956). Rocker, an anarchist, arrived in Britain on 1 January 1895 and settled in the East End, where he learned Yiddish and in October 1898 became editor of the paper *Arbiter Fraint* (*Worker's Friend*).[10] Rocker was not the only gentile radical who became editor of a Yiddish newspaper. Another gentile, a Russian Marxist named Beck, edited the paper *Die Neue Zeit* from 1904 to 1908. In the Jews' history of segregation, Rocker saw a greater radical potential than that found in Christian society, since in his view, Jews had through exclusion and necessity developed a high level of co-operation and self-regulation, and with this in mind, he focused his attention on the Jewish immigrants in the East End.[11]

The notion that there was a connection between Judaism and revolutionary politics was satirised by Israel Zangwill in *Children of the Ghetto* (1892), through the character of Melchitsedek Pinchas, who proclaims:

> Our great teacher, Moses, was the first Socialist. The legislation of the Old Testament – the land laws, the jubilee regulations, the tender care for the poor, the subordination of the rights of property to the interests of the working-men – all this is pure Socialism!... Socialism is Judaism and Judaism is Socialism, and Karl Marx and Lassalle, the founders of Socialism, were Jews... Yes, brothers, the only true Jews in England are the Socialists. Phylacteries, praying-shawls – all nonsense. Work for Socialism – that pleases the Almighty. The Messiah will be a Socialist.[12]

As this passage suggests, there were Jews who spoke of radical politics in quasi-religious terms, and to some immigrants Rocker represented a secular 'rabbi'. The anarchist Sam Dreen worked closely with Rocker in the East End before the First World War, and in an interview in 1969, recalled that,

> He united us, filled us with revolutionary ardour, inspired us with his clear thinking and wide knowledge, his love and understanding of art and literature and the values of culture. Rocker was our rabbi![13]

Another man, a baker named Kosoff, made a similar observation: 'He was my Rabbi! If it wouldn't be for the Club I might never have read a book.'[14] If some of the Jewish immigrants saw Rocker as their political 'rabbi', it must be noted that he did not 'preach' anarchism as such (although he gave lectures on history and politics), but instead initiated real improvements for immigrants, through education, unionisation and the provision of practical resources for the community. His efforts, however, were partly shaped by the desire to transform Jewish immigrants in accordance with his own political vision, and by a sense of their inherent capacity to make that transformation. It is this idea of the transformative potential of Jews that connects him to the Christian conversionists who operated in the East End during the nineteenth century. Like the conversionist societies, the anarchist clubs offered much-needed practical resources to Jewish immigrants, but these came with ideological strings attached. Just as some Christian proselytisers emphasised the similarities between Judaism and Christianity in their conversion rhetoric, Rocker was attracted by the perceived similarity between the principles of Judaism and those of anarchism, as expressed by Lieberman. In the conversion of the Jews, evangelical Christians saw the means of their own salvation, and in the Jews of the East End, Rocker saw the potential for creating an anarchist society. Rocker, however, was no 'millennial' anarchist, but saw anarchism as a stage in the progression of human society, as he noted in his memoir:

> My innermost conviction was that Anarchism was not to be conceived as a definite closed system, nor as a future millennium, but only as a particular trend in the historic development towards freedom in all fields of human thought and action, so that no strict and unalterable lines could therefore be set down for it.[15]

Accordingly, Rocker was less concerned with the 'conversion' of immigrant Jews to anarchism than with making immediate improvements to their quality of life. He focused his efforts on providing educational and recreational facilities in the East End, and helped to found the anarchist club in Jubilee Street, which opened on 3 February 1906. In December 1910 the journalist Philip Gibbs visited the club to assess the anarchist threat, and observed: 'These alien anarchists were as tame as rabbits. I am convinced that they had not a revolver among them. But out of that anarchist club in the East End come ideas.'[16]

The 'ideas' Gibbs referred to seem to have come from the national press rather than the 'alien anarchists', and by 1910 *The Times* was denouncing 'aliens' as violent troublemakers. A number of incidents had fuelled this, one of which was the 'Tottenham outrages', when on 23 January 1909, two Jewish men, Jacob Lepidus and Paul Hefeld, stole the payroll for Schnurmann's rubber factory in Tottenham. The police opened fire and a constable was killed, three others wounded and fifteen bystanders injured. Lepidus was killed and Hefeld received a head wound. *The Times* reported that it had been 'thoroughly established' that the thieves were 'members of the Russian revolutionary party, whose headquarters are known to be in London', and the two men were thought to be 'engaged in conveying revolutionary literature' from Russia to the West.[17] There seems to have been some confusion regarding the men's political allegiances, however. In one report they were identified as members of the Lettish Socialistic Revolutionary Party, and later by 'A member of the Russian revolutionary movement' as 'probably belonging to a Russian society known as Bolsheviky...the most extreme section of the Democratic party'. Lepidus was also described as 'a member of a notorious Russian revolutionary family'.[18] Ultimately, it was not the particulars of the revolutionary movements to which Jews belonged that were important, but the association itself, and it was this on which *The Times* traded in its appeals to popular antisemitism. An article published in the paper in 1911 described aliens, the majority of whom would, at that time, have been Jewish, as 'the waste products – the undesirable members of society', which the nations must eliminate or absorb. The article also referred to 'alien' involvement in the 'white slave traffic'.[19]

The 'Tottenham outrages' were followed by another incident that linked Jews with anarchism in the popular imagination, the 'Houndsditch murders' of 17 December 1910, in which three policemen died during the robbery of a jeweller's shop. Explosives and ammunition were found at an address in Gold Street, Stepney, where the thieves had been staying, along with papers in Russian and Yiddish, which led the police to conclude that the men concerned were members of 'a dangerous group of Anarchists'.[20] An article in *The Times* linked the violence to immigration, noting that 'the secretiveness and aloofness of the alien population' assisted anarchists, who could quickly blend in with the 'swarms of foreigners' in east London.[21] By January 1911, Chief Rabbi Dr Adler felt obliged to issue a statement to the effect that anarchism and Judaism were not alike, and to insist that it had been proved 'beyond doubt' that the Houndsditch murderers were Jews 'neither by race nor by faith'.[22] In fact, one of the men involved was a Jew, named Gardstein, who was killed during the robbery. Whether or not Gardstein was an anarchist, however, is unclear, although he had connections with the Italian anarchist Enrico Malatesta, who was arrested after the incident but later released.[23]

Despite flimsy evidence, the association between Jewish immigrants and anarchists persisted, as the coverage of the 'Siege of Sidney Street' shows. On 3 January 1911, police, disguised as 'Jewish pedlars', and a detachment of Scots Guards surrounded a house in which two men fitting the description of those involved in the Houndsditch incident were living. A siege ensued and after nearly seven hours of shooting the building caught fire and the men died. Winston Churchill, then Home Secretary, visited the scene, ensuring that the press gave the case a high profile, and the matter provoked calls for the amendment of the 1905 Aliens Act and for the police to be armed. Once again *The Times* appealed to popular antisemitism, noting of the onlookers that 'one could not fail to be struck with the fact that in nearly every case they were of the Semitic type', and reinforcing the political connection by referring to the two dead men as 'anarchists' throughout.[24] This assumption was perhaps partly based on the fact that Sidney Street ran immediately parallel to Jubilee Street,[25] where the anarchist club was located, and the article included a map showing this, but as investigations proceeded it became less clear that the dead men had been revolutionaries. Police found steel tubes in the house, which they initially identified as 'bomb-cases', but these were later proved to be leather cutting tools for use in button-making.[26] The inquest identified the men as 'Fritz Svaars' and 'Josef'. The causes of death were described as suffocation and shooting, and a verdict of justifiable homicide recorded.[27]

None of the men involved in these incidents was a proven member of the anarchist movement, and on only one occasion did Jewish members of the Jubilee Club plot violent activity, which Rocker intervened to prevent. This occurred in November 1909, when he discovered that the club had been infiltrated by *Okhrana* agents (the tsarist secret police) who had persuaded some young Russians to bomb the Lord Mayor's Show.[28] As *The Times'* coverage of these incidents shows, however, accuracy was not important in creating and maintaining a popular association between Jewish immigrants and radical political movements. Stories of 'alien' troublemakers appeared in the national press until 1914, when the anarchist movement in Britain was destroyed by the outbreak of the First World War. Rocker and other anarchist leaders were interned as 'enemy aliens', and the *Arbiter Fraint* was closed down by the British government in 1915.

As the war progressed, the image of the 'alien anarchist' gave way to that of the 'pro-German Jew', still an international figure but now with pronounced German sympathies, who attempted to use a network of Jewish financial power against the Allies. At the Foreign Office, fears were focused on British and American Jewish bankers, whose German connections and political influence were exaggerated, but whose financial support was vital to the war effort. By 1915 the Allies were seeking a war loan from, among others, the American Jewish banker Jacob Schiff, but were hampered in this by neutral Jewry's opposition to tsarist anti-semitism. Schiff was of German origin and agreed to extend a loan to Britain and France, but refused to lend money to Russia until the situation of Russian Jews was ameliorated.[29] As Russia's ally, Britain attempted, under pressure from the Anglo-Jewish journalist and diplomat Lucien Wolf, to secure the reform of Russia's anti-Jewish laws, but with little success.[30] It was subsequent political events that improved the position of Russian Jews. On 23 February (8 March) 1917 a revolution broke out in St Petersburg, in which some members of the military joined forces with the revolutionaries. This was followed by the abdication of Tsar Nicholas II in March 1917 and the formation of a provisional government, led initially by Prince Lvov, and later, in July, by Prime Minister Alexander Kerensky. By April 1917 Jews in Russian territory were emancipated, and the required American–Jewish financial support was forthcoming.[31] But the provisional government was short-lived and in August General Kornilov led anti-liberal forces in an attempted coup. This, too, was defeated, and another revolution occurred on 24–25 October (6–7 November), in which the Bolshevik party seized control.

Britain now feared not only the withdrawal of its ally from the war but also the spread of revolution. With the abdication of the tsar, the overthrow of the liberal Kerensky government, and the attack on the Russian Orthodox Church, Bolshevism could easily be construed, by those inclined to do so, as the latest international 'Jewish' attack on the Christian nation-state. Exaggerated reports of Russian Jews' Bolshevik sympathies were supplied by Robert Wilton, Petrograd correspondent to *The Times* and supported by the paper's editor Henry Wickham Steed. Political anxiety in Britain began to focus on the 'revolutionary Jew', agitating for the overthrow of the monarchy and parliamentary democracy. One possible way to deter Russian Jewry from supporting Bolshevism, in the eyes of the British government, was to pledge British support for Zionism. In the spring of 1917 Sir Mark Sykes of the Foreign

Office had entered into discussions with Zionist leaders, having been persuaded by Chaim Weizmann that an appeal to Zionist feeling would secure the support of neutral Jews for the Allies and deter Russian Jews from revolutionary politics.[32] Weizmann argued that antisemitism was linked to assimilation and would be eradicated through the creation of a Jewish homeland in Palestine. Lucien Wolf, who with Israel Zangwill had been involved in the Jewish Territorial Organisation (ITO) in 1905, now felt that Zionist activity could arouse xenophobia, provoke expulsions in Eastern Europe, and undermine the civil rights of assimilated Jews.[33] Wolf favoured continuing to negotiate for legal reform in Russia, but as Mark Levene has observed, Weizmann's perspective was more expedient, allowing the British to make a gesture of support for Jewry while avoiding confrontation with its ally over the persecution of Russian Jews.[34] It also offered the important illusion that government-endorsed 'Zionism' would deter Russian and East End Jewry from supporting the revolution.

Jews in both Russia and Britain held diverse views regarding revolutionary politics, but the complexity of their political identifications went largely unreported in the British national press. In Russia, orthodox Marxists regarded antisemitism as a product of capitalist society, and argued that efforts to preserve Jewish culture under socialism would simply maintain the 'ghetto' identity and invite antisemitic attack. The Jewish *Bund*, founded in 1897, was an anti-Zionist socialist organisation that disputed this, and sought to preserve a degree of Jewish cultural autonomy within the Russian socialist movement.[35] There were more Jews in the moderate Menshevik party than among the Bolsheviks, but it was the image of the 'Bolshevik Jew' that caught the popular imagination in Britain.[36] As the Bolsheviks gained support in Russia, fears were aroused in Britain, not least by the Northcliffe press, which owned *The Times* and the *Daily Mail*, that revolution would spread through the Jewish immigrants in the East End, already regarded as political troublemakers as a result of the publicity given to the earlier involvement of some Jews in anarchism.

How much truth was there in the construction of the 'revolutionary Jew' that emerged in wartime Britain? Prominent Jews in the development of European revolutionary politics included Moses Hess (1812–75), Karl Marx (1818–83), Ferdinand Lasalle (1825–64), Edouard Bernstein (1850–1932) and Rosa Luxemburg (1871–1919). The most notorious Russian revolutionary

Jew was Leon Trotsky (born Leo Bronstein, 1879–1940), a figure who prompted some to view all Jews as likely communist sympathisers. In Britain, the most prominent Jewish revolutionary was Maxim Litvinov (1876–1951), an immigrant from Russia and a member of the British Socialist Party. Litvinov was deported from Britain in September 1918, and was succeeded by Theodore Rothstein. When Rothstein was prevented from returning to Britain from Moscow in 1920, members of his family continued the Anglo-Soviet links. Jews were also involved in the Communist Party of Great Britain, and the Social Democratic Federation. Right-wing opinion associated the rise of the International Labour Party (ILP) with the Bolshevik coup, and Emmanuel Shinwell (1888–1986), who in 1922 became the first Jewish Labour MP, was dubbed the ILP's 'Jewish Bolshevik' for his role in the 'Red Clydeside' unrest in 1919.[37]

Most of the Jewish radicals in wartime Britain were immigrants, and as a result, concern over the 'revolutionary Jew' focused on the immigrant population. With recent memories of life under the tsars, some Jewish immigrants did become active in the socialist and communist movements, partly owing to a suspicion of state authority developed under the tsars, and partly because they had little parliamentary representation. There were no Jewish MPs representing East End constituencies in 1917, although Joseph King, Liberal MP for north Somerset, defended the Jews against the proposed Conscription Bill, and as a result earned himself the nickname 'King of the Jews',[38] which suggests a combination of religious and political themes in fears regarding Jewish immigrants. Jewish political groups in First World War Britain included the Marxist Jewish Social Democratic Party (the *Bund*, which became affiliated to the British Socialist Party after 1917), *Poalei Zion* (the Labour Zionists), and the Committee of Delegations of Russian Socialist Groups.[39] Other groups were formed with the aim of representing the collective interests and defending the rights of Jewish immigrants. Of these, the Foreign Jews' Protection Committee against Compulsion and Deportation (FJPC), founded in June 1916, was the most radical. After the Bolshevik coup, some of the most committed Jewish radicals returned to support the new Russia, and their departure meant that Jewish radicalism in the East End was far from the threatening presence described in the national press.

On the whole, the Jewish press in Britain was critical of communism during and after the war, aware of the danger for Jews of overtly supporting revolutionary politics at a time when 'aliens' were regarded with suspicion. Reporting on wartime events for a Jewish readership proved a delicate task, as discussion of issues affecting Jews in the Diaspora fuelled accusations of 'internationalism', and could lead to conflict with the censor. Like the Anglo-Jewish press, the Yiddish papers wrote optimistically of the liberal 'Kerensky revolution', but regarded Bolshevism with mistrust, owing to its hostility towards both Jewish nationalism and religion.[40] Despite the caution of the Jewish press in its coverage of revolutionary politics, however, the image of the 'Bolshevik Jew' persisted.

An alternative construction of Jewish political identity, and one that had the official support of the British government, was of 'the Jew' as Zionist, the antithesis of Bolshevik internationalism. This held a number of advantages for the British. A 'Zionist' approach to the political 'Jewish question' would facilitate the conscription of Russian Jewish immigrants – who had understandably been reluctant to fight in alliance with the tsar – and would allow Britain to expand its imperial territory through the proposed annexation of Palestine (General Allenby's troops were amassed at Sinai for this purpose by April 1917). Plans for the formation of specifically Jewish battalions in the British army were announced in June 1917 and aroused much debate. Jews in Britain were suspicious of the government's motives, having historical reason to be mistrustful of gentile 'solutions' to the 'Jewish question', the most recent example being the religious conversionist societies of the nineteenth century. What appeared to be happening in 1917 was that Jews were being subjected to another conversion drive, this time political, as the British government began to proselytise on behalf of Jewish nationalism.

The dialectical relationship between religion and politics in the Christian state was noted by Marx in 1843, when he wrote, 'The so-called Christian state...has a political attitude to religion and a religious attitude to politics.[41] In other words, under certain conditions the politics of the Christian state may become evangelical and its religious discourses political, presenting particular difficulties for Jews within the population. In the Christian state, Jews represented a perceived obstacle and a threat to fantasies of religious, cultural and national homogeneity, all of which became more important under wartime conditions. The obstacle and threat they appeared to represent in 1917 was as a people whose 'difference' was not contained within its own national borders, but dispersed around the world, representing a threatening heterogeneity and a means for the spread of revolutionary politics, then widely perceived as 'Jewish'. Fears regarding this were linked to the Jewish messianic tradition, with its promise of social and political reform, and in Britain this gave rise to the idea that Jewish immigrants could be attracted to the 'false messiah' of Bolshevism, and support revolution. The government's response, in what was becoming an increasingly simplistic discourse regarding Jewish collective political identity, was to promote Zionism as the 'good' Jewish political identity, and to set about 'converting' Britain's immigrant Jews, in particular, to nationalism, by means of the Jewish Legion and the Balfour Declaration. (British-born Jews were also under pressure to support the legion, and the issue proved divisive, but government anxiety was focused on the immigrant population.) As a result of this, Jews in Britain became caught in an ideological struggle between Bolshevism and Zionism that, for those whose sympathies were neither nationalist nor internationalist, made any other political self-definition very difficult.

'THE VOICE OF GOD'

It was a Jewish soldier, Acting Corporal Issy Smith, who won the first Victoria Cross of the Great War, in August 1915.[42] Yet in spite of this, the years 1914–18 were a period in which the loyalty and patriotism of Jews living in England was the subject of debate. In response to the climate of mistrust, the *Jewish Chronicle* published lists of Jewish volunteers for the army,[43] but regardless of the high rate of enlistment among Jews in Britain, their patriotism remained under suspicion. When conscription was introduced in the spring of 1916, some 25–30,000 Russian-born Jews of military age were strictly speaking ineligible, since they were not British subjects. The War Office decided in May 1916 to allow these men to enlist, but they were wary of fighting in alliance with the tsarist regime, having left Russia as a result of persecution. Those who refused to enlist were threatened with deportation, and in an attempt to resolve the problem, it was suggested that an all-Jewish regiment be formed. Vladimir Jabotinsky (1880–1940), a writer, orator and linguist originally from Odessa, and an ardent Zionist, had been campaigning for this since 1915, but with little success. It was not until the spectre of the 'Jewish Bolshevik' emerged, combined with the need to conscript immigrants, that the idea was taken up by the War Office. The proposed Jewish Legion would be deployed in Palestine, forming part of the British government's 'Zionist' policy, in conjunction with the talks between the Foreign Office and Zionist leaders that eventually produced the Balfour Declaration. As a result of these negotiations, unenlisted Jewish immigrants were faced with a choice of returning to Russia at short notice, or being conscripted into the legion, and the families of those who elected to return to Russia would remain in Britain, unsupported by the state.

As Mark Levene has noted, once the British government had announced its plans for a separate Jewish regiment, 'there was a marked sympathy for Zionism among those journalists who had been most persistent in their accusations of corporate Jewish sabotage, disloyalty, and treason'.[44] Religious themes were introduced into the debate over the Legion, and *The Times* speculated that the proposed Jewish unit would bring about the restoration of Israel as described in the Bible. An article published in August 1917 opened with the statement, 'There is an ancient Jewish prophecy which says that the Jews will be led back to their own land by a man of another race.'[45] The fulfilment of prophecy by this means called for a Moses figure, a commanding officer for the Jewish soldiers, and an Irish Protestant, Lieutenant-Colonel John Henry Patterson, was selected for this role. Patterson was a professional soldier and big game hunter who had served in Africa before the war. During this time he had written two books describing his experiences, *The Man-Eaters of Tsavo* (1907) and *In the Grip of the Nyika* (1909), titles which suggest the author as imperial adventurer, braving the dangers of the remote dominions of the British Empire. Forming a Jewish regiment and taking it to Palestine represented a mix of imperial trailblazing, military campaign history, and biblical prophecy fulfilled, and it was a project that excited him, as his memoirs show.

Patterson had been cast as 'Moses' once before, as commander of the Zion Mule Corps at Gallipoli during the Dardanelles campaign (1915–16). The corps was a transport unit composed of Jews who had fled Palestine when war broke out, and volunteered for the British army. The unit served at Gallipoli from 26 April 1915 to 9 January 1916, when the British retreated. It was disbanded in March 1916, but its brief existence was sufficient to prompt biblical comparisons. Patterson's Gallipoli memoir describes how, in an address to the newly formed Jewish unit, the Grand Rabbi of

Alexandria explicitly linked him to the leader of the ancient Israelites:

> The Grand Rabbi then delivered a stirring address to the new soldiers, in which he compared them to their forefathers who had been led out of Egypt by Moses, and at the end he turned to me and presented me to them as their modern leader.[46]

Patterson himself made no claims to be a modern Moses, preferring to cast the Zionist leader Chaim Weizmann in this role. Instead, his memoirs suggest an identification with Jewish military leaders, men like Judas Maccabeus, who led the Jews against Rome in 166 BCE, and Simon Bar Kokhba, who led a three-year revolt against Hadrian in 132 CE. Indeed, prior to the First World War, Patterson's only knowledge of Jews had been biblical:

> When, as a boy, I eagerly devoured the records of the glorious deeds of Jewish military captains such as Joshua, Joab, Gideon and Judas Maccabeus, I little dreamt that one day I, myself, would, in a small way, be a captain of a host of the Children of Israel![47]

As prospective commander of the proposed Jewish regiment, however, Patterson effectively became the British government's Zionist missionary to the Jews, attempting to persuade the leaders of Anglo-Jewry and the English Zionist Federation that their interests were foremost in its plans. In his account of the Palestine campaign, published in 1922, he described one of his unsuccessful 'conversion' attempts:

> I tried to do what in me lay with certain of the leaders of Zionism, and spent some time endeavouring to enthuse a devoted and spiritual Jew who was deeply interested in the Restoration; indeed, I thought I had won him over to the cause of the legion, for at times during our conversation his face lit up at the possibilities unfolded to him, but, alas, after I left him, I fear he fell away from grace![48]

Under the British government's 'Zionist' proposal, rather than being converted to Christianity, as in the millennial narrative, the Jews were to be 'normalised' through entry into nationhood. As members of a separate Jewish regiment, their position would not be dissimilar to that of the 'Hebrew–Christians' in nineteenth-century proposals for the religious conversion of the Jews. The 'Hebrew–Christians', of which there were few, were converts who remained segregated within the Church, as a reminder to both Christians and Jews of their significance in the fulfilment of the millennial narrative of the conversion of the Jews prior to the second coming. Patterson's role in this government-instigated political transformation of the Jewish people into a nation was to recruit and train Jewish soldiers and lead them into Palestine. This represented the fulfilment of an imperial rather than a millennial narrative, in which 'Jewish brains, Jewish capital, and Jewish workers' would establish a colony in Palestine that would 'loyally carry out the policy of the Imperial Government' and also help protect British interests in Egypt.[49]

The Jewish community was divided over the issue of what many saw as the military segregation of Jews through the proposed legion, and it was feared that a 'ghetto regiment' would be the result. The *Jewish Chronicle* noted that there were many other 'friendly aliens' in Britain at the outbreak of the war, besides immigrants from Russia. Jews everywhere were fighting for their countries of adoption, not for a 'Jewish nationalist' cause, and unless the War Office had a strategic need for a specifically Jewish regiment, the legion would serve no other purpose than that of segregation.[50] The Grand Order of the Israel Friendly Society, meeting in London in August 1917, regarded the Jewish regiment as a 'calamity' for Jews in Britain, whose patriotism was beyond question, the Order itself having contributed £22,000 to war loans, and lost 15 men on the battlefield.[51] The English Zionist Federation believed that the formation of a Jewish Legion would prompt the Turks to attack Jews in Palestine, and the Conjoint Foreign Committee, headed by Lucien Wolf, argued that Jewish collective identity was religious rather than political, and disputed the existence of a Jewish nationality.[52]

Other voices were raised in criticism of the plan, and the *Daily News* published an article by the Liberal peer G. W. E. Russell, which backed Wolf's position, and argued that however well-intentioned the proposal for a Jewish regiment might be, it was impractical and unnecessary. Russell pointed out that British Catholics and Methodists were not being invited to join separate regiments, and insisted that neither should British Jews. Modern

Jewry, he argued, was not a political but a religious community, and to illustrate his point, gave an account of a conversation with a Jewish friend on the subject of war and patriotism:

> A Jewish friend of mine said the other day to a pacifist who tried to appeal to him on racial grounds: *'I would shoot a Jewish Prussian as readily as a Christian Prussian, if I found him fighting under the German flag.'*[53]

Despite the controversy and criticism aroused by the proposal, the War Office announced its decision to form a Jewish regiment on 8 August 1917, the day before the final deadline for those returning to Russia. Immigrants serving in the Jewish regiment would be automatically naturalised after their initial three months' training, at no personal expense. A committee was formed to implement the decision, chaired by Lord Rothschild, with the writer M. J. Landa as Honorary Secretary. There were also plans for the creation of a Jewish Medical Corps and a regimental band, and it was proposed that a separate training camp be set up approximately 40 miles outside London, with kosher kitchen facilities.

Throughout September 1917, Lord Derby met with several deputations from British Jewry to discuss the title and insignia of the regiments for Jews, and the conditions of service. In response to concerns over the use of the term 'Jewish' in identifying the soldiers, Lord Derby stated that there would be no special treatment; they would be given numerals and would wear the general service badge.[54]

Furthermore, it was acknowledged that Jewish troops must fight where they were needed.[55] The regiment came into being on 24 August 1917, and *The Times* noted with approval that the War Office had received 'hundreds' of applications for transfer from Jews serving in other battalions in the British army.[56] According to Patterson, however, few Jewish officers wished to transfer, although non-commissioned officers were more enthusiastic. As a result recruiting was slow and it took four months to form one battalion.[57] Eventually three regiments were formed: the 38th, 39th and 40th Royal Fusiliers. They became known as 'the Judaeans' and wore the *menorah* as part of their regimental insignia.

During the debate over the conscription of 'aliens' and the formation of the Jewish Legion, Cabinet Ministers had been meeting with the Zionist leader Chaim Weizmann to discuss policy for creating a Jewish homeland in Palestine. The result of this was the Balfour Declaration,[58] which was formally issued on 2 November 1917, too late for its anticipated prevention of the Bolshevik party's rise to power by appealing to the national rather than the (exaggerated) revolutionary sympathies of Russian Jewry. The Declaration went through five drafts before the final version was approved on 31 October 1917.[59] The first, Zionist draft, of July 1917, read:

1 His Majesty's Government accepts the principle that Palestine should be reconstituted as the national home of the Jewish people.
2 His Majesty's Government will use its best endeavours to secure the achievement of this object and will discuss the necessary methods and means with the Zionist Organisation.

The draft that followed this in August 1917, written by Foreign Secretary Arthur Balfour, reproduced the first crucial point almost verbatim, and stated the government's readiness to 'consider any suggestions on the subject which the Zionist Organisation may desire to lay before them'.[60] After this, however, the document went through three further drafts, in which the statement regarding the Jews' claim to Palestine as a national homeland became increasingly diluted and the government's position more ambiguous. The next draft, made by the Conservative Lord Alfred Milner (1854–1925), who joined Lloyd George's War Cabinet in 1916, gave the government's view that 'every opportunity should be afforded for the establishment of *a* home for the Jewish people *in* Palestine'.[61] With his Cabinet colleague the Conservative Leopold Amery (1873–1955), Milner produced another draft on 4 October 1917, which changed the government's position again, from accepting the Jews' claim to Palestine to viewing it 'with favour', and spoke of 'a national home for the Jewish *race*'.[62] Even as it appeared to identify the Jews as a distinct national group (the term 'race' at the time was frequently used in this regard),[63] the language of this third draft retreated from the earlier statement that Palestine should become their homeland. The Milner–Amery draft did, however, acknowledge some of the wider issues, including the concerns both of Palestine's Arab population and Anglo-Jewry, noting that the Declaration should not 'prejudice the civil and religious rights of existing non-Jewish communities in Palestine', nor should it affect the 'rights and political status enjoyed [by Jews] in any other country'.

Like the Jewish Legion, the Balfour Declaration created divisions among Jews in Britain, many of whom resented the expectation that they should automatically become Zionists. As Leonard Stein describes it,

> There was...a kind of pro-semitism which to some Jews looked like the opposite – the pro-semitism which put all the emphasis on the distinctiveness of the Jews and seemed almost to imply that emancipation had done them a wrong by blurring their identity as a nation.[64]

The Declaration was politically expedient, however, for both the War Cabinet and the Zionist leaders. The 'Zionism' of the British government was a response to a variety of problems with which it was faced in 1917. These included fears of the spread of 'Jewish Bolshevism'; the need to conscript non-naturalised Jewish immigrants in the East End; the potential loss of Russia as an ally and the desire for imperial expansion in the Middle East. To the Zionists, it offered the official support of a Western government for Jewish settlement in Palestine, and the possible resolution of the 'Jewish question'. Both Lloyd George and Arthur Balfour realised that the creation of a buffer state in Palestine, administered by Jews but ultimately subject to British authority, would not only help regenerate the empire but also safeguard Britain's interests in Egypt, which had become a British Protectorate in December 1914. But besides its political expediency, the Declaration also appealed to the religious sentiments of British Cabinet ministers. Weizmann remarked upon this as early as January 1915, in a report submitted to the Local Government Board, in which he referred to a meeting with Herbert Samuel in December the previous year:

> He [Samuel]...thinks that perhaps the Temple may be rebuilt, as a symbol of Jewish unity – of course in a modernised form. After listening to him, I remarked that I was pleasantly surprised to hear such words from him; that if I were a religious Jew I should have thought the Messianic times were near...He added that these ideas are in the mind of his colleagues in the Cabinet.[65]

Colonel R. Meinertzhagen, Chief Political Officer to the Egyptian Expeditionary Force (EEF) in Palestine, also noted religious sentiment among British politicians with regard to Zionism. According to Meinertzhagen, Lloyd George's support for the Declaration and the Legion was 'influenced entirely by sentiment and by his belief in the Old Testament'. Of Balfour, Meinertzhagen states that his 'real motive was to remedy the unsatisfactory state of the Jews in the world'.[66] As Leonard Stein has observed, 'Balfour was not moved by any mystical ideas about the return of the Chosen People to the Holy Land.' He did, however, express the view that Christians owed much to the Jews, and on several occasions stated that the Christian nations should make reparations to the Jewish people for their treatment of them.[67] Yet as Conservative Prime Minister in 1905 he had been largely responsible for the Aliens Act, which appeared to target Jews fleeing the pogroms in Russia. A similar ambivalence is identifiable in the 'Zionist' Declaration of 1917. Although portrayed as a gesture of support for the Jews, it was also a reaction to the fear of collective 'Jewish power', and the desire to restrict or control it. As Mark Levene has observed,

> the origins of the Balfour Declaration are to be located less in the wartime policies and strategies of Britain in the Middle East and more in the murky waters of modern anti-Semitism. At the bottom of the pool was the fear that a collective, potentially conspiratorial Jewry knew something which the rest of the world did not know, and could manipulate it accordingly for its own ends.[68]

In fact, the British were manipulating Zionism as part of a propaganda battle with Germany, also interested in appealing to Russian and North American Jewry through the creation of a Jewish protectorate on Turkish territory.[69] In the rhetorical context of 'holy war', the return of the Jews to Palestine took on immediate religious significance, as *The Times'* coverage of the debate over the Jewish Legion demonstrates. As one of the commanders of the Jewish Legion, Patterson described his view of the impact of Balfour's statement upon British Jewry: 'By pious Jews it was regarded as little short of the Voice of God, bringing their long-cherished aspirations within sight of fulfilment.'[70]

Indeed, Chaim Raphael recalls the excitement that the Palestine campaign generated in his local synagogue:

General Allenby's campaign to win back the Holy Land from the pagans was a situation they were completely at home with. It had happened before with Abraham, Isaac and Jacob, and then again with Joshua and King David. I knew the place-names myself from the weekly Bible readings, and listened eagerly. Sons of our congregation were actually in the British Army with Allenby, fighting like the old children of Israel. It was almost as if the Messiah was on his way.[71]

Patterson's account of the Palestine campaign was consistent with this view, framing the formation of the Jewish Legion and its deployment in Palestine as a modern re-enactment of the biblical Exodus story, a British-led military ingathering of the Jews and their return to the Promised Land.

The Jewish troops left Southampton and sailed for Egypt on 5 February 1918. A Sabbath service was held on board ship, in which Patterson suggested to his men that as long as they had the Ark of the Covenant, 'neither submarine nor storm would trouble us'. They arrived safely in Alexandria on 28 February, although the ship, the *Leasoe Castle*, was torpedoed and sunk on her next voyage.[72] Alongside the biblical allegory, there is also a suggestion of what might be termed 'Zionist eugenics' in Patterson's account of this modern 'return to Canaan', which links Patterson's use of the Exodus narrative to then contemporary preoccupations with the 'racial' strength of nations.[73] Proximity to Palestine is portrayed as having marked beneficial effects on the health of the previously sickly Jewish troops:

> within a few weeks of our arrival in Egypt, no one would have recognized in these bronzed and well set up men, who walked about with a conscious look of pride in themselves and their battalion, the pale, pinched, miserable looking conscripts who joined up at Plymouth.[74]

Patterson's narrative quickly returns to the biblical context, however, noting that on leaving Egypt on 5 June 1918, the men entered Palestine to the sound of trumpets and prayers. As the modern Israelites crossed the Sinai Desert in trucks, the flames belching from the engine funnels reminded Patterson of the Old Testament and 'the wanderings of the forefathers of these men in this very Desert, who in their night journeys were always guided by a pillar of fire'.[75] In Patterson's account, then, it is not the British so much as the Jewish soldiers, albeit led by the British, who are in a privileged relation to God, a view that contrasts strongly with the clerical and civilian assertion that it was Christians who enjoyed divine favour during the war. In the context of Palestine, it was once again the Jews who were the 'chosen of God' and received his support. Patterson's sense that the Jewish Legion enjoyed divine protection was confirmed when a 'sign' appeared on the road to Jericho:

> a huge black column of fine dust, whose top was lost in the Heavens, arose in front of us and gyrated slowly and gracefully as our vanguard, leading us onwards to our bivouac on the banks of a cool and pleasant brook, where it vanished. I felt that this was a good omen for our success in the Jordan Valley, for it was a case of the Children of Israel being led once more by a pillar of cloud.[76]

But perhaps the passage that most clearly illustrates Patterson's view of the Palestine campaign as predestined is the following, in which he interprets the date of the Turkish defeat (20 September 1918) in numerological terms:

> Everybody knows that the Jewish era differs from the Christian era, but perhaps not so many are aware that the Jewish year 5679 corresponds to the year 1918 of our era. A peculiarity of the Hebrew language is that every numeral has a special meaning other than that connected with time or figures. In the dim and distant past, when seers, sages, and scribes were devoutly engaged in evolving such things, was it even then pre-ordained that this crowning victory – this victory which will surely hasten the restoration of Israel – should take place in the year 5679? However that may be, it is certainly extraordinary that the figures 5, 6, 7, 9, being interpreted, should mean Ha-atereth – 'Crown of Victory'.[77]

Whether or not his gematria and Hebrew are correct, this passage reveals Patterson's attraction to the notion that a divinely ordained synchronisation of British and Jewish destinies was occurring during the war, rather than a convergence of political interests with regard to Palestine. This notion of the linked destinies of Britons and Jews connects with British Israelism, of which there is an element in Patterson's Gallipoli memoir. Without overtly subscribing to the claims of British Israelism, he expressed an interest in this viewpoint, observing that,

> by many it is held that the British people are none other than some of the lost tribes; moreover we have taken so much of Jewish national life for our own, mainly owing to our strong Biblical leanings, that the Jews can never feel while with us that they are among entire strangers.[78]

Patterson's attraction to this idea seems to have been based more on affinity with the Jews than rivalry, however, since British Israelism aims to supplant the Jews as the 'chosen people of God', and was more frequently found in marginal religious discourse. But in the context of 'holy war' such ideas found their way into the mainstream, especially with regard to the Palestine campaign and the prospect of Christian control of the holy places. The beauty of the Palestine campaign, the Jewish Legion and the Balfour Declaration – from the viewpoint of the British government – was that they appealed to both imperial and religious sentiments, which had become intertwined through the popular rhetoric of 'holy war' and the construction of Germany as an apostate nation. Jews became caught in a propaganda battle between Britain and Germany over Zionism as a means of securing neutral Jewish support, and one of the results was that millennial themes became mapped onto political designs in a war between rival imperial powers. In this context, Chaim Weizmann manipulated the situation to Zionist advantage, while the British government and press appealed to prophecy to justify their actions.

In conclusion, then, the fears of political unrest that had been associated with the pre-war 'alien anarchist' became transferred during the war onto the constructed figure of the 'Bolshevik Jew'. Jewish immigrants in the East End remained the focus of political anxieties, as a result of two revolutions in Russia in 1917 and exaggerated accounts in the British press of the support of Russian Jews for Bolshevism. In response to such concerns, the British government mobilised another construction of Jewish collective political identity, that of the 'Zionist Jew', and attempted to use the Jewish Legion and the Balfour Declaration as a means of controlling and containing the perceived 'Jewish' political threat. Zionists seized the opportunity and negotiated as far as possible a specific and beneficial role for the Jews in the war between imperial powers, while members of the League of British Jews campaigned against the Legion, fearing that as a 'ghetto' regiment it would be vulnerable to persecution. From the British government's point of view, the Jewish units represented a means of accessing unused and much needed resources of manpower, which would also serve Britain's imperial interests in the Middle East.

The political motives behind the formation of the Jewish Legion and its involvement in the Palestine campaign were widely discussed in religious terms, as *The Times* spoke of the restoration of Israel, and members of the Cabinet viewed the campaign at least partly from a millennialist perspective. On Lloyd George's part, there was a desire for the fulfilment of biblical prophecy, and in Balfour's case, the wish to atone in some way for the historical suffering of the Jews at the hands of Christians. For the most part, however, the decision appears to have been a matter of political and military expediency, couched in the rhetoric of prophecy.

It was perhaps inevitable that a largely Christian nation, at war, and contemplating the conscription of Jews for service in Palestine, should invoke the Bible and prophecy with regard to its political decisions. The government's 'Zionist' project, as a response to the threat of 'Jewish Bolshevism', bore some of the hallmarks of a conversion drive, and may arguably be regarded as such. In the climate of xenophobia generated by the war, Jews were cast as 'aliens' and pressured to support government-endorsed Zionism, and Jewish refugees in the East End were offered a choice between returning to Russia at short notice without their families, or serving in the Jewish Legion. The legion was thus established partly through coercive means, by exploiting both antisemitism and Zionism, while the 'bait' for enlistment was the promise of naturalisation papers for immigrants at government expense. Through the 'Zionist' policy of the British government, the Jews were to be transformed into a national group with a homeland – in keeping with then contemporary constructions of nationhood – in a project which although it eventually brought self-government and a homeland for the Jewish people, initially served British political and imperial designs. But the wording of the Balfour Declaration was ambiguous, referring to the possibility of a Jewish homeland in Palestine rather than Palestine as the sole national territory of the Jewish people. This lack of clarity in the terms of the Declaration, and the military opposition to its aims (to be discussed in Chapter

6), resulted in Palestine being 'twice-promised' by the British, to both Jews and Arabs, and the effects of this are still visible today.

NOTES

1   The *Protocols of the Learned Elders of Zion* were compiled from various sources by Sergey Nilus, and first appeared in Russia in 1905. They were published in Britain as a series of articles in the *Morning Post*, 12–30 July 1920, and revealed as a forgery by Philip Graves in *The Times* in August 1921.

2   Ragussis, *Figures of Conversion*, p. 3.

3   Some of the material in this chapter has been published as an article entitled 'The politics of the "last days": Bolshevism, Zionism, and "the Jews"', in *Jewish Culture and History*, Vol. 2, No. 2, 1999, pp. 96–115.

4   Robert S. Wistrich, *Revolutionary Jews from Marx to Trotsky* (London: Harrap, 1976), p. 4.

5   Robert Owen, Charles Fourier, Pierre-Joseph Proudhon, Friedrich Engels, Karl Kautsky, Jean Jaures and Vladimir Ilyich Lenin are all examples of prominent radicals who were not Jewish.

6   Cheyette, *Constructions*, pp. 268–9.

7   Karl Marx, 'On the Jewish Question', 1843, in David McLellan (ed.), *Karl Marx: Selected Writings* (Oxford: Oxford University Press, 1977; reprinted 1990), p. 59.

8   Marx, 'Jewish question', p. 58.

9   This passage, from *Vpered!* No. 16, 1 September 1875, p. 505, is quoted in Rocker, *The London Years*, p. 116.

10   See Rocker, *London Years*, pp. 179–80.

11   In fact, the initial Jewish membership of the anarchist movement was low, partly because the idea of 'free love' associated with anarchism was counter to Jewish teaching. See William J. Fishman, *East End Jewish Radicals, 1875–1914* (London: Duckworth, 1975), p. 256.

12   Israel Zangwill, *Children of the Ghetto: A Study of a Peculiar People* (1892, reprinted Philadelphia: Jewish Publication Society of America, 1938), p. 245.

13   Interview with former anarchist Sam Dreen, Milwaukee, 18 October 1969. In Fishman, *Jewish Radicals*, p. 254.

14   Interview with former anarchist W. Kosoff, 21 September 1973. In Fishman, *Jewish Radicals*, p. 267, n 17. Kosoff was referring to the anarchist club at Jubilee Street, Stepney, which opened in February 1906, and was occasionally frequented by the prominent anarchists Kropotkin and Malatesta.

15   Rocker, *London Years*, p. 145.

16   Philip Gibbs, quoted by Joseph Leftwich in his introduction to Rocker, *London Years*, p. 23.

17   'Alien robbers run amok', *The Times*, 25 January 1909, p. 9.

18   'Anarchist society at Tottenham', *The Times*, 26 January 1909, p. 7.

19   'The expulsion of aliens: an intricate problem', *The Times*, 11 January 1911, p. 10.

20   *The Times*, 29 December 1910, p. 6.

21   'Anarchists in London: high explosives and crime', *The Times*, 29 December 1909, p. 8.

22   Chief Rabbi Dr Adler, quoted in *The Times*, 9 January 1911, p. 8.

23   Fishman, *Jewish Radicals*, p. 288.

24   *The Times*, 4 January 1911, p. 8.

25   Sidney Street and Jubilee Street are located in Stepney, off the Mile End Road.

26   *The Times*, 10 January 1911, p. 8.

27   *The Times*, 19 January 1911, p. 6.

28   Fishman, *Jewish Radicals*, p. 269.

29   See Mark Levene, *War, Jews, and the New Europe: The Diplomacy of Lucien Wolf 1914–1919* (Oxford: Oxford University Press, 1992), pp. 56–9.

30   Levene, *War, Jews, and the New Europe*, pp. 65–74.

31 Levene, *War, Jews, and the New Europe*, p. 132. 'Russian Jewry', as a result of Russian expansion and the partition of Poland in the late eighteenth century, in fact included Jews of Lithuanian, Byelorussian, Ukrainian, Bessarabian, Moldavian and Polish origins. These were grouped in the Pale of Settlement, which during the First World War became part of the war zone. See Kadish *Bolsheviks and British Jews*, p. 2.

32 Levene, *War, Jews, and the New Europe*, p. 133.

33 Levene, *War, Jews, and the New Europe*, p. 112. The ITO sought a Jewish homeland within the British empire. The annexation of Palestine, however, a key element in the British government's 'Zionist' project, meant that British imperial territory could be expanded.

34 Levene, *War, Jews, and the New Europe*, p. 129.

35 The formation of the anti-Zionist Jewish *Bund* coincided with the development of political Zionism. Theodor Herzl's influential work *Der Judenstaat* was published in 1896, and in 1897 the first Zionist Congress was held in Basle.

36 See Kadish, *Bolsheviks and British Jews*, p. 110.

37 Kadish, *Bolsheviks and British Jews* (1992), pp. 230–6.

38 Joseph Banister, *Our Judeo-Irish Labour Party* (London: Joseph Banister, 1923), quoted in Kadish, *Bolsheviks and British Jews*, p. 48.

39 Kadish, *Bolsheviks and British Jews*, p. 202.

40 Kadish, *Bolsheviks and British Jews*, p. 189.

41 Marx, 'Jewish Question', p. 48.

42 David Cesarani, *The Jewish Chronicle and Anglo-Jewry 1841–1991* (Cambridge: Cambridge University Press, 1994), p. 118.

43 *Jewish Chronicle*, 28 August 1914; 16 October 1914; 11 September 1915; 17 December 1915; 26 November 1915.

44 Levene, *War, Jews, and the New Europe*, p. 120.

45 *The Times*, 8 August 1917, p. 3.

46 Lt-Col J H Patterson, *With the Zionists in Gallipoli* (London: Hutchinson & Co., 1916), p. 35.

47 Lieutenant Colonel J. H. Patterson, *With the Judaeans in the Palestine Campaign* (London: Hutchinson, 1922) pp. 33–4.

48 Patterson, *With the Judaeans*, pp. 27–8.

49 Patterson, *With the Judaeans*, pp. 247, 276.

50 *Jewish Chronicle*, 7 September 1917, p. 5.

51 *The Times*, 7 August 1917, p. 5.

52 For a full discussion of the divisions among Jewry over Zionism, see Levene, *War, Jews, and the New Europe* and Stuart A. Cohen, *English Zionists and British Jews: The Communal Politics of Anglo-Jewry, 1895–1920* (Princeton, NJ: Princeton University Press, 1982).

53 G. W. E. Russell, article in the *Daily News*, 17 September 1917, published as a pamphlet in 1917. Emphasis in the original.

54 *The Times*, 1 September 1917, p. 3.

55 *The Times*, 13 September 1917, p. 3.

56 *The Times*, 14 September 1917, p. 7.

57 Patterson, *With the Judaeans*, p. 25.

58 Arthur Balfour (1848–1930) was Conservative Prime Minister from July 1902 to December 1905. In 1917 he was Foreign Secretary in Lloyd George's coalition government.

59 Ironically, Lucien Wolf's 1916 'formula' for the appeasement of neutral Jewish opinion with regard to Russian antisemitism formed the basis of the Declaration. Wolf's formula proposed that if Palestine should come under French or British control, the civil and legal rights of Jews resident there should be guaranteed and immigration facilitated. See Levene, *War, Jews, and the New Europe*, p. 92.

60 All five drafts of the Balfour Declaration are reproduced as an Appendix in Leonard Stein, *The Balfour Declaration* (London: Vallentine Mitchell, 1961, reprinted in Jerusalem: The Magnes Press, the Hebrew University and London: Jewish Chronicle Publications, 1983), p. 664.

61 Stein, *Balfour Declaration*, my emphasis.

62 Stein, *Balfour Declaration*, my emphasis.
63 See G. R. Searle, *Eugenics and Politics in Britain 1900–1914* (Leyden: Noordhoff International Publishing, 1976), p. 39.
64 Stein, *Balfour Declaration*, p. 163.
65 Chaim Weizmann, Report to the Local Government Board, January 1915, quoted in Stein, *Balfour Declaration*, pp. 138–9.
66 Colonel R. Meinertzhagen, diary entry dated 23 July 1921, *Middle East Diary*, p. 103.
67 Stein, *Balfour Declaration*, pp. 149, 156, 158.
68 Mark Levene, 'The Balfour Declaration: a case of mistaken identity', in *The English Historical Review*, Vol. 107, 1992, p. 70.
69 Levene, 'The Balfour Declaration', pp. 70, 55.
70 Patterson, *With the Judeans* (1922), p.17.
71 Chaim Raphael (Chaim Pruss), *A Coat of Many Colours: Memoirs of a Jewish Experience* (London: Chatto & Windus, 1979), p. 23.
72 Patterson, *With the Judeans*, p. 50.
73 Broadly speaking, eugenicists saw a correlation between the general health of the nation and Britain's status as an imperial power, and argued that environmental changes alone were not enough to achieve optimum 'national efficiency', and that a biological strategy was needed. The Eugenics Education Society (EES) was founded in London in 1907–08. It launched its journal, the *Eugenics Review*, in 1910, and prior to 1914 sponsored numerous lectures to teachers and physicians. Membership of the EES included prominent medical professionals, although the *British Medical Journal* was critical of the movement, and it was sometimes attacked in the national press. Eugenics appealed to a number of clergymen, including William Ralph Inge, Dean of St Paul's Cathedral 1911–34, and had some influence in political circles (Arthur Balfour was Honorary Vice-President of the EES in 1913, and the Tory William Joynson-Hicks was a member, as was Neville Chamberlain). Some Jews, such as Dr Sidney Herbert, for example, were involved in the EES, and a committee was formed in 1913 to investigate what Jewish culture, with its tradition of endogamy, could contribute to eugenics. See Searle, *Eugenics and Politics*, pp. 9–33.
74 Patterson, *With the Judeans*, p. 53.
75 Patterson, *With the Judeans*, p. 69.
76 Patterson, *With the Judeans*, p. 98.
77 Patterson, *With the Judeans*, p. 149.
78 Patterson, *With the Zionists*, p. 32.

6

The Imagery of Crucifixion in Relation to the War

In 1917, Max Plowman, a second lieutenant with the 10th West Yorkshire regiment, published a critical account of the war entitled *A Subaltern on the Somme in 1916,* under the pseudonym 'Mark Seven'.[1] He was particularly disturbed by Field Punishment Number One, in which the offending soldier was tied, with arms outstretched, to a stationary object and left without food or water for several hours at sunrise and sunset, symbolising a full day on the cross.[2] The front cover of his book shows a silhouette of a soldier tied to a gun wheel in crucifixion pose, his head drooping as if near to death. Plowman described an incident in which a soldier was given this punishment for falling out on a march after claiming to have glass in his feet, and observed that 'Quite possibly the boy is a liar; but wouldn't the army do well to avoid punishments which remind men of the Crucifixion?'[3]

While the military authorities framed 'crucifixion' as punishment, clerical representations of the soldier as a 'Christ' figure focused on his noble self-sacrifice for the greater good. The men who died in the first two years of the war were volunteers – conscription was not introduced until 1916. When addressing volunteers bound for the Front, clergymen appealed to the new recruits to emulate Christ, in his willingness to sacrifice himself for others and his bravery when facing death. Some members of the clergy viewed the sacrifice of men in terms of atonement for 'national sins': Germany had sinned, but so, too, had Britain, and as a result the judgement of God had been brought upon both nations. In this usage, the soldier's suffering was idealised and glorified through comparison with that of Christ, his 'crucifixion' gaining religious significance rather than the criminal associations of the military punishment.

Another function of the crucifixion trope during the war was to demonstrate the brutality of the Germans, as in the atrocity story of the 'Crucified Canadian' (1915), in which it was alleged that German soldiers engaged in the ritual murder of Allied officers. In what was widely portrayed as a 'holy war', the 'Crucified Canadian' story provided 'evidence' that the enemy was hostile to Christianity. It is this association between crucifixion and ritual murder committed by the 'enemies' of Christianity that reveals the ancient blood libel and the figure of 'the Jew' as subthemes that were present by implication in religious representations of the war.

The blood libel derives from the Jews' alleged role in the crucifixion of Christ, as described in the New Testament. Over the centuries this has given rise to the belief that Jews' hatred of Christianity is such that they feel compelled to re-enact the crucifixion by engaging in the ritual murder of Christians. Allegations of this kind have been made since the medieval period, and originated, according to the historian Gavin Langmuir, in an incident at Norwich in 1144, when the body of a Christian boy was found at Easter, and Jews were blamed for his death.[4] There were also stories of Jews attacking the Eucharist; fantasies, Langmuir has argued, that were a response to ideological doubt, their function being to assert the 'truth' of the doctrine of transubstantiation, the idea that the Eucharist constituted rather than symbolised the body of Christ.[5] Such stories expressed not only religious doubt, but also an irrational fear of attack by a religious 'other', which under certain conditions erupted in violence by Christians towards Jews. This fear of attack did not die out in the Middle Ages, but continued into the modern period: in 1903 a Russian Jew named Mendel Beilis was put on trial on charges of the ritual murder of a Christian. He was acquitted, but the allegations sparked the Kishinev pogrom later that year.[6] In June 1916 the *Jewish Chronicle* reported that following the disappearance of a Christian girl in the village of Maidan-Alexandrovsk in Russia, local Jews had been accused of her ritual murder. The Jewish community had braced itself for a pogrom, but eventually it was discovered that the girl had taken employment in a neighbouring village.[7] In May 1916, the *Chronicle* reported that 31 Jews resident in Lubar, near Kiev, were to stand trial accused of organising a pogrom against Christians in September 1913. The trial revealed that the event had been a demonstration by local Jewish traders against the erection of a stall by a Christian in a particular area of the local market.[8] And in Ireland in 1916, the *Catholic Bulletin* published an article entitled 'Ritual Murder among the Jews', which, according to the *Jewish Chronicle*, was 'a re-hash' of blood libel allegations. 'Even in England', the editorial observed, 'there is a little group assiduously at work to bring odium upon Jews and stir up ill-feeling against them'.[9]

In Britain, pre-war fears of a 'Jewish' attack generally took secular expression, but the religious origins of this anxiety remained discernible. In the campaigns against 'white slavery', for example, the fear of attack became sexualised, and focused on the perceived corruption and enslavement of British Christian womanhood by 'Jewish' procurers. There were also medical versions of the fear of attack by Jews, often expressed in ways that echoed older, religious beliefs. As Sander Gilman has observed, the medieval Christian view of the Jew as devil, identifiable by the 'cloven hoof', is found in the nineteenth century, updated and secularised, in discussions of the inherent difference of the 'Jewish foot', which was believed to affect the gait and supposedly render Jews identifiable by their movements.[10] Gilman also notes that beneath the medical rhetoric and the trope of the diseased 'Jew' lay a secular version of the blood libel, whereby,

> The Jew's role in literally destroying the life of Christians, whether through the ritual use of Christian blood or the mass poisoning of wells in order to cause the Black Death becomes the Jew's biological role as the transmitter of diseases.[11]

One of the diseases commonly associated with Jews in Europe at the start of the twentieth century was syphilis, despite the fact that where studies were carried out, Jews showed a lower rate of infection than did gentiles.[12] The spread of tuberculosis was another source of anxiety, and in July 1914, *The Times* reported that Dr D. L. Thomas, medical officer for Stepney, had recorded a high and increasing rate of tuberculosis among Jews.[13] According to Thomas' figures, Jews were more likely to contract tuberculosis than gentiles but less likely to die of it; therefore their role was as carriers of the disease. Most of the chronic cases in Stepney, he added, were Jews: 'They cough and expectorate quantities of sputum laden with tubercle bacilli, and are the centre of infection for many years.' Implicit in Thomas' medical language is the fear of attack through disease: being apparently more able to withstand tuberculosis than gentiles, Jews would spread contagion but survive, thus becoming dominant.

During the First World War irrational fears of a 'Jewish' attack on the Christian body continued, but although they remained secular in focus, being directed towards political and military enemies, these fears became more Christian in their mode of expression. The crucifixion trope was integral to this expression of embattlement, as this chapter aims to show. The first part examines clerical representations of the soldier as a 'Christ' figure, and the imagery of crucifixion in military punishment. This is followed by an example of the ritual murder charge in the context of war and a discussion of its ideological function during a period of crisis. The latter part of the chapter focuses on the development of the figure of 'Judas' in relation to these wartime uses of the crucifixion narrative, and in reactions to the rise of Bolshevism in Russia. The final section discusses the Palestine campaign of 1917–20, and the memoirs of the men who served in the Jewish Legion. The discussion returns to the two images of the soldier as 'Christ' – the idealised figure of self-sacrifice and the criminal enduring punishment by a military power – that reached an ironic convergence in events in Palestine in 1920.

CHRISTIAN SOLDIERS

On 9 August 1914, Henry Wace, Dean of Canterbury, informed a congregation of newly recruited servicemen that 'The soldier who sheds his blood on the battlefield in a righteous cause, and with a righteous purpose, is doing the very thing that Christ did, and he may be assured of Christ's approval and blessing.'[14] Such rhetoric, besides claiming divine approval for the war, also implied that the 'crucifixion' of the soldier – his death in battle – had a redemptive function with regard to the nation. Direct comparisons of the kind made by Wace were commonly used to glorify the almost certain death of the combatant in a war which produced casualties on an unprecedented scale. One function of the comparison between the soldier and Christ was that it allowed the political causes of the war to be elided, with the soldier becoming the champion of Christianity rather than the expendable instrument of an imperial power. This view was chiefly adopted by members of the higher clergy. In his book *The Spiritual Pilgrimage of Jesus* (1917), the academic theologian James Robertson suggested that it was not politics but 'sin' that had caused the war, and the death of the soldier was a case of life given for life ... when the flower of a country's manhood, fresh young lives in the bloom of youth, innocent in large measure of the crime, go down to death upon the battle-plain, bearing the penalty of the black sin-mass – the creation of the older generation, – which bursts volcano-like, and devastates the world with war.[15]

Even those clergymen who expressed regret at the conflict between two Christian powers used the imagery of crucifixion to illustrate their views. In a paper entitled 'Christianity and war' William Temple declared,

> Members of the body of Christ are tearing one another, and His body is bleeding as it once bled on Calvary, but this time the wounds are dealt by His friends. It is as though Peter were driving home the nails, and John were piercing the side.[16]

Temple used the crucifixion as a metaphor for the sacrifice of Christianity itself in the conflict between imperial powers, but the image of Christ on the cross was also used to represent both the heroism and suffering of the nation at war. The Bishop of London referred to the war as 'the Nailed Hand against the Mailed Fist' when appealing to the patriotic instincts of his congregations, and drew explicit comparisons between the nation going to war and Christ's contemplation of the cross, urging his listeners to show the same brave spirit.[17] Women, too, were encouraged to view the loss of their loved ones in terms of the crucifixion narrative. Elma Paget, wife of the Bishop of Stepney, described the war as a collective 'Calvary', in which women were, 'called upon to give. It is perhaps at this moment that we realize fully all that is meant by the 'pain and peril of child-birth', as we take our place with Mary on the hill of sorrow.'[18]

In a similar vein, an anonymous poem, published in a collection of popular war songs and poetry entitled *Songs of the Last Crusade* (1917), encouraged women to think of their dead in terms of heroic sacrifice, their reward in heaven being greater than any that was possible on earth, in the lines

> Comfort ye, women by the sepulchre,
> Our dead live greatly – what were this world's loss
> If He that gave His youth upon the Cross
> Had lived his long, long life ... a carpenter?[19]

The notion that in dying for his country the soldier was emulating Christ was more common among civilians than soldiers, many of whom found that their faith was undermined by the experience of war and became cynical regarding the rhetoric of crucifixion and resurrection used by non-combatants. George Coppard, an infantryman in the Queen's Royal West Surrey regiment and later a gunner in the Machine Gun Corps, recalled that in the context of war the Christian festivals lost their meaning:

> The next day was Good Friday. Being an old choir boy of Brighton and Croydon parish churches, my thoughts turned to the Christian meaning of that day, and of the several three-hour services I had attended in the past on Good Fridays. All that was over and seemed meaningless.[20]

The poet Wilfred Owen, who before the war had considered training for the priesthood, made cynical and parodic use of religious imagery in his letters from the Front. The rhetoric of 'pulpit professionals' which portrayed the war as a Christian venture served only to highlight the actual teachings of Christ, which were incompatible with violence, and in order to justify the war, omissions from Christian doctrine were necessary. Pure Christianity, he argued, 'will not fit in with pure patriotism'; therefore Christians had 'deliberately *cut* some of the main teaching of their code'.[21] A letter to his mother, written on Easter Day 1918 included a parody of a familiar evangelical passage: 'God so hated the world that He gave several millions of English-begotten sons, that whosoever believeth in them should not perish, but have a comfortable life.'[22]

Here, the death of the soldier in war becomes a travesty of Christian teaching, and represents betrayal by those at home. Like the clergy he criticised, Owen used Christian imagery, but in a different manner, to point to the war as a departure from Christian principles. This theme is also found in Owen's war poetry, which takes a dissenting stance with regard to the glorification of the war through romantic and religious themes. One of his most savage attacks occurs in the poem 'Parable of the Old Men and the Young', which uses Old Testament rather than crucifixion imagery to suggest that by continuing to send men to the Front, the British government was actively defying the will of God. The following is an extract:

> Then Abram bound the youth with belts and straps,
> And builded parapets and trenches there,
> And stretched forth the knife to slay his son.
> When lo! an Angel called him out of heaven,
> Saying, Lay not thy hand upon the lad,
> Neither do anything to him, thy son.
> Behold! Caught in a thicket by its horns,
> A Ram. Offer the Ram of Pride instead.
> But the old man would not so, but slew his son,
> And half the seed of Europe, one by one.[23]

Owen uses the Abraham and Isaac story to suggest that in moral terms, humanity has de-evolved rather than evolved over the centuries, to the extent that men will now sacrifice not only their own sons, but those of others. Abraham obeyed his God and halted preparations for sacrifice, unlike the modern imperial powers, which perpetuated human sacrifice on a mass scale. The imagery suggests that the proponents of 'Christian warfare' have lost contact with the divine, and cannot hear the angel pointing out an alternative sacrifice, that of pride. Since pride is what governs them, they will not sacrifice it, and instead betray not only their God but also their sons, by sending them to the slaughter.

Another of Wilfred Owen's poems, 'At a Calvary Near the Ancre', continues the theme of the betrayal of the soldier, in this case attacking the clergy, who are cast as the 'Devil' to the soldier's 'Christ'. The poem also links the clergy to the disciples who denied Christ prior to the crucifixion, a device that emphasises the aspect of betrayal. Unlike the disciples, however, their actions are prompted not by fear, but nationalism and a misunderstanding of the principles of Christianity. In portraying the war as 'holy', they are denying both Christ and Christian teaching, and preaching a doctrine of nationalist hatred:

> Near Golgotha strolls many a priest,
> And in their faces there is pride
> That they were flesh-marked by the Beast
> By whom the gentle Christ's denied.
>
> The scribes on all the people shove
> And bawl allegiance to the state,
> But they who love the greater love
> Lay down their life; they do not hate.[24]

The reference to the 'scribes', those not directly involved in the war who nevertheless 'bawl allegiance to the state', invokes military drill and the voice of the sergeant-major, the effect of which is to highlight the incompatibility of Christianity and belligerent nationalism. The soldier is indeed Christ-like, in his willingness to die if necessary, while beneath the Christian rhetoric of the non-combatants is the desire for blood. In the context of the analogy between the crucifixion narrative and the war, they become the crowd calling for the death of Jesus. The priests, exempted from combat, 'stroll' in a place of death that is both sacred and mundane, such is the scale of the loss of life in this modern conflict. The last verse juxtaposes civilian warmongering and hatred of the enemy with 'the greater love' that prompts the soldier to enlist, and alludes to the gulf between soldiers and civilians, particularly the clergy, in terms of attitudes to the war, and to Christianity itself.

Siegfried Sassoon, who knew Wilfred Owen, and wrote an introduction to a collection of his work published in 1920, also used Christian imagery in his war poetry.[25] Sassoon was of Sephardic Jewish ancestry but was estranged from his father's side of the family, partly as a result of the latter's marriage to Theresa Thornycroft, a gentile, in 1883. Siegfried was baptised into the Anglican Church at an early age, but as he grew older, began to question his faith.[26] Some of his early poems express enthusiasm for the war,[27] but this quickly gave way to a more cynical and satirical tone, in which Christian imagery is used to underscore the pointlessness of the conflict.[28] In a poem entitled 'They', he attacks the Bishop of London's rhetoric of redemption through war, and the notion that the soldiers were engaged in,

> the last attack
> On Anti-Christ.[29]

Another poem, 'Via Crucis' (1916), contrasts the religious significance of the death of Christ with that of the soldier, making the point that unlike the latter, 'Jesus had a purpose for His pain.'[30] 'The Redeemer' portrays a soldier, one of a party laying planks in the trenches, in crucifixion pose,

> leaning forward from His burdening task,
> Both arms supporting it.

This 'Christ' is not a divine figure, but distinctly mortal, and wears 'No thorny crown, only a woollen cap'. Yet like Christ, he is prepared to sacrifice himself for others, and is,

> not uncontent to die
> that Lancaster on Lune may stand secure.[31]

The final lines of the poem juxtapose these images of heroic suffering with blasphemy, however, as 'Christ' drops the planks, and curses:

> And someone flung his burden in the muck,
> Mumbling: 'O Christ Almighty, now I'm stuck!'.

The use of blasphemy continues in 'Stand-to: Good Friday Morning', as the soldier seeks to escape his sacrificial destiny and 'prays' for a 'Blighty' to deliver him from the war:

> O Jesus, send me a wound to-day,
> And I'll believe in Your bread and wine,
> And get my bloody old sins washed white![32]

In the poem 'Enemies', Sassoon links the death of the soldier with the crucifixion through the desire for revenge that is provoked by both. In response to the death of his fellow-combatant, the speaker has killed several Germans. A conversation takes between the dead, in which the German soldiers explain to the speaker's friend that this was done for his sake. The first dead soldier is thus portrayed as a 'Christ' who is puzzled by the murders committed in his name:

> He stood alone in some queer sunless place
> Where Armageddon ends. Perhaps he longed
> For days he might have lived; but his young face
> Gazed forth untroubled: and suddenly there thronged
> Round him the hulking Germans that I shot
> When for his death my brooding rage was hot.
> He stared at them, half-wondering; and then
> They told him how I'd killed them for his sake –
> Those patient, stupid, sullen ghosts of men;
> And still there seemed no answer he could make.
> At last he turned and smiled. One took his hand
> Because his face could make them understand.[33]

Here, the soldier is Christ-like because like Christ, the significance of his sacrifice has been misunderstood, and others have been killed in his name. The soldier and Christ are therefore linked though the vengeful response of the living to their deaths. Thus the poem implies a parallel between the soldier who kills the Germans in reaction to the death of his fellow-combatant, and the Christian whose zeal is driven by a desire to avenge the crucifixion (a response which, during the crusades, was enacted upon Jews in Europe).[34] The dead soldiers, both British and German, are also Christ-like in that they exemplify the principles of love and forgiveness, but this is lost on the living.

Both Wilfred Owen and Siegfried Sassoon, then, used religious imagery to parody the use of Christian themes as moral justification for the war and to suggest that religious representations of the conflict were not only inappropriate, but hypocritical. Owen uses biblical imagery to show how far the Christian state and its religious and military authorities have departed from Christian teaching in their enthusiasm for the war. His soldiers, however, retain a heroic aspect in their 'greater love' and their readiness to die for their country, while Sassoon's 'Christian' soldiers endure mundane and pointless suffering, and it is their brutalised humanity rather than their 'divinity' that is emphasised. Both writers use religious imagery to express alienation from Christian doctrine and its use with regard to the war, and contempt for religious authorities. Although they share the clergy's comparison of the soldier with Christ, their use of this trope is subversive and parodic, and the soldier-Christ becomes the critic and accuser of the Church and state.

But army life produced another form of religious parody, through the apparent use of the crucifixion theme in military discipline, in which the connection between the soldier and Christ was their shared punishment and humiliation. As noted in the introduction to this chapter, Max Plowman was critical of Field Punishment Number One, which explicitly evoked the crucifixion. Whether Plowman's objections were to the harshness of the punishment or a matter of religious sensibility is unclear, but to a religiously devout soldier the punishment would very likely have appeared blasphemous and inappropriate. Plowman used crucifixion as a universal theme, extending the image of the soldier's Christ-like suffering to include German prisoners of war, who were kept in a cage which was 'like a poultry-run, only laced in disordered strands with wire that is "barbed" after the pattern of the crown of thorns'.[35]

The barbed wire around the prisoners became the modern equivalent of the crown of thorns, 'worn' collectively by the German soldiers in their compound. Pilate-like, Plowman felt sympathy for the men, and wanted to go inside the compound to apologise and explain to them 'that the beastly necessities of the times have driven us to means we abhor', but could not.[36] Instead, he published his memoir in 1917, as a form of critical testament to the war, in which the soldier as 'Christ' became a universal figure that crossed national and imperial boundaries, and in which the imagery of crucifixion became a marker of the human capacity for cruelty.

THE DEVELOPMENT OF THE FIGURE OF 'JUDAS'

If the British soldier was Christ-like, whether as an image of heroic suffering or humiliation, then a Judas figure was required for allegorical coherence. Sir Owen Seaman, editor of *Punch*, allocated this role to the Kaiser, in the poem 'The Wayside Calvary',[37] which was published on the first anniversary of the war. The first verse draws a comparison between the war and the crucifixion, in terms of the loss associated with both:

> Now with the full year Memory holds her tryst,
> Heavy with such a tale of bitter loss
> As never Earth has suffered since the Christ
> Hung for us on the Cross.

The rest of the poem deals with the theme of the Kaiser's alleged rejection of Christianity in favour of ruthless imperial expansion, and portrays the German emperor as the very antithesis of Christ, 'Who died that men might live', whereas he 'live[s] that men may die'. Finally, these themes coalesce in the figure of Judas, as the Kaiser is accused of betraying Christ in the final verse:

> Ah, turn your eyes away; He reads your heart;
> Pass on and, having done your work abhorred,
> Join hands with JUDAS in his place apart,
> You who betrayed your Lord.[38]

The atrocity story of the 'Crucified Canadian', which circulated in Britain in May 1915, developed the idea of the German 'Judas' further.[39] The story was covered by *The Times'* Paris correspondent, who noted:

> Last week a large number of Canadian soldiers … arrived at the base hospital at Versailles. They all told a story of how one of their officers had been crucified by the Germans. He had been pinned to a wall by bayonets thrust through his hands and feet, another bayonet had been driven through his throat, and, finally, he was riddled with bullets. The wounded Canadians said that the Dublin Fusiliers had seen this done with their own eyes, and they had heard the officers of the Dublin Fusiliers talking about it.[40]

Subsequent versions of the story were even more graphic. In May 1915, *The Times* reported that the victim was a sergeant and that

> Bayonets were thrust through the palms of his hands and feet, pinning him to the fence. He had been repeatedly stabbed with bayonets, and there were many punctured wounds in his body… There is room for the supposition that the man was dead before he was pinned to the fence and that the enemy in his insensate rage and hate of the English, wreaked his vengeance on the lifeless body of his foe.

The article also claimed that 'written depositions testifying to the fact of the discovery of the body are in possession of British Headquarters Staff'.[41] Eventually, the matter was discussed in the Commons, where the Unionist MP Mr Houston (Liverpool, West Toxteth) asked Mr Tennant, Under-Secretary of State for War, whether he was aware that 'the Germans had removed the figure of Christ from the large village crucifix and fastened the sergeant, while alive, to the cross; and whether he is aware that the crucifixion of our soldiers is becoming a practice of the Germans'.[42] Mr Tennant replied that the War Office knew of no such behaviour, but that he would investigate the matter. This story, like the other wartime atrocity stories, aimed to show the depths of depravity to which the Germans had sunk. Unlike the other stories, however, it portrays the Germans not only as non-Christian, but as actively hostile to Christianity, and places them in a role historically allocated to Jews. In this respect it can perhaps be viewed as a military version of the blood libel: the charge of the ritual murder of

Christians that had previously been levelled at Jews, but in this case became displaced onto Germans. As previously noted, Gavin Langmuir has argued that the medieval stories of Jews attacking the Eucharist were prompted by Christian doubt regarding the doctrine of transubstantiation. Their function was to demonstrate the veracity of that doctrine, by showing the threat that the Eucharist represented to non-believers, such that they attacked it as the body of Christ. Thus the 'truth' of Christian doctrine is demonstrated to the doubter through the threat which it is portrayed as representing to Jews.[43] The story of the 'Crucified Canadian' seems to function in a similar way. The year of 1915 was a year that brought zeppelin raids, the use of poison gas by the German army, the Bryce report on atrocities and the sinking of the *Lusitania*.[44] In this context, the myth of the 'Crucified Canadian' may be read as expressing a crisis of faith in the notion of 'holy war'. This is met with a fantasy of how threatening the Germans find the Allied soldier, such that they feel compelled to commit a ritualised murder which echoes the crucifixion. This story would provide the civilian, if not the soldier, with reassurance that Germany recognised the spiritual and moral power of the Allies, and that self-sacrifice was not futile. It also served to arouse a spirit of revenge, not only for the alleged crucifixion of the Allied soldier, but for that of Christ himself, and enabled propagandists to marshal aspects of religious antisemitism in support of the war, by conflating 'German' and 'Judas' in the image of the enemy as 'deicidal'.[45]

In 1917 the use of the crucifixion narrative as a metaphor for the events of the war took another turn, and began to focus on the threat of betrayal from within. The *Daily Graphic* quoted Mr Ben Tillet MP (Labour, North Salford) as saying that Britain was 'being crucified between the Prussian and the food profiteer', the latter being considered 'far more deadly than the German and his guns'.[46] The real threat, then, came not from Germany, but from within Britain itself; an idea that was to become increasingly important as the crucifixion theme developed in relation to wartime politics, and the element of betrayal in the story came to the fore. War profiteers came from a variety of social groups,[47] but in the pages of *Punch*, the profiteer was frequently represented as 'Jewish', particularly in cartoons. In accordance with then contemporary 'racial' stereo-types, he was an overweight figure with a long nose, wealthy but mean, richly dressed and smoking a cigar. Sometimes the caption underscored the 'racial' imagery, by giving the profiteer the lisping 'Jewish' voice, with its inability to pronounce 'w' or 's'.[48]

Political radicalism represented another means of attack from within, and the pre-war image of the 'alien anarchist', often associated with the Jewish immigrant from Eastern Europe, was discussed in Chapter 5. After the 1917 revolutions in Russia, the image of the 'Jewish' revolutionary emerged, and acted as a repository for fears associated with the concentration of Jewish immigrants in London's East End. The 'Jewish Bolshevik' represented the route by which Bolsheviks would take over Britain, as they had taken power in Russia in November 1917. Whereas previously, Jewish immigrants had been solicited as supporters of the 'crusade' against Prussian militarism (and simultaneously portrayed as the pro-German financier and spy), they now began to be cast in the guise of 'Judas', the political betrayer of the Christian nation. Increasingly, the conflict between capitalism and communism was portrayed as a struggle between the forces of 'good' and 'evil'. Articles in the British press portrayed Bolshevism as a 'Jewish' politics, and warned that Britain would follow Russia into chaos unless this threat was controlled. Victor Marsden, Russian correspondent for the *Morning Post*, published articles stating that Russia was controlled by Jews who were themselves controlled by Germany, thereby fuelling fears that Russia would negotiate a separate peace with Germany and Britain would lose an ally.[49] This was precisely what happened, as in December 1917 the Bolshevik government began peace talks with Germany, and the Treaty of Brest–Litovsk was signed on 3 March 1918.

The theme of an alliance between Jews, Bolsheviks and Germans gained momentum and was taken up by other journalists. An article in *The Times*, one of a series entitled 'Russia to-day', noted that although the repressive policies of the *Okhrana* had impoverished large numbers of Jews, they had not succeeded in preventing a few from 'invading the professions, capturing finance and trade, and monopolizing the Press'.[50] Robert Wilton, one of the Russian correspondents for *The Times*, produced regular articles in which he blamed that country's political instability on the Jewish population. He also published two books on this theme. The first of these, *Russia's Agony* (1918), gives a portrait of the vengeful 'pseudo Jew', who had rejected Judaism and sought an alternative in revolutionary politics.[51] Wilton suggested that in league with Germany, 'pseudo Jews' had gradually gained control of Russia, through the universities, banks and the press, a situation that, he implied, could occur in Britain. In 1920 he published *The Last Days of the Romanovs*, in which he set out to tell 'the true story of the martyrdom of Nicholas II, ex-tsar of Russia, and of his wife and family'.[52] This reiterates the charge that Jews in Russia were under German control, but adds a new dimension, drawing a parallel between the death of the tsar at the hands of 'Bolshevik Jews' and the crucifixion of Christ. Religious imagery is used to portray the imperial family as Christian martyrs, and chapter eight, which describes 'the last stage of their earthly pilgrimage', is entitled 'Via Crucis'.[53] Describing the scene at the prison, Wilton draws an analogy between Tsar Nicholas II and Jesus in the garden of Gethsemane, and suggests that such was the piety and self-possession of the doomed monarch, that one of his guards underwent an experience of 'conversion':

> He had begun with hatred in his heart...He watched the crowned enemy of mankind, the 'drinker of the people's blood,' as he walked about the garden, and listened to him exchanging simple, homely words with the other warders. His notions began to waver. This was not a bad man: he was so human, so kindly, just a man like other men, and even better.[54]

The tsar and his family were killed at Ekaterinberg in July 1918. Wilton extended his crucifixion analogy, and stated that the Bolsheviks had erected a monument in Moscow dedicated to Judas Iscariot.[55] By relating the crucifixion to the death of a monarch and the seizure of power by 'Jews', Wilton updated the central Christian narrative of betrayal and crucifixion, and brought it into political discourse, creating what I have termed the figure of the 'Bolshevik Judas'. The *Morning Post* expanded on this theme, introducing the idea of the 'thirty pieces of silver' paid to Judas as blood-money, and reported that according to sources at the *Berne Tagblatt*, Russian revolutionaries had deposited large sums of money in Swiss bank accounts.[56]

But if the revolution was orchestrated by 'Jewish Bolsheviks', it was, according to Wilton, financed by 'Jewish capitalists'. In this respect, his account of events in Russia and their cause neatly demonstrates Bryan Cheyette's analysis of the dual, often contradictory nature of images of 'the Jew', a figure that 'can be constructed to represent both sides of a political or social or ideological divide'.[57] Wilton claimed that the revolution was masterminded and controlled by 'Bolshevik Jews', yet also asserted that the Soviet regime was funded by 'X', a German Jewish banker based in Petrograd.[58] Thus 'the Jew' could be both Bolshevik and capitalist, and the implication was that what united the two was their shared hatred of Christianity. In this respect, both could be cast as the enemy of the Christian nation.

The extent of Wilton's influence among the general British population is unclear, but *The Times* was widely read: the paper's circulation increased from an average of 145,000 at the outbreak of the war, to 278,000, as readers avidly followed the events of the conflict.[59] As an agent for British military intelligence in Russia, Wilton's bulletins had some impact at the Foreign Office.[60] His writing provoked criticism, however, not only from Jews and Russians in Britain, but also from members of the British government's intelligence and propaganda department at Wellington House.[61] John Buchan, the popular novelist who was in charge of propaganda production during the second half of the war, wrote to Geoffrey Robinson at *The Times* to express the view that Wilton should exercise more caution in his reports.[62]

To summarise, in the Christian rhetoric that was widely used in relation to the war, it was the image of the Allied soldier as 'Christ' that dominated. But where there is a 'Christ', for narrative and metaphorical coherence, there must also be a 'Judas', the betrayer and the target for revenge. Sir Owen Seaman, the editor of *Punch*, proposed the Kaiser for this role, suggesting in his poem 'The Wayside Calvary' that in allegedly rejecting Christianity in favour of imperial expansion, the German emperor had committed an act of betrayal comparable to that of Judas. The Labour MP Ben Tillett used the imagery of crucifixion in relation to the food profiteer and his effect on the nation. More broadly, antisemitic imagery was used to represent both the Germans and the profiteer, in the sense that the former were portrayed as hostile to Christianity (in the rhetoric of German 'apostasy' and the story of the 'Crucified Canadian'), and the latter represented as unscrupulous and materialistic, their desire for wealth stronger than their patriotism. But it was not until the Russian revolution and the death of the tsar that the figure of 'Judas' gained substance and stature, as the 'Bolshevik Jew', the betrayer of the Allies through the Brest–Litovsk Treaty, and the political enemy of the Christian nation. The figure of the 'Bolshevik

Judas' represented the threat of betrayal and attack from within, and this fear was present in reactions in Britain to the revolution that took place in Russia in October/November 1917, in which the Bolsheviks took power. As discussed in Chapter 5, the Foreign Office and the British government reacted to the rise of Bolshevism in Russia by promoting 'Zionism' as the political alternative for Jews, through the Balfour Declaration and the deployment of the Jewish Legion in Palestine. These developments were given prophetic significance by *The Times*, certain politicians and some members of Anglo-Jewry, through allusions to the Exodus narrative. But despite the support of the British government for a Jewish homeland in Palestine, and the brief emergence of the Exodus analogy in popular rhetoric with regard to the Jewish troops in Palestine, it was British, Christian interests that prevailed in that country. Under British occupation, the Jews who had returned to Palestine as soldiers in the British army were discriminated against, and in one case criminalised, in an uncanny parallel with events that occurred in Roman-occupied Palestine, during the first century CE.

VIEWS ON PALESTINE

Many of the men who joined the Jewish Legion upon its formation in the summer of 1917 did so under duress. The War Office gave Russian Jewish immigrants very little time in which to decide whether to leave their families in Britain and go to Russia to fight, or be conscripted into the Jewish battalions. Despite claims made in *The Times* regarding the enthusiasm with which Jewish soldiers responded to the legion,[63] recruiting was slow.[64] One soldier who was keen to join the Legion, however, was the artist and writer Isaac Rosenberg.

Rosenberg served with the Bantam battalion of the 12th Suffolk regiment in France. In his letters home he compared the hardships of trench life with the crucifixion, and described his own suffering as exceeding that of Christ. In 1918 he wrote to his patron Edward Marsh, saying 'what is happening to me now is more tragic than the "passion play". Christ never endured what I endure. It is breaking me completely'.[65] In this respect, his writing is consistent with other soldiers' use of the crucifixion trope as an index of personal suffering. But Rosenberg's work combined both Old and New Testament themes, a strategy which, according to his biographer Joseph Cohen, was designed to enable him both to draw on and transcend his background, and to present himself as an English poet with Jewish heritage, rather than a solely 'Jewish' writer.[66] The following is an extract from a poem entitled 'Creation', written in 1913, which illustrates this approach:

> Moses must die to live in Christ,
> The seed be buried to live to green.
> Perfection must begin from worst.
> Christ perceives a larger reachless love,
> More full, and grows to reach thereof.
> The green plant yearns for its yellow fruit.
> Perfection always is a root,
> And joy a motion that doth feed
> Itself on light of its own speed,
> And round its radiant circle runs,
> Creating and devouring suns.[67]

Here, Rosenberg seems to draw attention to the transitory nature of the dominance of any set of ideas, and suggest that each informs the next, in a constant process of development. The idea of shifting and cyclical religious authority was something that Israel Zangwill had engaged with in 1912, in a play entitled *The Next Religion*. This dramatised the foundation of a new 'religion of science', which was like Christianity in its incorporation of aspects of Judaism, yet would supersede it.[68] The Lord Chamberlain banned the play from public performance in Britain. In 'Creation', Rosenberg uses the figures of Moses and Christ to illustrate the development and interrelation of sets of beliefs and the processes by which they are established and inform one another, thus Moses is the 'root' of the green 'plant' of Christianity. The imagery of circles and growth cycles suggests that Judaism and Christianity co-exist in a complimentary and developmental relation to one another.

The antisemitism he encountered at the Front, however, prompted Rosenberg to alter his approach. In a letter to the author Sydney Schiff, written in October 1915, he wrote that 'my being a Jew makes it bad amongst these wretches'. Shortly afterwards, he wrote to Edward Marsh, saying that his senior officer 'has me marked – he has taken a dislike to me I don't know why'.[69] Rosenberg's writing began to focus more on the figure of Moses.

His play *Moses*, written in 1916, dramatises the events leading up to the incident briefly referred to in Exodus, in which Moses kills an Egyptian whom he discovers beating a Hebrew slave (Exodus 2:11–13).[70] Rosenberg draws on this part of the story to create a rebellious, anti-messianic and individualist figure. In the opening scene of the play Egypt is in the midst of a famine, and the young Moses is supervising the building of the sixteenth pyramid, when Pharaoh sends an edict which orders him to draw the slaves' back molars, to prevent them from eating and thus conserve food. Moses seizes this opportunity to test both Pharaoh's feelings for him and his own power, and decides to ignore the edict:

> I have a way, a touchstone!
> A small misdemeanour, touch of rebelliousness;
> To prick the vein of father, monitor, foe,
> Will tell which of these his kingship is.
> If I shut my eyes to the edict,
> And leave the pincers to rust,
> And the slaves' teeth as God made them ...
> Pharaoh will speak, and I'll seize that word to act.
> Should the word be a foe's, I can use it well,
> As a poison to soak into Egypt's bowels,
> A wraith from old Nile will cry
> 'For his mercy they break his back'
> And I shall have a great following for this.
> (lines 70–76, 77–83)

The slaves, for their part, are uncertain whether Moses is a messianic figure, and the play includes a debate over messianism that takes place between the Old and Young Hebrew slaves.[71] These two characters may be read as representing what Jody Elizabeth Myers has identified as the two main views of religious messianism historically held by Jews. The Old Hebrew represents 'passive messianism', the belief that the Jews' exile will end through supernatural intervention rather than human agency, while the Young Hebrew advocates a more pragmatic and 'active messianism', whereby 'signs' of the impending messianic age were to be acted upon, and efforts made to speed its arrival.[72] The Young Hebrew argues that Moses is indeed a messianic figure:

Is not Miriam his sister, Jochabed his mother?
In the womb he looked round and saw
From furthermost stretches our wrong...
He fears our fear and tampers mildly
For our assent to let him save us.
(lines 255–257, 267–268)

This is met with scepticism by the Old Hebrew, who reminds his companion that there have been other supposed deliverers, all of them false:

I have seen splendid young fools cheat themselves
Into a prophet's frenzy; I have seen
So many crazed shadows puffed away,
And conscious cheats with such an ache for fame
They'd make bonfires of themselves to be
Mouthed in the squares, broad in the public eye.
And whose backs break, whose lives are mauled, after
It all falls flat?
(lines 294–301)

Moses' 'will-to-power' is personal, however, and the Hebrew slaves are not so much 'his' people as the instruments of his own rebellion against Pharaoh. In this respect, he is arguably more of a Nietzschean than a messianic or Zionist figure, concerned with his own liberation and empowerment rather than that of the slaves. Rosenberg's dramatisation of the emergence of Moses' desire for power suggests he was influenced by some of Nietzsche's ideas, and according to his biographer, Joseph Cohen, he had read some of his work.[73] *Moses* is, amongst other things, a narrative of individual revolt against an oppressive régime that is not worthy of respect. With regard to Rosenberg's war experience, the play's corrupt Egyptian culture is perhaps comparable with the harsh conditions and injustice of military life, in which severe penalties were imposed for disciplinary offences. If Christ was an index of the suffering of the soldier, then in Rosenberg's play, Moses becomes a figure of resistance. The context of *Moses* is not the collective flight of the Jews from Egypt, but the rebellion and liberation of Moses the individual, and possibly relates to Rosenberg's own frustrated attempts to transfer from his regiment. The play was written in 1916. In August that year, Rosenberg made enquiries about joining the Camouflage Corps, led by the artist Solomon J. Solomon,[74] and in the spring of 1918 he wrote to the Ministry of Munitions regarding a transfer on health grounds. He also applied for a transfer to the Jewish Legion around this time.[75]

Despite Rosenberg's interest in the Legion, however, *Moses* is not a Zionist drama. Only in his later poems was the desire for escape connected to the idea of a Jewish homeland, as in his last work, 'Through These Pale Cold Days', written in 1918:

> Through these pale cold days
> What dark faces burn
> Out of three thousand years,
> And their wild eyes yearn,
>
> While underneath their brows
> Like waifs their spirits grope
> For the pools of Hebron again –
> For Lebanon's summer slope.
>
> They leave these blond still days
> In dust behind their tread
> They see with living eyes
> How long they have been dead.

This poem and two others, 'The Burning of the Temple' and 'The Destruction of Jerusalem by the Babylonian Hordes' (both written in 1918) express anger and sadness at the loss of a homeland and a longing to return to it. 'The Destruction of Jerusalem' is an image of the invasion of the city by an 'alien' power, and apparently refers to the Babylonian capture. Since this poem was written in 1918 by a young

Jewish soldier who had tried unsuccessfully to transfer to the Jewish Legion, however, it is tempting to read it in connection with the British capture of Jerusalem, led by Field Marshal Allenby in December 1917. Rosenberg's application for transfer was never processed, and he was killed in action on 1 April 1918.

Rosenberg's desire to join the legion seems to have been at least partly prompted by the need to escape from the harsh conditions of trench life and the antisemitism he encountered among ranks and officers. There was also hostility towards Jewish troops in Palestine, however, as the memoirs of the men who served with the legion show. In a war against German imperialism, the British government had appealed to political Zionism in order to mobilise Jews for its own imperialist designs in the Middle East. As a result, the Jewish Legion was the only group within the British forces in the Great War that pursued its own nationalist agenda, with government support. But the Balfour Declaration represented a threat to the authority of the British administration in Palestine and the reaction to this was discrimination, which came from the very pinnacle of the military hierarchy. Patterson, one of the commanding officers of the Jewish Legion, described this in biblical terms, casting Field Marshal Allenby as 'Pharaoh' in a conflict over continuing recruitment for the Jewish battalions in March 1918:

> Alas! it seemed that another Pharaoh had arisen who knew not Joseph; and once again we would be expected to make bricks without straw, and become hewers of wood and drawers of water. Instead of this new unit being helped and encouraged, we were...made to feel that we were merely Ishmaelites, with every hand uplifted against us.[76]

While Patterson focused on the military 'ingathering of the Jews' and the 'restoration of Israel' (as discussed in Chapter 5), the Egyptian Expeditionary Force (EEF) made repeated attempts to disperse the Legion, which, by 1918 numbered over 5,000 men. The first was a proposal to break up the battalions into labour units. Twelve of Patterson's men expressed support for this idea, a number he thought appropriate, 'as it was one for each tribe', but ultimately only two transferred.[77] On another occasion, plans were secretly made to attach the Jewish unit to two West Indian battalions, with a commander already appointed, thus removing Patterson from the scene. While his men were on active service, Patterson found it difficult to obtain replacement clothing for them, 'although it was freely handed out to other units'. Appeals were useless, and 'the policy adopted by the local Staff was to keep us as "wandering Jews," pitched from one Brigade to another, in a continuous round of General Post'.[78] Indeed, according to Patterson, in three months the Jewish units were attached to no less than 12 different sections of the British army.[79] The campsites allocated to them were usually inferior to those assigned to other troops, as, for example, on the regiment's arrival at Ramallah on 9 August 1918: 'It was midnight when we got to our camp, where we found that someone had carefully chosen a site for us which was literally one mass of stones.'[80]

The men spent over seven weeks in the Jordan valley during August and September 1918, the hottest time of the year, whereas other units had been stationed there for a maximum of one week. At one time, the battalion, although more than 2,000 strong, was without a medical officer for over a year. Patterson fought back, however, and his most effective weapon was to threaten resignation. This he did repeatedly, and since no other officer would command a regiment that was internally divided over Zionism and faced hostility from staff officers in Cairo, this strategy brought results. Perhaps the most dramatic victory was what he describes as 'The Fall of Goliath', which occurred on 16 July 1919, when 'Goliath', or 'General Z', insulted Jewish soldiers, assaulting one of them during Patterson's absence. The men made an official complaint and insisted that the general apologise publicly to the entire battalion, which he did, but the petty discrimination continued. Eventually, Patterson informed Allenby and 'General Z' was removed from command. More frequently, however, the men found that their best defence was to substitute their Fusiliers badges for others when they were outside the camp limits, thus evading unwanted attention.

Lieutenant Vladimir Jabotinsky had instigated the legion and served with Patterson's regiment; his memoir of Palestine was published in Hebrew in 1945. Unlike Patterson, he did not use biblical metaphors, but preferred to draw comparisons between the Palestine campaign and Garibaldi's drive for Italian unification, a goal that was eventually achieved in 1870. Perhaps the most interesting aspect of Jabotinsky's memoir is not his choice of historical parallels, however, but the way in which he engages with notions of national and 'racial' psychologies. The characteristics of which Jabotinsky was critical were psychological rather than 'racial', which meant that both Jews and gentiles could exhibit behaviour that conformed to unflattering stereotypes. He argued that both groups were capable of developing a 'ghetto' mentality, as in this assessment of the psychology of the English 'ruling caste':

> that caste is a world of its own, distinct from the rest of English humanity, deaf and proud of its deafness, unimagina-tive and proud of it. Do you want an exact parallel to their outlook? Take the old Ghetto. Other days, other customs, but

the same fanaticism of 'We are chosen,' the very same disregard for the world outside, 'Pooh!' to everything new.[81]

The 'average Englishman', Jabotinsky argued, was opposed to 'any big, far-reaching project, and also to sentimentalism'.[82] The Balfour Declaration and the Jewish Legion smacked of both and provoked resistance. A preferable project was the promotion of the 'Greater Arabia', or 'Arabophilia' as Jabotinsky called it. This was in his view a British fantasy of Oriental primitivism, in which the Zionist Jew appeared as an unwelcome modernising force threatening to corrupt the Arabic 'Eden' of the Middle East. While the British government's 'Zionism' may have gathered popular support amongst Britain's civilian population, to many in the EEF the Jew was not a romantic figure, but one who threatened change and disruption. As Jabotinsky put it,

> They had seen Jews, both rich...and poor, in Whitechapel; quite sufficient for them to realize that the idea of the National Home had nothing to do with 'picturesque' Chasidim with curls (which they could certainly have 'swallowed,' for they are not Jew-haters) but with modern Jews, wearing trousers on their legs and hats on their heads, and with European ideas under those hats. An end to all the *couleur locale!*[83]

The Middle East was to remain a museum to British fantasies of Oriental primitivism, or the desire for 'the perpetuation of the caravan and the harem', and the Balfour Declaration threatened this.[84]

Another possible threat to the Zionist project in Jabotinsky's view was the 'altogether curious psychology' of the 'tailors', the Russian immigrants recruited from Britain. These men performed their duties conscientiously, but without enthusiasm, and, it seemed, lacked the pioneer spirit essential to Zionism. A 'gathering of exiles',[85] they were, in Jabotinsky's view,

> Inspired by nothing, loving nothing except their homes, their wives and their children somewhere in Whitechapel or Leeds, indifferent to Zionism, indifferent to Palestine...I saw nothing of any collective life among them. They had no common interests, held no meetings, displayed no tendencies to any kind of unification.[86]

It was not only the 'tailors' who lacked Zionist enthusiasm. The Anglo-Jewish lawyer Horace B. Samuel entered Palestine in 1918 'as a Zionist' and an officer in the 38th Royal Fusiliers, the battalion under Patterson's command, but gradually became disillusioned with the nationalist project.[87] During the British occupation he served as a military magistrate and then set up a private legal practice. In 1928 he left Palestine for Britain. His account offers a cynical view of the various performances of identity given by the key players in the Jewish Legion. Published in 1930, after 'a discreet interval', his memoir assesses Zionist achievement in what he described as 'the British-cum-Arab-cum-Zionist-cum-Missionary-cum-League-of-Nations Palestine'.[88] Samuel claimed impartiality, to the extent that he once represented the London Society for the Promotion of Christianity among the Jews in a dispute with the widow of a Hebrew Christian. Having demonstrated his professional detachment, Samuel gave the following summary of what Palestine meant to its various inhabitants during and after the war:

> To the supporters of missionaries it is a place where all the Jews should be converted into Christians. To the Zionist it is the scene of the building up of the National Home. To the British Imperialist it is the scene of the last crusade, another base for protecting the canal, and an important stage in the new air-way to India. To the believers in the League of Nations it is one of the most important of the Mandated Territories. To the Arabs and their backers it is a place where the native inhabitants of the country have been handed over *en masse* to be placed under the heel of hordes of alien immigrants (*sic*).[89]

In contrast with Patterson's memoir, which presented an image of Jewish solidarity in the face of discrimination, Samuel identified a confusion of motives among the men who joined the Jewish battalions, in which a hierarchy of Anglo-Jewish officers commanded a mass of soldiers hailing from Russia, Egypt, Palestine and parts of eastern Europe. In addition, Samuel observed a 'racial' hierarchy within the Jewish military community in Palestine, in which both Ashkenazic and Sephardic Jews regarded Levantine Jews as inferior to themselves, and 'As for the Yemenite Jew, ... he was rated a nigger pure and simple, and bullied accordingly'.[90] Besides these internal divisions, Samuel felt that the Jewish soldiers were manipulated not only by the British military administration, but also by their commanding officers and the Zionist leaders. Jabotinsky is portrayed as a posturing figure, 'the most picturesque and melodramatic nationalist that ever performed upon the Zionist stage';[91] a fanatical propagandist who urged the soldiers on with the words 'We are not merely a regiment – we are a political performing company!'[92] Jabotinsky, according to Samuel, saw himself as 'some Jewish D'Annunzio', a comparison that implies an autocratic element in his character.[93] Weizmann is given similarly unflattering treatment, and 'with his Mephistophelian face and subtle sinister charm', is portrayed as manipulative. Samuel describes one of his visits to the Jewish troops:

> I well remember how he addressed them. Lolling at a table, with his hands deep in his trouser pockets, he just spoke to them easily and racily and familiarly, in their own and his own native Yiddish...The audience responded to a man... As he walked across the camp, the men, like rats after the Pied Piper, just followed, to the long drawn out wistfulness of the *Hatikvah*.[94]

Samuel satirised the performances of identity, political and religious, which seemed obligatory for Jews serving in Palestine during the Great War, and revealed their comic elements. He resisted the display of ardent political Zionism expected by Jabotinsky, and mocked the theatrical piety of the Reverend Falk, chaplain to the Jewish Legion. Falk produced the Jewish national flag 'on every possible occasion', and ostentatiously observed the dietary laws of Judaism.[95] Many of his charges did not, and despite Patterson's efforts to ensure the men had kosher food, Samuel recalls 'Jewish lines littered with bacon tins'.[96] Jewish nationalism was in Samuel's view atavistic, and he described the Zionists as 'modern reactionaries'.[97] Whereas in 1922 Patterson had imagined the future Palestine as a modern utopia, built on the hydro-electric potential of the Jordan river, in 1930 Samuel viewed the 'conversion' of Jewry into nationhood as a primitivising process in its initial stages, which in practice meant that intellectuals worked as agricultural labourers. Patterson had focused on the religious and military history of Palestine, and avoided discussing its political future, but Samuel argued that the two themes were impossible to separate in a country whose politics had always been shaped by competing religious claims. Politics *was* religion in Palestine, and this was especially clear in the use of the synagogue and the Hebrew language in enforcing conformity to the construction of Jewish national identity.[98]

The ideological and coercive aspects of establishing cultural homogeneity in Palestine would perhaps have been excusable if the result had been a homeland for world Jewry, but Samuel argued that the division between eastern and western Jews remained intact. Most Jewish immigrants to Palestine came from central or eastern European countries, 'where there is little assimilation either in practice or in theory'.[99] For Western Jewry, Palestine was a 'charity' to which they donated, and a commodity, for religious tourists and for novelists in particular, who could 'pay a flying visit to Palestine, like Mr. Ludwig Lewisohn, and embody the results in a book'.[100] National identity, he argued, was an unnecessary luxury, which in the case of Palestine involved the sacrifice of cultural and material necessities. Western Jews were best advised to support Palestine financially, and to continue to enjoy the pleasures of civilisation in Europe, giving the idealists the chance to develop Jewish national culture into 'something mid-way between failure and maximum success'.[101]

Private Roman Freulich, by contrast, felt that Jewish national life had begun during the Palestine campaign, in the tents of the Jewish Legion. Freulich, an American, joined the 40th battalion of the Royal Fusiliers after hearing an English soldier speak about the Jewish Legion in New York City in early 1918. He left for Palestine with the first group of American volunteers on 28 February that year.[102] His account of the campaign, entitled *Soldiers in Judea*, was published in 1964, and draws on Patterson's memoir. Freulich, however, casts neither Weizmann nor Patterson as 'Moses', but Ben Zvi, future second President of the state of Israel, who is described as having parted the waters of a *wadi* with a pile of rocks so that the soldiers could cross without getting their feet wet.[103] Apart from this one allusion to the Old Testament, Freulich avoids Patterson's explicitly biblical reading of the campaign. Instead, his introduction focuses on the history of rebellion associated with Palestine: the Maccabean revolt against Seleucid rule and the recapture of Jerusalem in 164 BCE, and the revolt against the Romans led by Simon Bar Kokhba in 132 CE. This was the history that had been partly repeated, with Jewish troops fighting against (Turkish) imperial power in Palestine in the Great War, and partly rewritten, with the recaptured territory being held and the eventual formation of the state of Israel in 1948.

After the First World War Freulich returned to the United States and worked as a photographer, and his book offers a number of prose 'snapshots' of events in Palestine, which are presented to the reader without 'captions' or any explanation of the way in which they are considered to be significant. Among the most striking of these is an image of the Anglo-Jewish sculptor Jacob Epstein, a private in the 38th battalion, modelling a human figure out of sand:

> It was late in the afternoon, when Private Jacob Epstein, the sculptor, began pouring a bucket of water onto a heap of sand. Then he kneaded the mixture, and in silent eagerness commenced to work. Before darkness fell, the sand sculpture was finished – the figure of a man writhing in silent agony.[104]

Freulich does not ascribe any explicit meaning to this moment, but the image lends itself to a number of interpretations. Epstein's writhing figure may represent Jewish national life in embryo, or symbolise the birth of Jewish national art, or the historical suffering of the Jews. It may also, perhaps, be a *golem* image, drawing on the legend of the Rabbi Judah Loew (1512–1609) of sixteenth-century Prague, who fashioned a humanoid creature out of clay and brought it to life, for the purpose of protecting the Jewish community.[105] Prior to the existence of a Jewish Legion, the *golem* was the legendary means by which Jews defended themselves against persecution. The sand sculpture, then, may perhaps be viewed as a double metaphor, not only representing the *golem* of legend, but also the Jewish Legion, which arguably performed the same function, that of defending the interests of the Jewish community in Palestine. According to the legend, once the danger was past, or if the rabbi appeared to be losing control of his creation, the *golem* was destroyed. This was done through the removal of an amulet, which served to identify the *golem* and contained the secret name of God that gave it life.[106] Ironically, unlike the *golem*, the Jewish soldiers were empowered by the removal of their 'amulets' or Fusiliers badges, an act that allowed them the freedom of movement enjoyed by other soldiers outside of camp limits, as they were no longer identifiable as members of the Jewish battalions. Since the Jewish soldiers were equipped to defend themselves, and did so, the function of Epstein's '*golem*' was symbolic only, and accordingly it had disintegrated by the end of the day.

The chief function of the legendary *golem* was to defend the Jewish community against attack, and the Jewish Legion, perhaps its modern 'equivalent', was subject to persistent discrimination by the British military administration and repeated attempts to bring about its dispersal. Within the battalions themselves, Patterson claimed that 'race' was never an issue, but Freulich identified antisemitism not only among staff, but also among the gentile officers and non-commissioned officers in the legion itself.[107] In addition, there were problems between Jewish and West Indian soldiers, owing to gambling losses by the latter.[108] There was one black soldier in the Jewish Legion, Bata Kindai Amgoza ibn Lo Bagola, or Lo Bagola as he was known. He claimed to be of the tribe of Ephraim, and entertained the men with stories of Africa which appeared to be largely based on white imperialist stereotypes, stories of, in Freulich's words, 'the Africa of tom-toms, strident chantings, barbaric matings, superstitions and brutality'.[109] In his memoir, *An African Savage's Own Story* (1930), Lo Bagola complained of 'racial' discrimination from men under his command at Kantara in Egypt.[110] While no autobiography or memoir can be regarded as a completely reliable source, Lo Bagola's is particularly unreliable: he was not born in Africa but Baltimore in 1887 under the name of Joseph Howard Lee, and his claimed Jewish ancestry is by no means certain.[111]

Freulich's account of the Palestine campaign, written after the formation of the state of Israel, is a nostalgic look at what its author viewed as the birth of the Jewish nation during the First World War. The diary of Private Paul Epstein, a Russian immigrant who was conscripted into the Jewish Legion in 1918, gives a very different view of military life in Palestine.[112] Epstein found conditions at the base camp at Rafa unsatisfactory: the food was of poor quality, and for entertainment there was only 'a very small recreation marquee for about 1000 men'. This contained 'books about Zionism and literature of that name', which, Epstein wrote, 'makes me feel fed up whenever I enter that show' (diary entry, 8 February 1919). The monotony was relieved only by the occasional concert, football match, or *shool* service. Epstein was religiously devout, and disappointed by the lack of piety among the Jewish troops and what he regarded as the over-emphasis on Zionism within the legion. Attendance at the voluntary services was low, and he noted that 'Particularly sad to me is the indifference, almost antagonism, with which the Jewish religion is regarded! It seems unthinkable –

Zionism without the Jewish faith, but such it is' (2 September 1919). Finally, the rate of demobilisation among the Jewish troops was very slow, and many were still in Palestine long after the war had ended. Epstein noted that on one occasion Jabotinsky attempted to persuade soldiers awaiting demobilisation to stay on for another six months, but received 'only 10 volunteers' (6 April 1919).

Jabotinsky's appeal to the men was partly in response to growing anti-Jewish feeling among the Arab population in Palestine, assisted by the open preference of some high-ranking British officers for the Arabs' claim to the land. Colonel Meinertzhagen, chief political officer to the EEF, identified Lieutentant Colonel H. B. Waters-Taylor and Brigadier General Ronald Storrs as particular culprits.[113] The British occupying forces in Palestine, like their Roman predecessors, sought to suppress rebellion and discontent in order to preserve their authority. But the situation was complicated. The Jews in Palestine had the support of the British government, in the (albeit ambiguous) Balfour Declaration – to which the military administration in Palestine was largely hostile – and the Arabs had been assured that their claim to the land would be respected and upheld. Both Jews and Arabs felt somewhat betrayed by the British, but it is the form that Lieutenant Jabotinsky's betrayal and punishment took that is of interest here. In August 1919 Jabotinsky wrote a letter to Field Marshal Allenby, in which he protested against military antisemitism and requested a personal interview. While awaiting a response, Jabotinsky was visited by a Jewish Staff-Major from General Headquarters who claimed to have been sent by Allenby, and who submitted a falsified report on he conversation between them. As a result, Jabotinsky was compulsorily demobilised on 29 August 1919, but remained in Palestine, forming a *Haganah*, a self-defence corps, in response to increasing hostility from both Arabs and the British administration. The situation reached a horrific climax in the 1920 Jerusalem pogrom. In that year, the Passover coincided with the Muslim festival of *Nebi Musa*. A large number of Arab pilgrims came to the city, and with the encouragement of some British Staff officers, incited violence against the Jews.[114] Three days of looting, murder and rape by Arabs followed, in which the gates of the city were blocked, preventing anyone from leaving or entering. Kept outside the gates, Jabotinsky and his men were helpless to intervene. The self-defence corps was declared illegal and Jabotinsky, as its leader, was charged with 'banditism' and sentenced to 15 years' imprisonment by the British military authorities. As part of his humiliation before beginning his sentence, Jabotinsky was marched through the streets of Jerusalem and Kantara, flanked by two Arab rapists, who were also given 15 years. Whether Staff officers were conscious of the parallels between Jabotinsky's humiliating parade through Jerusalem and Jesus' journey to Calvary in the company of two thieves is unclear.[115] There was, however, a precedent for military punishment with Christ-like overtones in Field Punishment Number One. Obviously, Jabotinsky's punishment was not an exact parody of the crucifixion, but it did appear to dramatise elements of the crucifixion story, namely, the leader of a group of Jews being viewed with suspicion by Palestine's military rulers, and his betrayal and public humiliation on trumped-up charges alongside common criminals. Eventually, after protest from, amongst others, Lieutenant-Colonel Patterson and Justice Louis Brandeis of the US Supreme Court, the War Office intervened to annul Jabotinsky's sentence, and after his release he became leader of the 'Revisionist' Zionist movement.

To conclude this chapter, in civilian, and especially clerical usage, the crucifixion trope related to the soldier as a figure of heroic self-sacrifice, although occasionally it was also applied to the nation at war. Such imagery was used to glorify the war itself, and to portray it as a moral and religious struggle rather than a political conflict. In a 'holy war', the imagery of crucifixion served to differentiate between the British and the Germans, asserting the 'Christian' identity of the one nation and the 'paganism' of the other, and idealising the sacrifice of men in the interests of a new order. The image of the soldier as 'Christ' took on a different meaning in military life, however. 'Crucifixion' was the means by which the military authorities expressed their power over the soldier, by separating him from the rest of the group through the humiliating Field Punishment Number One. Combatants made cynical use of Christian themes in their letters and other writings to attack the notion of 'holy war' and the rhetoric of salvation used by some clergymen. Religious imagery was used to express alienation from Christian doctrine as a result of war experience, and to portray the soldier's suffering as mundane rather than expiatory.

For coherence and completion the crucifixion narrative relies upon a 'Judas' figure and the war provided a series of candidates for this role. One of these was the Kaiser, portrayed by Sir Owen Seaman, editor of *Punch*, as having betrayed Christ through his alleged renunciation of Christianity. Another was the German soldier, whose hatred and fear of the Allied soldier was 'demonstrated' by the story of the ritual murder of the 'Crucified Canadian'. But it was the Bolshevik revolution that produced the most enduring and compelling figure of the betrayer of the Christian nation. This figure was not just 'Judaised' by association with 'pagan' Germany, but explicitly constructed as 'Jewish', in keeping with the antisemitism embedded in the New Testament account of the crucifixion. Robert Wilton's direct comparison of the tsar with Jesus and the Bolsheviks with Judas is one of the most striking examples of this.

After the revolution of October 1917 the image of the 'Bolshevik Jew' allowed the notion of the Jews' hostility towards Christians to be translated into political terms. This gave the fear of attack by 'Jews' an immediacy and currency that directly influenced government policy and gave rise to the Balfour Declaration and the Jewish Legion. The Declaration and the Jewish battalions met with hostility from the staff at the General Headquarters in Cairo, as the memoirs discussed above show. The men who served in the Jewish Legion used a mixture of imagery to describe their experiences and impressions of Palestine, much of it deriving from the Old Testament and from Jewish history. Patterson drew comparisons between the staff officers and the pharaohs of ancient Egypt, with regard to their treatment of the Jews. Freulich referred to the history of Jewish resistance to occupation by the Greeks and the Romans, and expressed pride in having been present at what he saw in retrospect as the birth of the Jewish state. But among all the historical parallels that were being drawn with regard to Palestine, perhaps the Roman occupation was the part of that country's history that was most graphically evoked under British control in April 1920. Uncannily, in its opposition to Jewish claims to Palestine, the British military administration seemed almost to emulate its Roman predecessors, in terms of the punishment it awarded to Lieutenant Jabotinsky. Without wishing to overstate the matter, I have suggested that by accident or design, Jabotinsky's betrayal and imprisonment as the leader of a band of Jewish dissidents, and his march through Jerusalem accompanied by two common criminals, appeared to dramatise elements of the crucifixion story, and bore a parodic resemblance to the punishment of Jesus by the Romans. In a war that was saturated with the imagery of crucifixion in relation to the soldier, it was perhaps military discipline that evoked the crucifixion most forcefully, in Field Punishment Number One, and in Jabotinsky's punishment. These were images of the soldier as 'Christ' that the civilian did not see. The crucifixion theme in military discipline revealed something that civilian use of such imagery sought to obscure and displace, namely, that the responsibility for the sacrifice of the soldier (and, by extension, the death of Jesus) ultimately rested with the ruling powers. In this respect, military use of the crucifixion trope could only add to the process of the decline of Christian faith that had begun in Britain before the war.

It is ironic that even as the Church was losing its sense of authority in national life, the tropes and central narratives of Christianity should develop a powerful secular significance and emerge in a wide range of popular interpretations of the war. This chapter has examined the function of the crucifixion story in relation to the conflict. Chapter 7 explores the use of another Christian grand narrative; that of the apocalypse as described in the Book of Revelation, and examines modern interpretations of this theme in relation to the war and the immediate post-war period.

NOTES

1　'Mark Seven', *A Subaltern on the Somme in 1916* (London & Toronto: J. M. Dent & Sons, 1917).
2　Field Punishment Number One was dropped by the British army in 1923.
3　'Mark Seven', *A Subaltern*, p. 30.
4　See Langmuir, *History, Religion, and Antisemitism*, pp. 298–300 for a discussion of the medieval origins of the blood libel.
5　Langmuir, *History, Religion, and Antisemitism*, pp. 249–51.
6　The Kishinev pogrom occurred in 1903, and brought widespread condemnation of tsarist antisemitism. Kishinev, in Bessarabia, was the one place in the tsarist empire in which Jews could own land.
7　*Jewish Chronicle*, 23 June 1916, p. 10.
8　*Jewish Chronicle*, 28 April 1916, p. 8 and 23 June 1916, p. 10.
9　*Jewish Chronicle*, 9 June 1916, pp. 5–6.
10　Sander L. Gilman, *The Jew's Body* (New York: Routledge, 1991), p. 39.
11　Gilman, *The Jew's Body*, p. 19.
12　Gilman, *The Jew's Body*, pp. 96–98.
13　*The Times*, 30 July 1914, p. 5.
14　Henry Wace, Dean of Canterbury, *The Christian Sanction of War*. Address at the Service of Intercession for the King's Naval and Military Forces, Canterbury Cathedral, 9 August 1914 (London: J. C. Thynne, 1914), p. 14.
15　Robertson, *The Spiritual Pilgrimage of Jesus*, p. 207. Robertson's lectures and book were aimed at fellow clergymen, but the book went through five editions from 1917 to 1922, which suggests it had a wider appeal.
16　William Temple, *Christianity and War*, Papers for War Time Series, No.1 (London: Humphrey Milford, Oxford University Press, 1914), p. 3. Temple (1881–1944) was the son of Archbishop Frederick Temple, and a prominent Anglican clergyman. He

was Rector of St. James' from 1914–1918, and Editor of the periodical *Challenge* from 1915 to 1918. He later became Canon of Westminster (1919–21), Bishop of Manchester (1921–29), Archbishop of York (1929–42) and finally Archbishop of Canterbury (1942–44). See Wilkinson, *The Church of England*, p. 343.

17   A. F. Winnington-Ingram, 'In time of war', sermon published in *Kaiser or Christ?*, pp. 3–9.

18   Paget, *The Woman's Part*, p. 4.

19   Anon, 'A Song of Comfort', 1917, in Ella McFadyen, *Songs of the Last Crusade*, p. 9.

20   Coppard, *With a Machine Gun to Cambrai*, p. 73. Coppard joined the Machine Gun Corps in February 1916 when his regiment broke up.

21   Wilfred Owen, letter to his mother of uncertain date, but probably 16 May 1917. In Harold Owen and Joan Bel (eds.), *Wilfred Owen: Collected Letters* (London: Oxford University Press, 1967), pp. 460–2.

22   Owen and Bell (eds), *Wilfred Owen*, p. 462.

23   Wilfred Owen, 'The Parable of the Old Men and the Young', in Edmund Blunden (ed.), *The Poems of Wilfred Owen* (London: Chatto & Windus, 1933), p. 57.

24   Wilfred Owen, 'At a Calvary Near the Ancre', in Blunden, ed., *Poems* (1933), p. 108.

25   Wilfred Edward Salter Owen, *Poems*, with an introduction by Siegfried Sassoon (London: Chatto & Windus, 1920).

26   See Jean Moorcroft Wilson, *Siegfried Sassoon. The Making of a War Poet: A Biography (1886–1918)* (London: Duckworth, 1999), p. 194. Wilson notes that in his early and middle years, Sassoon identified more with the Thornycroft side of the family, although he began to romanticise the Sassoons after meeting his paternal grandmother at the age of eight and after the death of his father (pp. 12, 13). As Wilson suggests, the poem 'Ancestors', written between 1908 and 1915, exemplifies Sassoon's exoticisation of his Persian ancestry, with its references to 'jewelled, merchant Ancestors', who 'barter monstrous wealth with speech subdued'. Siegfried Sassoon, 'Ancestors', in *Collected Poems* (London: Faber & Faber, 1947), pp. 46–47.

27   Examples of Sassoon's early poems which express the glory and excitement of war include 'France' and 'To Victory'.

28   Sassoon's war poetry does not make use of Old Testament themes, although one might perhaps have anticipated their use given his developing interest in his Jewish ancestry. Equally, however, the absence of Old Testament imagery might suggest ambivalence in this respect. He was posted to Palestine in the spring of 1918, and initially felt alienated from the members of the Jewish Legion, but gradually began to identify with the country. His diary for that period includes the observation '*c'est la guerre* – in an Old Testament environment', plus a list of 'Birds seen in Judaea...'. He quickly returned to the Western Front, however, arriving at Marseilles on 7 May 1918. See Rupert Hart-Davis (ed.), *Siegfried Sassoon Diaries 1915–1918* (London: Faber & Faber, 1983), pp. 216, 223, 233, 245.

29   Siegfried Sassoon, 'They', in *Collected Poems*, p. 23.

30   'Via Crucis' appears in Sassoon's diary, dated 1916. See Hart-Davis (ed.), *Siegfried Sassoon Diaries*, p. 102.

31   Sassoon, 'The Redeemer', in *Collected Poems*, pp. 16–17.

32   Sassoon, 'Stand-to: Good Friday Morning', in *Collected Poems*, p. 24.

33   Sassoon, 'Enemies', in *Collected Poems* (1947), p. 26.

34   See Armstrong, *Holy War*, pp. 52–3. As Armstrong notes, the official Church doctrine during the crusades was that the Jews had forfeited their 'chosen' status as a result of their alleged role in the crucifixion of Christ, but that they were to be spared. Forced conversion was officially discouraged, but popular crusaders, disowned by the Church, overlooked this, and reacted to the orthodoxy that the Jews were a 'deicide people', and therefore deserving of punishment.

35   'Mark Seven', *A Subaltern*, p. 27.

36   'Mark Seven', *A Subaltern*, p. 28.

37   Roadside calvaries were a familiar part of the topography of war zones in France. As Paul Fussell notes, they were often located at crossroads, and in one case, in a valley on the Somme. See Paul Fussell, *The Great War and Modern Memory* (Oxford: Oxford University Press, 1975, reprinted 1977), p. 118.

38   Sir Owen Seaman, 'The Wayside Calvary', in *Punch*, 4 August 1915, p. 102.
39   This atrocity story was the subject of a television programme, entitled 'The Crucified Soldier' (Director: Jonathan Dent), and shown on Channel 4, Thursday 12 December 2002, 9–10pm. The programme included an interview with Jack Davis, a war veteran who recalls the rumour, and commentary from various academics. The programme claims to have identified the victim of the alleged crucifixion, naming him as Sergeant Band of the 48th Highlanders of Canada, but the evidence is far from conclusive.
40   'Torture of a Canadian Officer', *The Times*, 10 May 1915, p. 7.
41   See *The Times*, 15 May 1915.
42   See *Hansard Parliamentary Debates*, Commons, Vol. 71, 14 April–19 May 1915, columns 1623–25, 2330.
43   Langmuir, *History, Religion, and Antisemitism*, p. 250.
44   The 'Crucified Canadian' atrocity story coincided with reportage of the sinking of the *Lusitania*, which was carrying around 250 Canadian passengers (*The Times*, 8 May 1915, p. 9); the publication of the Bryce Report (*The Times*, 13 May 1915, p. 6), and anti-German rioting in Liverpool (*The Times*, 10 May 1915, p. 10) and London (*The Times*, 12 May 1915, p. 10).
45   The story of the 'Crucified Canadian' was finally denied by General March in Washington in 1925. See Arthur Ponsonby, *Falsehood in War-Time: Containing an Assortment of Lies Circulated throughout the Nations during the Great War* (London: George Allen & Unwin, 1928), p. 93.
46   'Pacifists and Profiteers', *Daily Graphic*, 12 November 1917, p. 8.
47   See Jean-Louis Robert, 'The Image of the Profiteer', in Jay Winter and Jean-Louis Robert (eds.), *Capital Cities at War: Paris, London, Berlin 1914–1919* (Cambridge: Cambridge University Press, 1997), p. 120.
48   On the notion of the 'Jewish voice', see chapter one of Gilman, *The Jew's Body*, pp. 10–37.
49   The apex of Victor Marsden's career as an antisemitic propagandist occurred in late 1920, when he translated the forged *Protocols of the Learned Elders of Zion* for publication by the Britons' Society.
50   *The Times*, 20 September 1917, p. 7.
51   Robert Wilton, *Russia's Agony*, (London: Edward Arnold, 1918), p. 60.
52   Robert Wilton, *The Last Days of the Romanovs* (London: Thornton Butterworth, 1920), p. 13.
53   Wilton, *The Last Days*, p. 76.
54   Wilton, *The Last Days*, p. 80.
55   Wilton, *The Last Days*, p. 148.
56   *Morning Post*, 26 July 1918, p. 6.
57   Cheyette, *Constructions*, p. 9.
58   Wilton, *The Last Days*, p. 131.
59   See Oliver Woods and James Bishop, *The Story of The Times: Bicentenary Edition 1785–1985* (London: Michael Joseph, 1983, reprinted 1985), p. 212.
60   See Levene, *War, Jews, and the New Europe*, p. 133.
61   See Peter Buitenhuis, *The Great War of Words: British, American, and Canadian Propaganda and Fiction, 1914–1933* (Vancouver: University of British Columbia Press, 1987) for details of the formation of the wartime propaganda unit at Wellington House and the writers involved.
62   See Colin Holmes, *Anti-Semitism in British Society 1876-1939* (London: Edward Arnold, 1979), p. 275, n 12. The letter from John Buchan to Geoffrey Robinson, dated 1 May 1917, is held in *The Times*' archives.
63   See *The Times*, 14 September 1917, p. 7.
64   Patterson, *With the Judaeans*, p. 25.
65   Letter from Isaac Rosenberg to Edward Marsh, March 1918, quoted in Cohen, *Journey to the Trenches*, p. 3.
66   Cohen, *Journey to the Trenches* (1975), p. 29.
67   Isaac Rosenberg, 'Creation', in Ian Parsons (ed.), *The Collected Works of Isaac Rosenberg* (London: Chatto & Windus, 1979) pp. 50–1.
68   Israel Zangwill, *The Next Religion. A Play in Three Acts*, 2nd edn (London:

Heinemann, 1912, reprinted 1925).

69   For the letter from Rosenberg to Sydney Schiff, see Ian Parsons (ed.), *Collected Works* (1979), p. 219. Letter from Isaac Rosenberg to Edward Marsh, October–November 1915, in Parsons (ed.), *Collected Works*, p. 225

70   All Rosenberg material comes from Isaac Rosenberg, *The Collected Works of Isaac Rosenberg*, Ian Parsons (ed.) (London: Chatto & Windus, 1979).

71   In this respect, the play is chronologically inaccurate, as the messianic expectation did not develop until much later, during the exile in Babylon. A faithful historical representation, however, does not appear to be what Rosenberg intended.

72   See Jody Elizabeth Myers, 'The Messianic Idea and Zionist Ideologies', in Jonathan Frankel (ed.), *Jews and Messianism in the Modern Era: Metaphor and Meaning*, Studies in Contemporary Jewry: An Annual 7 (New York and Oxford: Oxford University Press, 1991), pp. 3–13.

73   See Cohen, *Journey to the Trenches*, p. 84. Rosenberg's possible use of Nietzsche is relevant because of the latter's criticism of Christian mores, and also because of the popular, civilian representation of Nietzsche, along with Treitskche and Bernhardi, as part of the 'unholy trinity', the 'prophets' of an 'apostate' Germany, discussed in Chapter 2. Nietzsche's writing on the Jews is notoriously complicated and has generated much debate, but see Jacob Golomb (ed.), *Nietzsche and Jewish Culture* (London and New York: Routledge, 1997) for a full discussion of the complexity of Nietzsche's attitudes towards the Jews, ancient and modern.

74   Rosenberg, letter to Edward Marsh, August 1916, in Parsons (ed.), *Collected Works* (1979), pp. 242–3.

75   Rosenberg, letter to Edward Marsh, postmarked 7 March 1918, in Parsons (ed.), *Collected Works*, p. 271.

76   Patterson, *With the Judaeans*, p. 57.

77   Patterson, *With the Judaeans*, p. 65.

78   Patterson, *With the Judaeans*, p. 84.

79   Patterson, *With the Judaeans*, p. 123.

80   Patterson, *With the 'Judaeans'*, p. 92.

81   Vladimir Jabotinsky, *The Story of the Jewish Legion*, trans. Samuel Katz (New York: Bernard Ackerman, 1945), p. 169.

82   Jabotinsky, *Jewish Legion*, p. 168.

83   Jabotinsky, *Jewish Legion*, p. 171.

84   Jabotinsky, *Jewish Legion*, p. 174.

85   Jabotinsky, *Jewish Legion*, p. 151.

86   Jabotinsky, *Jewish Legion*, p. 159.

87   Horace B. Samuel, *Unholy Memories of the Holy Land* (London: Hogarth Press, 1930), p. 1.

88   Samuel, *Unholy Memories*, p. 7.

89   Samuel, *Unholy Memories*, p. 6.

90   Samuel, *Unholy Memories*, pp. 19–20.

91   Samuel, *Unholy Memories*, p. 8.

92   Samuel, *Unholy Memories*, p. 13.

93   Samuel, *Unholy Memories*, p. 9. Gabriele D'Annunzio (1863–1938) was an Italian nationalist and writer, who fought in the Great War and in 1919 occupied Fiume and set himself up as a dictator, remaining there until 1921.

94   Samuel, *Unholy Memories*, pp. 13, 15–16.

95   Samuel, *Unholy Memories*, p. 15.

96   Samuel, *Unholy Memories*, p. 19.

97   Samuel, *Unholy Memories*, p. 254.

98   Samuel, *Unholy Memories*, p. 268. A tax was levied upon all members of the Jewish community, which was used to maintain a salaried Rabbinate. This was in Samuel's view analogous to the trade unions' political levy, in the sense that although it was not strictly compulsory, any secession would have to be made public, thereby discouraging open dissent in favour of an appearance of solidarity.

99   Samuel, *Unholy Memories*, p. 257.

100   Samuel, *Unholy Memories*, p. 260.

101   Samuel, *Unholy Memories*, p. 276.

102   Roman Freulich, *Soldiers in Judea: Stories and Vignettes of the Jewish Legion* (New York: Herzl Press, 1964), p. 31.

103   Freulich, *Soldiers in Judea*, p. 63.

104   Freulich, *Soldiers in Judea*, p. 65.

105   See Frederick Thieberger, *The Great Rabbi Loew of Prague: His Life and Work and the Legend of the Golem: With Extracts from his Writings and a Collection of the Old Legends* (London: East and West Library, 1955).

106   It is of interest at this point to recall Patterson's view of the meaning of the Balfour Declaration to pious Jews, as the 'Voice of God' (Patterson, *With the Judaeans*. To extend the analogy of the legion as '*golem*', then, while the Balfour Declaration did not create the Legion, it certainly validated its existence.

107   Freulich, *Soldiers in Judea*, p. 143.

108   Freulich, *Soldiers in Judea*, p. 167.

109   Freulich, *Soldiers in Judea*, p. 199.

110   Bata Kindai Amgoza ibn Lobagola, *An African Savage's Own Story* (London: Alfred A. Knopf, 1930), p. 360.

111   On Lobagola's origins, see David Killingray, 'LoBagola and the making of "An African Savage's Own Story"', in Bernth Lindfors (ed.), *Africans On Stage* (Bloomington, IN: Indiana University Press, 1998). See also Jeffrey Green, *Black Edwardians: Black People in Britain, 1901–1914* (London: Frank Cass, 1998).

112   The diary of Private Paul Epstein, 1918–19, may be found in the rare books section of the Hartley Library, University of Southampton, Britain, under the shelfmark MS 1124 AJ15/8. All further references will be given in the text.

113   Meinertzhagen identifies Lieutenant Colonel H. B. Waters-Taylor and Brigadier-General Ronald Storrs as particular culprits. See Meinertzhagen, *Middle East Diary*, pp. 82, 86.

114   Meinertzhagen, *Middle East Diary*, pp. 81–3.

115   See Luke 23:32.

7

The Apocalyptic Imagination

In a letter to a friend, dated 14 November 1914, the Scottish poet Charles Sorley[1] gave his opinion of Israel Zangwill:

> I admire him enormously and like him about as much. He reminds me often of the author of *Revelation* in his outbursts of revolting sensuousness (he too is fully capable of imagining heaven as inhabited by four beasts and four and twenty elders) varied occasionally by really beautiful passages, but he is far more humorous and witty than St. John the Divine. *Dreamers of the Ghetto* is his best. I love Jews – of a type.[2]

Sorley used the Revelation narrative – a dramatic vision of the end of the world in which the forces of 'good' and 'evil' struggle for supremacy – as an example of a tendency towards 'excess' that he perceived in Jews, and to suggest that 'outbursts of revolting sensuousness' were a 'Jewish' trait. In doing so, he subscribed to the then contemporary perception that Jews were creatures of dual nature, capable of extremes of both 'good' and 'bad'. Sorley cast Zangwill as a 'good' Jew, the quality of whose writing was only occasionally marred by the supposedly 'racial' tendency to 'excess', as exemplified in Revelation.[3] In fact, the imaginative excess that Sorley associated with 'Jewish' writing came mostly from gentiles, in the rhetoric of 'apocalypse' that was frequently used to describe the war and the changes it brought. Apocalyptic imagery, drawn directly from Revelation, was central to the widespread portrayal of the war as a cataclysmic struggle, and was also used with regard to the political developments of the post-war years. Even more than the trope of 'crucifixion', that of 'apocalypse' captured the public imagination, and the language of 'apocalypse' was used to describe the scale of the war and its impact, and to express excitement and apprehension at the changes that would follow. Members of the clergy focused on the themes of judgement and the triumph of Christianity; politicians spoke of the war's capacity to 'purge' national life and unite the British in making a fresh start, and soldiers drew on Revelation to convey the devastation of their surroundings, but without the redemptive optimism of the civilian perspective.

Christian apocalyptic allocates a particular role to the Jews in the 'last days' and differentiates sharply between 'good' and 'bad' Jews; the former being converts (or potential converts) to Christianity and the latter the servants of Antichrist, who will perish in the prophesied cataclysm. The concept of 'Antichrist' is integral to the Christian apocalyptic tradition, and takes two main forms. First, there is the definition given in the letters of St John, that of Antichrist as one who denies the divinity of Christ: 'The man who denies that Jesus is the Christ – he is the liar, he is Antichrist.' (1 John 2:22) This is repeated in St John's second letter, in which Antichrist pertains to a deceiver, or a false doctrine: 'There are many deceivers about in the world, refusing to admit that Jesus Christ has come in the flesh. They are the Deceiver; they are the Antichrist' (2 John: 7). Then there is the personification of Antichrist found in early Christian writings, as an individual under the control of Satan, whose appearance would immediately precede the second coming. The origins of this figure are found in the Johannine and Sibylline prophecies, which foretold the overthrow of a demonic king by a Jewish military and religious leader.[4] These texts, written by Jews for use as conversion tools, were produced around the same time as Daniel (between 167 and 164 BCE) and like Daniel, may be viewed as a response to the rule of Antiochus Epiphanes, under which Jews were persecuted. Christian narratives of redemption drew on the evil monarch featured in Daniel and the Johannine and Sibylline texts, but gradually this powerful figure became portrayed as 'Jewish'. This was partly owing to religious rivalry, as Church and Synagogue competed for converts before the Roman empire was Christianised in 400 CE, and partly a reaction to the Jews' perceived failure to recognise Jesus as the Messiah. As a result, some of the early Christian theologians linked the figure of Antichrist with the Jewish messianic expectation, and warned that when he appeared, Jews would follow him into battle against Christianity (according to Iranaeus, for example, Antichrist would be a Jew of the tribe of Dan). The association between Jews and Antichrist was further developed in medieval drama, in the miracle and mystery plays that depicted their destruction at the start of the millennium. The politics of the Reformation in Europe gave rise to another collective image of evil incarnate, in Lutheran representations of the papacy.[5] The papal image of Antichrist is found at the margins of early twentieth-century religious discourse, but the wartime rhetoric of apocalypse was mainstream and secular and the constructions of 'Antichrist' reflected the political anxieties of the period.

Apocalyptic imagery was used in relation to events such as the Bolshevik revolution, the rise of the labour movement and widespread unemployment and unrest. This secular apocalyptic, like its religious counterpart, tended to reproduce the polarised representations of 'good' and 'bad' Jews that are found in millennial thinking. In anti-Bolshevik propaganda in particular, 'Jews' were cast as either the potential allies or the ruthless enemies of the Christian state. This chapter considers the use of apocalyptic imagery in the portrayal of the war as a battle between 'good' and 'evil', and examines the representation of these forces. It also explores the hopes and fears associated with the post-war period and the roles that popular discourse ascribed to 'Jews' in the political and social reconstruction of Britain.

'ARMAGEDDON'

During the First World War the imagery of apocalypse became common to both marginal and mainstream religious discourse, as millennialists and leading clergymen alike spoke of the war as 'Armageddon', a battle between 'good' and 'evil' that would usher in a new order. 'Armageddon' seemed an appropriate metaphor for the scale of the conflict between the rival powers and the degree of destruction and slaughter it provoked, and was also useful in demonising the enemy. The difference between clerical and millennialist engagement with the Revelation narrative, however, was that the latter took Revelation literally, and regarded the events of the war as 'signs' of the fulfilment of prophecy, while the clergy made selective and rhetorical use of the language of apocalypse, and the 'millennium' they anticipated took the form of a stronger Church and a more devoutly Christian post-war society.

Even before the outbreak of war there was speculation among millennialists that the 'last days' were near, and groups such as the

Prophecy Investigation Society (PIS) met regularly to discuss 'signs' of the second coming of Christ.[6] The society was a marginal Protestant group that formed part of the Dispensationalist movement, which had begun in Britain in the 1830s under the leadership of John Nelson Darby, of the Plymouth Brethren. Although by the 1860s dispensationalism had become a popular movement in the United States, in Britain it remained a peripheral influence.[7] Dispensationalists view history as divided into several eras, and regard the dispersion of the Jews as an interruption in the chronology given in Daniel 9: 24–5, of the '70 weeks' which will elapse before the rebuilding of Jerusalem and the anointing of the Messiah. According to dispensationalism, as long as Jews are dispersed, this chronology cannot be resumed and redemption cannot occur. Once the Jews have returned to the Holy Land, however, the Seventh Dispensation, the 'time of the end', the second coming and salvation, will begin. To some members of the society, the events of 1912 indicated that this time was close at hand. In a collection of papers first published in 1913, members of the Women's Branch identified irrigation work in Mesopotamia (Iraq) as a 'sign' of the prophesied building up of Babylon prior to its destruction.[8] Since 1905, the British engineer Sir William Willcocks had been in the Middle East conducting surveys for a number of irrigation projects, including the one in Mesopotamia, then a province of the Ottoman empire. Returning to London in 1912, he published an account of his findings and on 10 June that year gave a lecture on the subject to the Royal Geographical Society. The title he chose was 'The Garden of Eden and its Restoration'. Willcocks identified the Garden of Eden as an early Jewish settlement on the upper Euphrates, which the inhabitants had been forced to leave when their irrigation channels collapsed. In describing this scene he attempted to provide an archaeological gloss on the biblical narrative of the Fall, suggesting that the tar deposits, or 'bitumen springs' that appeared in the suddenly arid landscape would have seemed to the departing Jews 'like flaming swords in the hands of the offended Seraphim'.[9] Despite his rationalist attempt to explain the Eden myth, Willcocks was a religious man, and his writing reflects both his faith and his profession; besides accounts of his engineering work in the Middle East, he also published translations of the Gospels in colloquial Egyptian.[10] By framing his account of early irrigation in Mesopotamia in the context of a recovered 'Eden', Willcocks was indirectly invoking the themes of apocalypse and millennium; dramatic and highly resonant images whose appeal was more than marginal. Millennialists would undoubtedly have been attracted by the apparently biblical significance of the Mesopotamia project, but as Willcocks' choice of title shows, the possible retrieval of a lost earthly 'paradise', if couched in scientific terms, would also have appealed to members of the Royal Geographical Society.

Another development that aroused millennial interest was Zionism. After the first congress of the World Zionist Organization, held at Basle in 1897, Jews began to return to Palestine and form small co-operative settlements. One of a number of books discussing the significance of Zionist settlement was Frank Jannaway's *Palestine and the Jews; the Zionist Movement an Evidence that the Messiah will soon Appear in Jerusalem to Rule the Whole World Therefrom*, published in early 1914, just before the outbreak of war.[11] Jannaway argued that the Jewish settlements in Palestine indicated that the second coming was imminent.[12] Although he did not call for the conversion of the Jews, Jannaway did refer to Jesus as the Messiah, and in an anecdote that suggests conversionist desires, recalled being directed to 'Christian Street' while souvenir hunting in Jerusalem, and finding it dominated by Jewish shops. For the Jewish colonies, however, he had nothing but praise, which is perhaps why his book was politely received by Jewish readers, despite the fact that it described the colonists' success as, 'an absolute fulfilment of those prophecies concerning the Jew and his land just prior to the return to earth of his Messiah, and which time is so frequently spoken of by the prophets of Israel as "The Time of the End"'.[13] But just as the Jews were returning to their land, so the forces of Antichrist were gathering strength, as prophesied. Jannaway identified Russia and Germany as 'Gog' and 'Magog' respectively, since both countries had recently bought land near the Mount of Olives and had installed consulates and troops.[14] This, along with Zionist settlement and the stockpiling of arms by the nations, meant that from the millennialist perspective, the world was preparing for Armageddon. Interpretative literature of this kind was not simply generated by the prospect of war, but was widely published during the late nineteenth and early twentieth centuries. Popular titles included two books by Dr Gratton Guinness, *Light for the Last Days* (1886, reprinted in 1888 and 1917) and *The Approaching End of the Age* (1878, reprinted in 1879, 1880, 1882 and 1918). Although there seems to have been some demand for such writing, it was also ridiculed, as in, for example, F. J. B. Hooper's *An Extinguisher for the Guinness 'Light for the Last Days:' and a Stopper for 'The Approaching End of the Age'* (1888). The impending war, however, added a certain immediacy to such interpretation. Initially, the idea of the coming war as the apocalypse prophesied in Revelation was confined to the fringes of Protestantism. Once war had broken out, however, the rhetoric of apocalypse began to enter into mainstream religious and political discourse.

Theological interest in the Apocrypha was not simply confined to marginal religious groups during the First World War. The Society for the Promotion of Christian Knowledge (SPCK) published a series of what might be termed 'pocket apocalyptic', in small, mass-produced editions of the Jewish apocrypha. The stated aim was to provide 'short, cheap, and handy text-books' of interest to the general reader as well as to theology students, and the books were described as 'important for the study of Christian origins'.[15] The majority of the books in this series were published during 1917 and 1918, which seems to suggest that theological interest in apocalyptic writing increased during the war, possibly in response to the conflict itself and the prevailing rhetorical climate.

Members of the Anglican clergy at all levels used the theme of 'Armageddon' to refer to the spiritual significance of the war, as a conflict between 'good' and 'evil' and a defence of Christianity against 'paganism'. Their use of apocalyptic language, however, was selective. There was, for example, little rhetorical engagement with the second coming, which follows 'Armageddon' in the Revelation narrative and references to 'judgement' and 'millennium' took the form of calls for the repentance of national 'sins' and the hope that a more devoutly Christian nation would emerge from the war. The Bishop of London's rhetoric typifies this approach. In sermons preached during the winter of 1914–15, Winnington-Ingram referred to the war as 'this Armageddon'[16] describing it as a 'Day of God', a supreme test of Christianity which was 'in many respects an anticipation of the Judgement Day'.[17] His rhetorical use of the 'Last Great Day' and 'Judgement' referred not to events at the end of the world, as in Revelation, but to periodic tests of Christian faith and endurance, the effects of which were cataclysmic, as he informed his congregation: 'When they come, everything is broken up in the world, everything is altered; boundaries, frontiers, all melt away – the whole world is put into the melting-pot.[18] From this a new order would emerge, but first, however, a 'holy war' must be fought.

On other occasions, the Bishop's rhetoric seemed to shift towards British Israelism, as when, in 1914, he informed civilian and military congregations that, 'Jerusalem is beautiful, standing as it does three thousand two hundred feet above the sea. But there is a more beautiful place than Jerusalem, and that is England.'[19] This statement suggests that England will emerge from the war as the 'new Jerusalem', the modern centre of Christian faith, with the English replacing the Jews as the 'chosen people'. But first they must become worthy of the responsibility. The Bishop of London hoped that the war would act as 'a purifying, cleansing draught',[20] which would unite the English, strengthen their faith, and return religion to the centre of national life. Other nations were being 'reborn' as a result of the war; the French, he argued, had abandoned their trivial interest in fashion and gaiety for patriotism and the Russians, too, had reformed: 'In a week the vodka was flung aside...the nation was unified, and the Tsar became the father of his people.'[21] England, too, could be strengthened through war, and must repent of her sins, in order to become fit to lead the Christian nations. In a sermon preached at St Paul's in July 1915, he called for national repentance in urgent terms, and declared 'it is only a new England, which has come back to her best self, which can save the world to-day'.[22]

Apocalyptic imagery can be effective in arousing both religious and national fervour at times of crisis, as Winnington-Ingram's successful appeals to Christian patriotism demonstrate. Despite drawing criticism from both government ministers and fellow-clergymen,[23] his sermons had great popular appeal and were widely published. Winnington-Ingram used the imagery of apocalypse and judgement not in anticipation of the second coming of Christ, but to demonise the Kaiser, defend Christian imperialism and aid military recruitment. As the content of his sermons shows, the language of apocalypse and redemption was not confined to marginal religious groups in wartime Britain, but was also present in mainstream discourse and had both religious and secular appeal. It is the secular use of apocalyptic imagery that I want to consider next.

Secular engagement with the theme of the war as a cataclysm that would precede a new order was immediate and enthusiastic. In a speech made in September 1914, Lloyd George anticipated the emergence of a new Britain, declaring,

I can see signs of its coming in the glare of the battlefield ... A great flood of luxury and of sloth which had submerged the land is receding, and a new Britain is appearing. We can see for the first time the fundamental things that matter in life and that have been obscured from our vision by the tropical growth of prosperity.[24]

The imagery is of the 'flood', the narrative of apocalypse found in Genesis, used here to suggest the war as a fresh start. Like the clergy, politicians made selective use of biblical imagery in relation to the war, according to the desired impact. The Old Testament provided Lloyd George with metaphors for what he perceived as the corrupted state of pre-war British society, while Winston Churchill chose a passage from Deuteronomy, in which Yahweh calls the nation of Israel to arms, to dramatise and justify Britain's entry into the conflict. In October 1911 Churchill was invited by then Prime Minister Herbert Asquith to go to the Admiralty. Foreseeing war, he accepted, and recalled the moment in his memoir:

> That night, when I went to bed, I saw a large Bible lying on a table in my bedroom ... I opened the Book at random, and in the ninth chapter of Deuteronomy, I read – Hear, O Israel: Thou art to pass over Jordan this day, to go in to possess nations greater and mightier than thyself, cities great and fenced up to heaven ... Not for thy righteousness, or for the uprightness of thine heart, dost thou go to possess their land: but for the wickedness of these nations the Lord thy God doth drive them out from before thee, and that he may perform the word which the Lord sware unto thy fathers, Abraham, Isaac, and Jacob.[25]

To Churchill, this 'seemed a message full of reassurance'.[26] Territorial expansion through war could be justified by means of the 'wickedness' of the nations targeted. Whether or not events happened as Churchill described, his reference to Deuteronomy in this context suggests a view of the British as the modern 'Israelites', in much the same way as Winnington-Ingram's assertion that the beauty and spirituality of England surpassed that of Jerusalem implied the 'chosen' status of the British. This tendency to appropriate parts of the Old Testament in support of Christian projects is also found among millennialists, who have sought from it evidence of proto-Christianity in their efforts to assert a Christian religious authority and to convert Jews.[27] Ultimately, however, it was Revelation that provided Christians with the justification they needed for a 'holy war', since analogies between the British and the 'Israelites' could hardly be sustained in a context in which Britain was being popularly portrayed as a Christian nation. The Revelation narrative provided an account of moral warfare which, unlike the tales of divinely sanctioned war in the Old Testament, privileged Christians. Accordingly, after its initial foray into the Old Testament, Churchill's memoir draws on Revelation for its content and structure, and chapter one, entitled 'The Vials of Wrath', portrays the war as an event of apocalyptic proportions:

> No truce or parley mitigated the strife of the armies. The wounded died between the lines: the dead mouldered into the soil...Cities and monuments were smashed by artillery. Bombs from the air were cast down indiscriminately. Poison gas in many forms stifled or seared the soldiers. Liquid fire was projected upon their bodies. Men fell from the air in flames, or were smothered, often slowly, in the dark recesses of the sea.[28]

The language and imagery of this passage compares directly with that of Revelation, chapter 16, which describes the loss of human life through the seven plagues unleashed upon the earth, in which unbelievers are scorched by the rays of the sun, all life in the sea is extinguished, and 'the cities of the world collapsed' (Revelation 16: 19). In other passages, Churchill used apocalyptic imagery to convey not the horror of the war so much as the drama of the conflict and the power of those involved. Aside from the accounts of the destruction, there is a tone of awe and admiration for the might of the participating nations in a war that brought them 'to the knowledge of their strength'. The 'vials of wrath', he wrote, 'were full: but so were the reservoirs of power'.[29]

Among civilians, the drama and spectacle of 'Armageddon' generated fear and excitement, as this letter by an anonymous woman, dated 1917, indicates:

> Harry and I were in the Zeppelin raid night before last in London, and it was most interesting and exciting...Guns were going off over us, so we charged up an alley, only to find

them worse at the other end. The smell of powder was exciting. We stood in a doorway, and Harry put an arm around me and I kissed him solemnly, and we waited to be exterminated.[30]

For those who wanted to see 'Armageddon' from the soldier's perspective, the War Office and the British Topical Committee made a series of films at the Front, which were publicised in the film journal *Bioscope* in 1916 under the title '"Peeps At the Hidden War": Official Pictures of Armageddon'. The article described the war as 'the greatest event in the world's history' and one that 'the ordinary citizen' was not allowed to witness:

> The most tremendous event that has ever shaken the earth is being waged in virtual secrecy. Save for brief official narratives and vague newspaper reports, the darkness of Armageddon has been unrelieved for the spectator by any really graphic verbal description of its dreadful yet heroic course.[31]

With titles such as *Liveliness on the British Front* and *The Eyes of the Army: With the RFC at the Front*, the films claimed to offer the public 'a marvellously graphic and intimate impression not only of real fighting, but also of the life of battlefield', and guaranteed 'absolute authenticity'.[32]

The ubiquity of the theme of 'Armageddon' prompted satire, at least initially. On 5 August 1914, A. A. Milne published an article in *Punch* which portrayed the war not as a Christian crusade in answer to God's will, but as a game of the pagan gods, played in response to the violent desires of humans.[33] The article describes how, when overhearing the views of one 'Mr Porkins', who felt that the British were 'getting flabby' and that war was the only solution, the gods of Olympia decided to grant his wish. From trivial beginnings and fuelled by the press, events escalated, until finally a world war broke out, providing humans with an outlet for their belligerence and the gods with entertainment. The following issue of *Punch* featured a cartoon in which an elderly woman, having taken the rhetoric literally, is unable to find 'Armageddon' marked on a map of the war zones. Returning to the shop where she bought the map, she says to the shopkeeper 'I've brought back this war map you sold me yesterday, Mr. Brown. It's not up to date. I've been looking all the morning for Armageddon, and can't find it marked anywhere.'[34] But satire of this kind quickly became unacceptable in the rhetorical climate of morally justified war by 'Christian' Britain against 'pagan' Germany. Occasionally, however, a dissenting voice was heard, often attacking the jingoism of the clergy, as in a letter from J. E. Symes to the editor of *The Nation* in December 1914, which appeared under the heading 'The Moratorium for the Sermon on the Mount'. Symes wrote:

> Sir – The clergy make excellent recruiting officers; but need they give up preaching that we should love our enemies?... we need not talk as if, to the eye of faith, angel wings were spreading from the shoulders of Thomas Atkins, and horns from the forehead of Fritz.[35]

In *John Bull*, a populist weekly with a nationalist and conservative bias, the editor Horatio Bottomley pointed out that the Germans, too, claimed divine support for their cause, and noted 'It really is very embarrassing – this perpetual invocation and praise of the Deity by both sides!'[36] This initial scepticism soon gave way, however, to prose that was worthy of Winnington-Ingram, such was its evangelical tone.[37] An article entitled 'The mills of God are grinding', published in September 1914, incorporated the themes of 'apocalypse', 'antichrist', 'judgement' and 'millennium', and read more like a sermon than an editorial. It is worth quoting at some length:

> To-day, we grope in darkness, almost despairing of our race. But there, far ahead, we see the faint light of a New World; behind it we discern the outlines of the Prince of Peace; and as we step warily, day by day, towards him, over and above all the din of battle ... we are conscious of an awful, never-ceasing sound. And there, before the light, we see at length the Mills of God – grinding, grinding, grinding; and beneath them, beyond all hope of rescue or escape, there writhes a mad Teutonic tyrant, with blood-guilt upon his head, the greed of conquest on his lips, and the doom of a People on his soul.
> Come, brother, let us turn our eyes to the light![38]

This may have been a satire on the imagery of apocalypse and millennium used by press, politicians and clergy, but whether or not the article was mocking the rhetoric of 'Armageddon', this passage suggests that in a very short time, the notion of the war as a conflict between the forces of 'good' and 'evil' had become an established, perhaps even orthodox, part of wartime civilian discourse.[39]

While in the early months at least, civilians tended to view the war in glorious terms, as a divinely sanctioned venture, soldiers saw little evidence of God's presence at the Front. Among combatants, the use of apocalyptic imagery was more often descriptive than moral, and served to convey the devastation of their surroundings. Describing a ruined cemetery at Fricourt, Second Lieutenant Max Plowman of the 10th West Yorkshire regiment (or 'Mark Seven' as he called himself) drew on the imagery of Judgement Day but without its underlying theme of resurrection, and wrote 'It looks as if it might have heard the Last Trump. Graves are opened and monuments of stone and beaded wire lie smashed and piled into heaps.'[40] The artist Paul Nash used the imagery of apocalypse not only to describe the horror of his surroundings but also as an indictment of civilian enthusiasm for the war. In a letter to his wife, dated November 1917, he wrote:

> Evil and the incarnate fiend alone can be master of this war, and no glimmer of God's hand is seen anywhere. Sunset and sunrise are blasphemous, they are mockeries to man, only the black rain out of the bruised and swollen clouds all through the bitter black of night is fit atmosphere in such a land. The rain drives on, the stinking mud becomes more evilly yellow, the shell holes fill up with green-white water, the roads and tracks are covered in inches of slime, the black dying trees ooze and sweat and the shells never cease . . . It is unspeakable, godless, hopeless. I am no longer an artist interested and curious, I am a messenger who will bring back word from the men who are fighting to those who want the war to go on for ever. Feeble, inarticulate, will be my message, but it will have a bitter truth, and may it burn their lousy souls.[41]

This is an image of apocalypse without the attendant themes of 'resurrection' or 'millennium'. There is no portrayal of the German troops or the Kaiser as the embodiment of 'evil', nor any suggestion of a 'new order' emerging from the devastation, only continuing and pointless death and destruction. In this letter, Nash is the soldier-prophet of the war as 'apocalypse', whose message is that there is no hope to be gleaned from this devastation. His hostility is directed towards those on his 'own side', the civilians who glorify the conflict but take no personal risks, and it is they, not the Germans, who are charged with responsibility for the war.

Others used 'Armageddon' in a more geographical sense, to refer to the Palestine campaign and specifically the capture of Jerusalem by the British in December 1917. Raymond Savage, who served with Field Marshal Allenby in Palestine, recalled that this event was widely viewed 'in relation to the prophecy of the Apocalypse for the great fight between Good and Evil', and that in celebrating the victory, 'the Chief selected the title of "Allenby of Armageddon" for himself'.[42] This anecdote suggests that senior and commanding officers were aware of the view of the war as the prophesied 'apocalypse' in Revelation, but did not take it seriously. More removed from the actual dangers of the war than the ordinary soldier, they could subscribe, however flippantly, to the idea of the war as a moral conflict and glorify it as civilians did. This difference in attitudes to and experience of the war is reflected in the ordinary soldiers' contempt for the military staff, as their letters and writings show.[43] For Allenby at least, the war did bring glory, and on his return to England, he was showered with honours, including the Freedom of the City of London. The average ex-combatant, however, returned to a society that had changed dramatically, and from which he felt alienated. Riots occurred among soldiers awaiting demobilisation at various camps in Britain and France during the spring of 1919. There were also demonstrations at the Victory Day parades of July that year by veterans who were angered by unemployment and what they regarded as a lack of sympathy among civilians towards the difficulties they faced in attempting to integrate into industrial society.[44]

This sense of alienation is reflected in fiction written by ex-soldiers, much of which is critical of the political and social changes brought about by the war, and nostalgic for a more stable society ascribed to the pre-war period. Wilfred Ewart's novel *Way of Revelation* (1921) draws upon themes from Revelation in its structure and content to portray the war as cataclysmic not only in the battle zones, but also with regard to English culture.[45] *Way of Revelation* suggests that in the absence of 'Englishmen' fighting at the Front, England became vulnerable to 'bohemians' and 'Jews', who preyed upon society for their own gain. Born in 1892 into a High Anglican family, Ewart served in the Scots Guards and wrote accounts of

trench life for *The Times* and *The Spectator*. In July 1918 he met
Stephen Graham at the Front, and they became friends.[46] Graham
had been one of the Russian correspondents for *The Times*, and in
1913, had accompanied Russian peasants on their annual pilgrimage
to Jerusalem, publishing an account of his experiences in 1914.[47] Like
his colleague Robert Wilton, Graham blamed Jews for events in
Russia, and it is possible that his views influenced the younger
Ewart, whose novel portrays 'Jews' and 'bohemians' as responsible
for the erosion of class certainties in Britain during the war.

Way of Revelation is divided into five parts, each opening with a
quotation from Revelation. The main character is Adrian Knoyle,
the son of 'a reputedly impecunious baronet' and for this reason
somewhat insecure in his class position (p. 10). Section one, entitled
'Illusion' relates to the 'full force of the class tradition in England',
soon to be shattered by war. Yet even before the war, the world of
privilege inhabited by Knoyle and his set is threatened by
modernity, in the form of rapidly changing values. This is
embodied in Gina Maryon, a young woman with 'pretensions to
advanced literary and artistic tastes' who mixes with artists,
'bohemians' and 'Jews', a group that Adrian refers to as the
'Maryonites' (p. 13). Adrian is both attracted and repelled by Gina,
but is more drawn to the aristocratic yet vulnerable Rosemary
Meynell, who, as the narrative progresses, becomes emblematic of
England and, drawn to the exotic, falls under the influence of
'foreigners'. Against the modernist and hedonistic 'Maryonites' and
the corruptible Rosemary are set the more traditional Ardens, in
Lady Arden and her daughter Faith Daventry, who possesses 'a
beauty that belongs peculiarly to England', that of 'fair hair, regular
features' and 'serenity', 'courage' and 'honesty' (p. 23). Adrian,
Gina, Rosemary and others are enjoying a weekend at the Arden
estate, when, just after dinner, war is declared. Later, walking
among the crowds in London, Adrian reflects that they 'cheered
their own peril, cheered the triumph of the anti-Christ, cheered the
downfall of the world' (p. 109). Yet he has to acknowledge that there
is something undeniably exciting about the prospect of war:

> It seemed to him then as though some Judgement, great and
> terrible – for all its sins and shames, for all that city's wrongs
> and self-inflicted woes – impended above himself, above her
> beside him, above the generality of mankind.
> Rosemary clung to his arm in these moments, thrilled and

wondering not less than he. And in these moments, they lived. (p. 199)

Adrian goes to the Front, described as a region where 'Men lived, physically and mentally...in the dim contorted regions of the anti-Christ' (p. 288). But rather than heralding the new order imagined by civilians, he sees the war as signalling 'something closer akin to the end of things than to their beginning' (p. 461). This is confirmed when during his leave he visits the self-made Lord and Lady Freeman at their country estate, in his sense that class relations are shifting, and that under 'the Freeman influence...the much-talked-of invasion of England had really begun' (p. 210). The novel suggests that it is through women, however, that a nation is most vulnerable to degeneration and corruption. In Adrian's absence, Rosemary has become involved with the dissolute 'Maryonites', and he views her choice of company – 'poets and comedians and Jews and foreigners' – with suspicion and mistrust. Rosemary eventually rejects Adrian for Harold Upton, a manipulative character and a non-combatant, and her decline accelerates. In keeping with the novel's concern about the effects of the war on England, the 1918 Victory Ball is also the scene of her death, the result of an overdose of drugs supplied by her new friends. Ewart seems to have modelled the fate of his fictional character Rosemary Meynell on the actual case of 22-year-old Miss Florence Leonora Stewart, an actress known by the stage name Billie Carlton, who died of a cocaine overdose after attending the Victory Ball, held at the Albert Hall in 1918. One of the witnesses at the inquest, the film actor Lionel Belsher, named a Mrs Adamoff, an Englishwoman married to a Russian, as the supplier.[48] The combination of drugs, 'foreigners' and the early death of a young British woman in this story became incorporated into Ewart's novel about the decline of society under the influence of 'foreigners' during the war. The fictional character Rosemary Meynell was made emblematic of England, and among her last words to Adrian are the lines '...if only you had never left me...That was the war' (p. 527). Her death becomes a metaphor for the infiltration and corruption of English society by plutocrats, profiteers and 'Jews' during the war, who, it is suggested, have taken advantage of the absence of patriotic 'Englishmen' to gain positions of power. At the end of the novel, the anxieties about national and social decline are resolved in the marriage between Adrian Knoyle and Faith

Daventry and England is secure once again. In the final scene of the novel the couple view the surrounding countryside from a hill in the Mendips, an idyllic setting, 'Hardly defiled by the railway, seldom touched by foot of tourist', with a Norman church below them and the scent of wild thyme everywhere (p. 531).

Way of Revelation incorporates a number of themes that were widely used in relation to the war. Apocalyptic imagery is used to describe the war landscape, but there is a parallel destruction occurring within English society as a direct result of the conflict. The marriage between Adrian and Faith and the rural idyll they inhabit may be read as the 'millennium' that follows the novel's 'apocalypse', in which, despite the undeniable impact of the war, the 'old order' has been preserved. The theme of a return to the land, expressed as an idealisation of rural life, was common in novels written by ex-soldiers. Such rural fantasies were encouraged, perhaps, by the proposals outlined in the Small Holding Colonies Bill for the settlement of disabled war veterans on the land. It was proposed that 6,000 acres in England and Wales and 2,000 acres in Scotland be used for this purpose. The Small Holdings Colonies Act was passed in 1916.

Wilfred Ewart's novel combines what may be broadly termed civilian and combatant perspectives on the war: there is much use of apocalyptic imagery, but this is descriptive rather than moralistic, and there are passages which depict the soldier as Christ-like, but as a suffering rather than a heroic or transcendent figure. It is the absence of a distinct figure of Antichrist as a foil to the 'Christian' soldier, however – so common in civilian rhetoric – that marks this novel as the work of a former combatant and reflects the cynicism with which soldiers regarded the notion of 'holy war'. In civilian engagement with the apocalyptic narrative, Antichrist was a central theme.

'ANTICHRIST'

The two main uses of the Antichrist theme during and after the war correspond to those found in the Christian tradition; namely, of Antichrist as a false doctrine or deceiver, and Antichrist personified, as a powerful figure of evil. In the early years of the war, popular rhetoric portrayed the Kaiser as the 'Beast' incarnate, or alternatively, as the servant of the devil. An example of this is found in a poem entitled 'The Kaiser's God', published in *John Bull* in 1914. The Kaiser is visited by 'A creature he mistook for God', who encouraged him to 'ravage peaceful Belgium', and then,

> vanished ere the Monarch, pale,
> Could see his God *possessed a tail!*[49]

But although the Kaiser was widely portrayed as an evil figure, the term 'Antichrist' was rarely applied to him directly. An exception to this is found in a sermon entitled *Anti-Christ and Armageddon*, by the Reverend A. H. T. Clarke, Rector of Devizes.[50] The author claims his text was published 'by request', although it seems unlikely that a sermon preached by a west country clergyman would have had a very large circulation, unlike those given by Bishop Winnington-Ingram and the higher clergy, which were reported in the national press and widely published. Clarke saw the war as a struggle between faiths, with Prussia, the Catholic Church and Islam as 'the triple combination let loose from hell' against the Anglican Church.[51] In his view, Antichrist was doubly personified, in the Kaiser and the Pope, who were linked through their common despotism, the former focusing on civil rule and the latter on religious domination.[52] Generally, however, the clergy refrained from identifying any individual as Antichrist, preferring instead to cast 'Prussianism' in this guise, and using the term in the sense of (German) militarism as a false doctrine. *Armageddon,* a sermon preached in 1914 by the Reverend H. C. Beeching, Dean of Norwich, is a typical example of this.[53] To Beeching, the war was a conflict between 'the final issues...of good and evil, right and wrong',[54] with the British fighting against 'a new religion of anti-Christ, [a] new God of Force and Falsehood'.[55] Winnington-Ingram used similar language, but characteristically went a little further, referring to the war as a struggle between 'Kaiser or Christ', and, by extension, Antichrist or England.[56] As the war progressed, the apocalyptic theme in its various interpretations began to circulate more widely, to the extent that in December 1917, Dr Fort Newton complained to the congregation at the City Temple, London, that the Book of Revelation had 'fallen into the hands of the puzzle-maker and the prophecy-monger', who used it as 'a kind of cryptogram to prove when the world is coming to an end'.[57]

The third year of the war, 1917, was a time of crisis for Britain: public support was waning, and there were food shortages, price increases and labour unrest. In addition, Britain's ally, Russia, went through two revolutions. The first of these, in February, met with measured support in Britain, as the provisional government introduced liberal reforms including the emancipation of Russian Jews. But as the Bolshevik party gained support and influence, it was feared that they would negotiate a separate peace with Germany, and that Britain would lose an ally. (This occurred when the Treaty of Brest-Litovsk was signed on 3 March 1918.) Having expressed measured support for the Kerensky revolution, the British national press began to portray Bolshevism as an anti-Christian politics dominated by 'Jews' under German control.[58] The link between communist revolution and Russian Jews became established partly because Marx was Jewish, and also because of press articles that exaggerated the involvement of Russian Jewish immigrants in pre-war anarchism and socialism, which had produced an association between the two in the minds of both gentiles and Anglo-Jewry. As Sharman Kadish has pointed out, however, those Bolsheviks who were Jewish had little in common with orthodox Jews living in the Pale. In addition, radical Russian Jews were divided over Bolshevism, and the Jewish *Bund* clashed with the Bolsheviks over the question of retaining Jewish culture within a socialist state. Such distinctions, however, were rarely acknowledged in Britain.

The Times and the *Morning Post* received their information on revolutionary Russia from Robert Wilton and Victor Marsden respectively, both of whom had spent years in Russia and had adopted extreme right-wing and antisemitic views which were reflected in their bulletins. On 11 October 1917, as part of its 'Russia To-day' series, *The Times* published an article which stated that the Russian press was more or less controlled by 'revolutionary Jews', who were working to bring the Bolsheviks to power.[59] At this point, however, the general view was that Russia's 'Bolshevik Jews' served the Kaiser. A collection of reports on Russia compiled from government sources and published by the Foreign Office in 1919 seemed to verify this, containing a number of assertions by consulate staff and other ex-patriates to this effect.[60] A telegraph from Sir E. Howard to Arthur Balfour (then Foreign Secretary), for example, dated August 1918, stated that most of the Bolshevik leaders were 'either fanatics or Jewish adventurers like Trotsky or Radek'.[61] Similarly, on his return to Britain in early 1919 after ten years in Russia, the Reverend B. S. Lombard, chaplain to the British interventionary forces in Russia, wrote to Lord Curzon (who replaced Balfour as Foreign Secretary in 1919)[62] to say that although Bolshevism 'originated in German propaganda', it was being 'carried out by international Jews'.[63] Gradually, the association between Bolshevism and Russian Jews began to link up with earlier fears relating to this group, and the theme of enforced prostitution entered into accounts of life in Russia. In January 1919 General Poole advised the War Office that a 'Decree for nationalisation of women has been put into force', and that there was 'evidence to show that commissariats of free love have been established in several towns, and respectable women flogged for refusing to yield'.[64] General Knox made a similar statement in a report from Vladivostock, dated 4 March 1919, claiming that women between the ages of 16 and 50 had been mobilised in order to minister to the sexual needs of the Bolsheviks.[65]

At this stage, it can be seen that representations of the Bolshevik régime were beginning to resemble pre-war sexual anxieties connected to Russian Jewish immigrants. The allegations of the sexual exploitation of women in Bolshevik Russia were similar to the 'white slavery' scares associated with Jewish refugees before the war, and the link between both these expressions of sexual anxiety was the figure of the 'Russian Jew'. The connection made between Russian Jews and the Bolshevik revolution re-awakened earlier fears regarding 'Jews' as procurers, and the sexual and political combined in representations of the international 'Jewish Bolshevik' who paradoxically demanded the 'nationalisation' of Russian women as sexual commodities. In fact this association had been made very shortly after the revolution, as a cartoon in *Punch*, dated 12 December 1917, shows (see Plate 5). In this image, the feared alliance between revolutionary Russia and Germany is framed as a sexual transaction, with Russia portrayed as a woman being forced by a Bolshevik into an embrace with the Kaiser. The Bolshevik 'pander', while not physically caricatured as 'Jewish', carries a bag of German gold, which, like the title, 'Betrayed', evokes the biblical Judas, and suggests that Bolsheviks had betrayed both Russia and the Allies in favour of pan-Germanism.

Anti-Bolshevik pamphlets published in Britain took up the theme of the exploitation of women, framing a threatening political ideology as a sexual attack on women as individuals and as a group. One pamphlet, published in 1919, warned newly enfranchised women that to vote for socialism would amount to their 'consenting to the destruction of [their] own family prospects'.[66] The writer referred to an 'Edict' which decreed that 'women of *any* rank, between the ages of 17 and 32' must 'register themselves with the local authorities as being at the (immoral) disposal of any citizen who chooses to apply for them'.[67] Former suffragette Christabel Pankhurst also urged women to vote against socialism, but for different reasons. Her pre-war writing and speeches had focused on the sexual exploitation of women in Britain, but she made no reference to their alleged 'nationalisation' under Bolshevism. Instead, as part of her morale-raising tour of wartime Britain she addressed workers on the subject of 'industrial salvation', and in October 1918 published a pamphlet under this title.[68] Bolshevism, she argued, was a German plot to ruin Britain's economy, and to participate in industrial action was to co-operate with political 'invasion'. Christabel inverted Marxist theory to produce her own solution to class conflict, arguing for the abolition not of the bourgeoisie but the proletariat, and suggesting that rather than taking control of the means of production, workers should increase production, thereby creating more wealth. This increased wealth, comprising 'comforts, refinements, and luxuries', would be distributed through the 'democratisation of property', as prices would drop, demand rise and the market increase.[69] As a result, a high standard of living would become 'as open to all, without distinction of class, as the free air of heaven'.[70]

Unlike many opponents of Bolshevism, Christabel Pankhurst avoided the political racism that was developing during 1917–18, and refrained from commenting on the 'racial' character of Bolshevik activists. Despite her connection with movements that expressed hostility or mistrust towards 'Jews', such as the anti-vice campaigns and the anti-communist lobbies, she does not seem to have been antisemitic herself. After the war, she exchanged the quasi-religious rhetoric of 'industrial salvation' for straightforward millennialism, in her book *The Lord Cometh: The World Crisis Explained*.[71] As a millennialist, however, she could hardly avoid the 'Jewish Question', and stated that this would be resolved by conversion, or 'the simple condition of faith in Jesus Christ – whereupon all distinction between Jew and Gentile disappears'.[72] Unusual as an anti-Bolshevik who was not an antisemite, Christabel also differed slightly from other millennialists in her attitude towards Jews. While many millennialists denounced 'Jews' for 'deicide', and asserted that they had forfeited their chosen status,[73] Christabel focused simply on conversion. Nor, unlike other millennialists, did she identify any group or doctrine as the servants or the embodiment of 'Antichrist'.

Not all millennialists regarded Jews as the chief threat to the establishment of the kingdom of God on earth, however, and Reformation tensions are apparent in the Reverend E. P. Cachemaille's interpretation of events.[74] Cachemaille addressed the Prophecy Investigation Society in 1921 and asserted that it was the Catholic Church and not the Jews that represented the 'Antichristian body' that threatened the post-war world.[75] He identified Pope Benedict XV (1914–22) as Antichrist 'posing as the Vicar of Christ on earth' and argued that the papacy, although professing Christianity, actually represented a latent world dictatorship.[76] The Kaiser, he asserted, had promised the Pope that Palestine would become a Catholic state,[77] and the 'final conflict' between good and evil would take place in Palestine between Britain and the Latin countries, led by the Pope, over possession of the holy places. In Cachemaille's view 'Bolshevik Jews' formed the third part of the 'Formidable Sect' that sought to dominate the post-war world:

> Not a few of the leaders of this Formidable Sect are apostate Jews, and their motive for destroying the Christian nations is said to be revenge for the wrongs that Judaism has suffered at their hands. But the Christianity the Jewish revolutionaries have chiefly known, and that has bitterly persecuted their race, is that of the Romish Church. So they will fulfil their purpose against her, and will then think that thereby they have destroyed Christianity, but it is only a parody of Christianity that they will have destroyed.[78]

Jewish revolutionaries, then, were ironically playing their predestined role in 'God's plans' for the world by helping to undermine a false Christianity. Cachemaille suggested that by attacking the Russian Orthodox Church (which in fact has Greek rather than Roman origins), the atheist Bolsheviks were in fact assisting in creating the conditions for the second coming.

While millennialists continued to anticipate the 'last days' after the war had ended, the British press invoked religious apocalyptic less frequently with regard to political events. But the themes of apocalypse and millennium did not disappear from secular life. A new form of apocalyptic writing appeared, which represented the 'Jewish' threat as an immediate danger to the Christian state. The document that became known as the *Protocols of the Elders of Zion* originated in Russia in 1905. The main source for the content of the *Protocols* was a satire on the French second empire by Maurice Joly, published in 1864 under the title *Dialogue aux Enfers entre Montesquieu et Machiavel*. Other sources included extracts from a novel entitled *Biarritz*, published in 1868 by Hermann Goedsche, a former Prussian postal worker who wrote under the name of Sir John Retcliffe.[79] The key moment in the novel is a chapter set in a Jewish cemetery in Prague, where a discussion takes place between the devil and the leaders of the 12 tribes regarding plans for world domination. This chapter was published as a pamphlet and circulated in Russia during the 1870s.[80] The *Protocols* were compiled from these and other sources by the writer and mystic Sergey Nilus, who in 1901 published a book entitled *The Great in the Small. Antichrist Considered as an Imminent Political Possibility*, which in its third edition, in 1905, incorporated the *Protocols*. A subsequent version entitled *He is Near, At the Door... Here comes Antichrist and the Reign of the Devil on Earth* appeared around the time of the Bolshevik revolution.[81] These titles make obvious allusions to Christian apocalyptic, but the document that reached Europe was secular, purporting to be the leaked minutes of a meeting of Zionist 'Elders', led by Theodor Herzl,[82] at the first World Zionist Congress held in Basle in 1897. Despite its secular presentation, the themes of the document remained apocalyptic and represented a distortion of the Jewish messianic tradition, in which plans were outlined for the destruction of Christian civilisation and the enthronement of a Jewish dictator-king who would avenge Israel's suffering. The *Protocols* circulated throughout the world, and reached the British army in Palestine in 1918. In his memoir *Trial and Error* (1949), the Zionist leader Chaim Weizmann recalls that General Wyndham Deedes handed him a sheaf of typewritten extracts from the *Protocols* and informed him that British officers read and believed them.[83]

The *Protocols* reached Britain in early 1920, brought by 'White' Russian officers spreading anti-Bolshevik propaganda, and the British Museum held a Russian copy from 1906. The document was published in January or February 1920 under the title *The Jewish Peril*. The publishers were Eyre and Spottiswoode, who, as Norman Cohn has noted, also published the Anglican Prayerbook and the authorised version of the Bible.[84] The authenticity and origins of the

Protocols were debated in *The Times* in May 1920[85] and also in *The Spectator,*[86] but the *Morning Post* was less reserved, and serialised the *Protocols* in the summer of 1920. In addition, Victor Marsden, the paper's Russian correspondent, prepared a new English translation, which was published that autumn as *The Cause of World Unrest* and included a preface by the editor, H. A. Gwynne. The way for the acceptance of the *Protocols* had been paved by earlier publications suggesting that 'Jews' were gaining ascendancy in Europe as a result of the war. In 1918, before the Armistice, an anonymous book entitled *England Under the Heel of the Jew* appeared, in which the author stated that contrary to popular belief, Germany was under the control of the Jews, as a result of its dependence upon international Jewish finance.[87] Similar views appeared in the British press and were given official 'confirmation' in a Foreign Office report published in 1919, in which various individuals asserted that 'Jews' were gaining power through the political chaos in Russia.[88]

The appearance of the *Protocols* in 1920 supplied conspiracy theorists with a suitably 'international' culprit for the threat represented by communism – with its hostility to nationalism and religion – in the Jews of the Diaspora, and replaced the earlier view that the Russian revolution had been controlled by the Kaiser. Part of the *Protocols'* impact was that, like the scriptural prophecies, they lent themselves readily to broad interpretation with regard to recent world events, and some readers, such as the members of the Britons' Society, founded in July 1919, regarded them as prophetic. As Norman Cohn has argued, the *Protocols* represented prophecy and apocalyptic updated and secularised and took the irrational Christian fear of the Jew in a new direction.[89] In them, the threat of destruction was more immediate than that represented by Antichrist in the Revelation narrative. They appeared at a time when the notion of 'Jewish domination' was already becoming established in Britain. During the war, the allegation that 'Jews' avoided enlistment while 'Englishmen' fought and died, had produced the figure of the 'Jewish profiteer', imagined as having exploited the situation to the extent that he now dominated the media, the entertainment industry and politics, as a result of his financial power.[90] This was the 'capitalist Jew', motivated by greed rather than political ideology. As Bryan Cheyette has observed, however, 'the Jew' can be constructed to embody contradictory opposites,[91] and in post-war Britain this figure was made to represent the threat of both unrestrained capitalism and international communism. According to the *Protocols*, the ultimate aim of the Jewish people was world domination, using any means necessary, and both the capitalist and communist 'Jew' could be regarded in this light; the one gaining control through financial power, the other gaining political influence by fomenting revolution among the dissatisfied working classes, and both united in their shared hatred of Christianity.

The *Protocols* may well have informed an article by Winston Churchill, published in the *Illustrated Sunday Herald* on 8 February 1920 under the title 'Zionism versus Bolshevism: A Struggle for the Soul of the Jewish People'. As Secretary of State for War from 1919 to 1921, Churchill organised the supply of British aid to anti-Bolshevik 'White' Russians, who were responsible for pogroms against Jews during the civil war. In the context of British military intervention in Russia, his article, which drew on the theme of the 'world Jewish conspiracy' and applied it to Bolshevism, supported the idea that Bolshevism was a 'Jewish' politics. Churchill described Jews as an exceptional people, who felt the 'conflict between good and evil' more intensely than gentiles and in whom the 'dual nature of mankind' was 'nowhere more strongly or more terribly exemplified'. One must, therefore, distinguish between 'good' and 'bad' Jews: 'national' Jews were patriotic and contributed to the economic wealth of their adopted countries, while 'international' Jews were apostates who reacted to persecution by plotting revolution. Just as the Jews had provided Christianity with its foundations, so they had created its evil, irreligious counterpart, in Bolshevism, which was portrayed in apocalyptic terms:

> It would almost seem as if the gospel of Christ and the gospel of Antichrist were destined to originate among the same people; and that this mystic and mysterious race had been chosen for the supreme manifestations, both of the divine and the diabolical.[92]

Churchill cited the antisemitic writer Nesta Webster's work on the role of the 'international Jew' in the French Revolution, and concluded his article by urging 'national' Jews to 'take a prominent part in every measure for combating the Bolshevik conspiracy', in order to 'vindicate the honour of the Jewish name'. Leopold Greenberg, editor of the *Jewish Chronicle*, responded with a leading article in which he attacked the growing 'cult' of the 'Jew-obsession disease', and expressed anger and concern over the fact that 'a prominent British statesman had adopted the hoary tactics of hooligan anti-Semites'.[93] Churchill's suggestion that Jews were torn between Bolshevism and Zionism was false, Greenberg argued, and he cited the 'Letter of the Ten' as a reminder of the dangers of engaging in superficial debate over the nature of Jewish political identity. The 'Letter of the Ten' was a response to articles in the *Jewish Chronicle* in March and April 1919, which had explored possible links between Bolshevik idealism and the principles of Judaism.[94] Rather than reply to the *Chronicle*, ten prominent figures in Anglo-Jewry signed a letter to H. A. Gwynne, editor of the *Morning Post*, the aim of which was to demonstrate the patriotism of British Jews and disassociate them from revolutionary politics. The letter was published on 23 April 1919. It backfired on two counts, causing an internal conflict among Jewry by appearing to differentiate between 'British' and 'foreign' Jews, and being easily construed as a tacit admission of Jewish support for Bolshevism.[95] Despite Churchill's rather simplistic assessment of the situation, then, in the climate of mistrust and suspicion, exacerbated by the *Protocols*, it was difficult for Jews to successfully refute the idea that they were pro-Bolshevik, since both silence and condemnation on their part were liable to misinterpretation.

Eventually the *Protocols* were exposed as a fake in *The Times* in August 1921, when Philip Graves identified their sources in Maurice Joly's play *Dialogue aux Enfers* and Sergey Nilus' mystical writings, and press fascination with them subsided. The Britons' Society continued to print and circulate copies and one of its members, Nesta Webster, produced two secular apocalyptic texts of her own, based on the themes of Jewish conspiracy in the *Protocols*.[96] The first, entitled *World Revolution: The Plot Against Civilization* (1921), claimed to bring 'scientific investigation' to post-war political unrest and argued that the origins of this could be traced back to the emancipation of the Jews following the French revolution.[97] The most diabolical and recent manifestation of the Jewish plan for world domination, however, was the Bolshevik revolution. Webster argued that despite having gained control of Russia, Bolshevik Jews had no specific political loyalty, but manipulated dissenters, mystics and radicals in their drive for domination. They could even appropriate antisemitism for their own ends, and Webster regarded German post-war antisemitism as simply a cover for an alliance

between German expansionism and Jewish internationalism.
Having seized Russia and taken financial control of Germany, the
Jewish apostate revolutionaries were now turning to England and
Webster called for an antisemitic crusade, urging the British
bourgeoisie to mobilise itself in a new war, this time against the Jews.
Like Bishop Winnington-Ingram, but with an overtly antisemitic
angle, she regarded England as Christianity's best hope against the
forces of 'paganism': 'It is because England, with all her
shortcomings... yet remains the stronghold of Christian civilization,
that the conspiracy has made her the principal point of attack. If
England goes the whole world goes with her.'[98]

Webster wrote another book, *Secret Societies and Subversive
Movements*, published in 1924, which expanded on the theme of the
'concerted attempt... being made by Jewry to achieve world-
domination and to obliterate the Christian faith', and claimed to
chart this through 19 centuries.[99] After discussing the 'immense
megalomania of the Jewish race'[100] and the extent, in her view, of
Jewish domination in Europe, Webster returned to apocalyptic
themes to end her book on a dramatic note. The 'Jewish conspiracy',
she argued, was simply the latest manifestation of the powers of
darkness:

> For behind the concrete forces of revolution – whether Pan-
> German, Judaic, or Illuminist –... is there not yet another
> force, still more potent, that must be taken into account? In
> looking back over the centuries at the dark episodes that have
> marked the history of the human race from its earliest origins
> – strange and horrible cults, waves of witchcraft, blas-
> phemies, and desecrations – how is it possible to ignore the
> existence of an Occult Power at work in the world?
> Individuals, sects, or races fired with the desire of world-
> domination, have provided the fighting forces of destruction,
> but behind them are the veritable powers of darkness in
> eternal conflict with the powers of light.[101]

In conclusion, it can be seen that secular use of apocalyptic
imagery continued after the war, specifically in relation to the threat
represented by Bolshevism and was found in marginal and, briefly,
in mainstream discourse. Like Churchill who quoted her, Webster
applied the rhetoric of 'apocalypse' and 'antichrist' to post-war
political events, and specifically to Jews, as the alleged followers of

an anti-Christian ideology. Such thinking was supported by the combination of political and apocalyptic themes in the *Protocols*, which seemed to 'confirm' the idea that Jews were a threat to the Christian nation. Mainstream interest in the *Protocols* decreased after their exposure as a forgery in 1921, but the idea of revolution as an attack on Christianity (which after all, had some basis in fact) continued into the post-war period.

'MILLENNIUM'

After the war, religious apocalyptic thinking returned once more to the margins and was confined to millennialists. Christabel Pankhurst thought that the second advent was very near and paradoxically cited the decline of faith as a 'sign' of this, stating that current world events represented 'fingerposts to Armageddon'.[102] Others felt that 'Armageddon' was past, and focused on dealing with its aftermath. The war had left many of the participating countries in a state of disarray, facing economic problems and unemployment. The sacrifices made by all class groups in Britain during the war merited, many felt, the construction of a fairer society to reflect those sacrifices. But falling export demands, foreign competition and the devalued pound (as a result of a return to the gold standard) meant that the British economy suffered and recovery was slow. Unemployment grew, reaching over 16 per cent of the population in 1921, and dissatisfaction was widespread.[103]

The expectations of the working classes, in particular, had changed as a result of the war. The process of mass democratisation was accelerating, as men over 21 and women over 30 gained the vote in 1918.[104] Women had entered the workforce and union membership had increased dramatically, reaching over 8 million in 1920.[105] Wages had risen during the war and many of the strikes in the immediate post-war period were a response to attempts by employers to bring wages back down to earlier levels. There were numerous cases of industrial action among miners, dockers and railwaymen, and even the London police went on strike in 1918. The Liberal government struggled to control the situation and in December 1918 entered into a coalition with the Conservatives. This government introduced further anti-alien legislation in 1919, which facilitated the deportation of non-naturalised Jews and their British-born children. The Jewish community fought back through the

Board of Deputies, but the legislation was implemented under the Conservative government formed in 1922, and particularly by Sir William Joynson-Hicks, Home Secretary in Stanley Baldwin's Cabinet in 1924.[106] Parliament was dissolved that December over Baldwin's attempt to introduce anti-unemployment tariffs and although the Tories were re-elected, support for Labour was growing, and Ramsay Macdonald formed the first Labour Cabinet in 1924. In addition to these rapid changes of government, two new parties were formed; the Communist Party of Great Britain in 1920 and the British Fascisti in 1923. As Samuel Hynes puts it, 'The British political spectrum had been stretched, leaving the centre less stable, and less certain.'[107]

Some working-class Jews, feeling unsupported by the Board of Deputies against anti-alienism and fascism and attracted by the ideals of the far left, joined the Communist Party, and the Jewish trades unions were also active against fascism.[108] Membership figures for the British Fascisti are unreliable, but Home Office sources indicate that in the late 1920s and early 1930s, members numbered between 300 and 400.[109] Support for the British Fascisti came from across the class spectrum and included aristocrats, members of the middle and working classes and ex-servicemen.[110] Lord Garvagh was the group's first president and other aristocratic members included the Earl of Glasgow, Lord Ernest Hamilton, Earl Temple, Lord de Clifford and Baroness Zouche.[111] The middle classes, too, were threatened by the rise of the labour movement and middle-class admiration for Mussolini's dictatorship was satirised in a cartoon in *Punch* dated 1922. This cartoon, entitled 'The Fascisti Spirit', shows a well-dressed member of the 'Middle-class Union (*fired by the example of Signor Mussolini*)' shopping for an appropriate outfit for a revolution, in which he will defend the interests of his own threatened class. The caption reads 'I want a black shirt, please, suitable for a bloodless revolution.' Support for fascism in Britain was limited, however, and the fascist groups remained marginal.[112]

The sense that the war had radically altered the social and political structure of British life was a recurrent theme in popular fiction and the press, and one that was treated with varying degrees of seriousness. In 1920 *Punch* published a 'guide' to assist American tourists in understanding the new post-war social order in Britain. In this cartoon, which both satirises and perpetuates anxieties regarding changes to the class structure of British society, rural areas no longer represent a place in which the 'old order' of aristocratic privilege is preserved, as in Wilfred Ewart's novel *Way of Revelation*. Instead, the countryside has undergone a 'revolution' whereby the former hierarchy has shifted, with 'Jews' and profiteers at the top and the gentry and clergy at the bottom. The former squire now lives in an almshouse, having been displaced by an overweight and racialised 'Jew', who ostentatiously puffs at a cigar. Likewise, the proprietor of the village shop is a richly dressed profiteer, the parson is clearly poverty-stricken and the war veteran is clothed in rags and employed as a bird-scarer. The oldest inhabitant of the village has a long, twisted beard and a hooked nose.[113] As Paul Rich has written, during the 1920s the fantasy of 'village' England

> served as a means for neutralising the concept of class warfare and emphasising the homogeneous nature of English society rooted in small town and village life, and spreading up through the shires and counties to... central government and the organisations of national power'.[114]

The *Punch* cartoon suggests that this structure has been infiltrated by class mobility at its deepest level, the village, and although intended to be humorous, it also reveals a fear that 'Jews', profiteers and the working classes were becoming dominant in British society, to the detriment of the aristocracy and the clergy in particular, and that something of 'British' identity was being lost in the process.

Among the Anglican clergy there was general support for workers' rights, and a widespread view that in failing to address inequality the Church had assisted the rise of socialism, and that in order to create a more just society the principles of Christianity should be applied to social and political life. This Christian idealism was found at the highest level of the Anglican Church, and also, to a lesser extent, among Nonconformists.[115] Aware that the war had revealed the shortcomings of the Church, the clergy sought to investigate the reasons why the anticipated religious revival had not occurred, and why Christianity failed to attract the working classes. In 1918 a series of reports was commissioned to investigate perceptions of the Church, which resulted in calls for moderate social and ecclesiastical reform.[116] The fifth report in this series, entitled *Christianity and Industrial Problems* argued for wage increases, a revision of the taxation system and the restriction of profits.[117] At a conference at Lambeth in 1920 Church leaders called for greater co-operation between labour and capital, and in the same year a Christian Social Crusade was initiated, led by Bishop Gore.[118] In 1923 the Standing Committee on Social and Industrial Questions was formed with the aim of promoting the Church's principle of 'co-operation', and was chaired by Bishop Winnington-Ingram.[119] But although there was general support for the idea of a more egalitarian society, the clergy, like any other group, were politically divided. Sympathies ranged from the avowedly socialist members of the Christian Socialist Union, to the hostility to labour shown by Bishop Moule,[120] who in 1919 criticised striking Yorkshire miners, and Bishop Henson,[121] who blamed the dispute on Bolshevism.[122] The more moderate Archbishop Davidson attempted to mediate in the 1919 railway strike and in the coal strike in 1921, but his efforts aroused hostility among more conservative clergymen and also within the government.[123]

The government did not want or need ecclesiastical intervention in politics, having made provision for the threat of mass unrest in the Emergency Powers Act of 1920, which allowed for a military-backed dictatorship to rule in the event of a general strike. High unemployment and industrial disputes continued to fuel fears of class revolution throughout the 1920s and in 1925 it looked as though the Emergency Powers Act would need to be implemented. In that year the coal owners demanded wage reductions and longer hours for miners. When these demands were rejected, a committee led by Sir John Anderson of the Home Office began to organise in anticipation of a general strike. Food and coal were stockpiled and the country was divided into districts to be ruled by civil commissioners with sweeping legal powers. The miners struck on 4 May 1926 and were joined by workers in the transport, building, steel, iron and printing industries. The General Strike ended on 12 May, but the miners stayed out for another eight months.[124]

Two novels, both published in 1926, take up the themes of rapid social and political change, and engage with the threat of revolution. Gilbert Frankau's *Masterson: A Story of An English Gentleman* addresses the issues of class privilege and political reform, and introduces the author's response to the international 'Bolshevik Jew', in the figure of Major Adrian Rose, DSO, a right-wing Anglo-Jewish politician and playwright.[125] Through its two central characters, Adrian Rose and John Masterson, the narrative presents an argument for co-operation between the 'Englishman' and the 'Jew' in the defeat of socialism and the reconstruction of post-war Britain. Like Rose, Masterson served in the First World War, but then went into voluntary exile in Abyssinia (Ethiopia). His father is a self-made man given to vulgar displays of wealth and on his death, Masterson returns to Britain to take up his inheritance. On arrival he encounters rapid modernisation and industrial unrest, and decides to settle the estate and leave, but his plans are thwarted by a combination of politics and romance. Mary Millward, once his sweetheart, is working near the estate, carrying on the family building business after the death of her father in the war, but is hampered in this by unionisation, which is depicted as causing a breakdown in employment relations even in rural areas. As an alternative to unionisation, *Masterson* argues for a quasi-feudal paternalism, a system in which landlords and landowners take responsibility for their tenants' welfare and the tenants, in return for this, are content to be ruled. This idea comes to Masterson while surveying his estate, in a flash of inspiration in which he realises the significance of his name:

> there came on John Masterson a fantasy, and by the light of that fantasy he seemed to see the meaning of his own name: Masterson – the son of the master – the one man bound, by very reason of his dead father's mastery over these men, to serve them until he died. (p. 214)

He begins by renovating one of his father's slum tenements, cancelling the tenants' rent arrears and redesigning the building to create habitable accommodation. He also acts as a force of moral authority among his tenants, warning a man found beating a child that if it happens again he will be evicted (p.287). A reunion with Adrian Rose, however (the two were at Eton), persuades him that this is not enough, and that change is needed at the national level. Rose is now a successful playwright with political ambitions, although these are thwarted by his impending divorce and cohabitation. An intense and volatile character, Rose is described as

> a forceful rock of a man, just over-long in the arm, and just over-broad in the shoulder, who looked, despite the jet-black moustache clipped to a tight line between the big, only slightly Hebraic nostrils and the big, though even less Hebraic, mouth, far more like an old-time prize-fighter than a modern playwright. (p. 85)

The mark of the 'Englishman', by contrast, is moderation, and Masterson is

> Not over-quick to perceive, yet never quite lacking in perception. Not over-imaginative, yet not wholly devoid of imagination. A man of quiet compromise rather than of flashing talent, of plodding purpose rather than of sudden intuition. (p. 9)

In *Masterson*, as in Charles Sorley's view of Revelation and Israel Zangwill's writing, with which this chapter opened, 'Jewishness' is signalled by 'excess'. But the narrative suggests that Rose's 'Hebraic excess', particularly his intense patriotism, is what Britain needs at this point of crisis. Frankau uses Rose and Masterson to portray 'Englishman' and 'Jew' as complementary opposites, each providing what the other lacks. Rose is politically astute and capable of providing inspired if eccentric leadership, but his credibility is weakened by the consequences of his sexual appetite, while Masterson attracts no scandal but lacks the firmness necessary to resolve his country's problems. Learning of Rose's sexual past, which includes several mistresses and two illegitimate children, Masterson, a celibate, views him as 'an animal – just a lustful animal' (p. 100). Like the 'Bolshevik Jew' who insists on the 'nationalisation of women', the sexual appetite of the right-wing 'Jew' becomes the marker of his difference. Yet although flawed, Rose possesses qualities portrayed as vital to Britain's success and in this virulently anti-socialist Jewish character, Frankau seems to be attempting to counter the stereotype of the 'Bolshevik Jew'. He is also attacking antisemitism, as becomes clear when Rose warns Masterson of the threat that Bolshevism represents:

> you can take it from me, as a Jew, that these Bolshevik Jews are the dregs of my race. And that the dregs of my race are just as much anti-Gentile as the dregs of yours are anti-Semite. That's the whole truth of Bolshevism; and the sooner the Christian countries wake up to it, the better. (p. 202)

Rose makes the point that gentiles, too, can be divided into 'good' and 'bad', thus the 'Bolshevik Jew' finds a counterpart in the anti-semite. Bolshevism, he suggests, is not so much political ideology as blind hatred, hence the comparison with antisemitism. 'Good'

Jews and gentiles are patriotic, co-operative and possess mutually complementary qualities, although the novel suggests that the 'good Jew' may have the advantage, in the gift of 'imaginative foresight' (p. 318), which allows him to predict the outcome of a situation. Rose has lost faith in parliamentary democracy and believes that Britain is faced with a choice between class revolution under Labour and an incompetent and ineffectual Tory party. Frustrated by his inability to enter Parliament owing to his marital situation, Rose has instigated the Fellowship of Loyal Citizens, a nationalist group that includes members of the British Fascists. Eventually, Rose's divorce becomes absolute and he is free to remarry and seek election. He wins the Thameside South seat, previously a Labour stronghold, for the Tories with a majority of 500 and takes his anti-socialist campaign to Parliament. The political acumen of the 'good' Jew will act as a stabilising force in British society, and the threat of revolution will be removed.

There is no such optimism in Ursula Bloom's novel *The Judge of Jerusalem*, also published in 1926.[126] Ursula Bloom was a parson's daughter, who grew up in Whitchurch, near Stratford-on-Avon. The family was friendly with the writer Richard Aldington (1892–1962), who in 1913 married the Imagist writer H.D. (1886–1961). The Catholic writer Marie Corelli lived nearby and was Ursula's friend until the latter asked her about rumours that she was divorced. She also met Guy Thorne, author of the best-selling novel *When It Was Dark* (1903). Thorne's novel features a Jewish millionaire who devises a plot to bring about the collapse of Christianity, and forces the British Museum into faking archaeological evidence to demonstrate that the resurrection of Jesus did not occur. Like Thorne's novel, *The Judge of Jerusalem* plays upon Christian paranoia and irrational fears of 'the Jew', and depicts a protracted struggle between the forces of 'good' and 'evil'. Bloom's novel, published in 1926, is set in the 1930s, in a post-revolutionary dystopia, in which northern Britain is run by revolutionary tribunals.[127] Like Frankau's *Masterson*, *The Judge of Jerusalem* proposes an idealised quasi-feudal society as an alternative to the growing Labour movement. In this type of post-war utopian fantasy, the landowner is responsible for the welfare of his tenants and the social group operates according to a distinct hierarchy, which is often portrayed as 'in harmony with nature', whereas socialism is represented as counter to this. Bloom's novel adds an extra dimension, however, by framing class revolution in terms of the crucifixion narrative; its two main characters, Andrew Stevens and Sir John Booth representing reincarnations of Pontius Pilate and Jesus respectively. Stevens is of lower middle-class origins, a grocer's son from the Midlands, and Booth is the local landowner. Their paths cross when the balance of power is inverted through revolution.

From childhood Andrew Stevens had ambitions to be a judge, but his father expects him to enter the family grocery business. Andrew capitulates, but continues to study law in his spare time. By 1911 he is an adolescent with an interest in socialism, which the narrative implies stems from a lack of religious faith. When war breaks out Andrew volunteers, but is rejected because he is lame. He lays in stores, anticipating food shortages, and later becomes the local food controller, effectively a 'profiteer'. After the war, the class war begins, and Andrew anticipates revolution and his own ascendancy. It is at this point that the novel's language becomes apocalyptic:

> These great tidal waves that flooded England – they were the aftermath of the War. He considered them critically. Waves of crime, waves of resentment, and the seventh wave – the greatest – would be the wave of revolution. When that burst the country would be swept off its feet by the tumultuous flood. When it burst power would come to him; then was the time to strike. (p. 111)

The revolution begins with strikes by railway and transport workers, followed by the engineers and shipbuilders. The unrest spreads to Liverpool, where the army and navy join the revolt. The revolutionaries, however, are unable to cope with power, and a reign of violence and terror begins. Andrew climbs a hill outside the town and looks towards the cathedral, which becomes a symbol of the impending martyrdom of the ruling classes, who in turn become synonymous with Christ:

> Everywhere the shadows seemed to be engulfing, every-where save the cathedral, and that seemed to be dripping with blood...It reared its battlements to the sky, its great tower defined against the night. Century after century so it had stood, red with the blood of martyrs, grey with the dust of saints; it stood for something that no man could touch, no war could sully; it stood for the hidden, intangible element in

life that had never been understood. It was not red with the blood of nations alone – it was empurpled with the blood of Christ.

The first knell of revolution had struck. (pp. 135–6)

In this explicit parallel between revolution and the crucifixion, Bloom portrays class revolution as a catastrophe akin to the death of Jesus. The modern 'Christ' is Sir John Booth, a local land and property owner, who is falsely charged with 'treason', and the revolutionaries become the Jews that in the New Testament story betray Jesus to the authorities and insist upon his death. Unlike popular images of the Bolshevik, Bloom's revolutionaries are not portrayed as Jewish; there is no need, because the analogy between the 'crucifixion' and class revolution already provides that association. Sid Field, a revolutionary and 'a foe disguised with a Judas-like friendship' (p. 220), sets a trap for Booth, but Andrew, by now a judge, discovers the plan and writes to warn him. Sid finds the letter and blackmails Andrew with it, insisting that he find Booth guilty at his trial, to which he agrees. The next day Andrew hears the evidence against Booth in the Hall of Judgement, and defers sentence. At the end of the day he has a vision, in which he seems to travel back in time, to the events preceding the crucifixion. He is Pontius Pilate, threatened with the loss of his procuratorship if there are any more rebellions amongst the Jews. He watches as Jesus is led into the Hall of Judgement:

> In front came Caiaphus and the elders, and behind them the prisoner, led by chains in the hands of angry-looking Jews. It seemed to Pilate that it was an age-old picture – the hostile crowd with their bestial faces and their raucous upraised voices, and their prisoner. (p. 258)

Looking at the prisoner, the judge is shocked: 'It was his eyes... They were not the eyes of a felon, they were not the eyes of a rabbi or a Nazarene... They were the impenetrable eyes of a god' (p. 259). Andrew awakes in the grocer's shop and recognises that he must atone for his part in both trials, that of Jesus and Booth, by way of self-sacrifice. The next day, he enters the Hall of Judgement for the trial, and sees from the papers on his desk that the revolution is failing. He acquits Booth and leaves the chamber, climbing the hill outside the town (an image of Calvary), where he sees the cathedral lit up by sunshine, representing the restoration of his faith. Having atoned for his part in the crucifixion by declaring Booth/'Christ' innocent, Andrew dies a peaceful death on top of the hill, just as the revolutionaries come to arrest him.

In the absence of a stable post-war government and with high levels of unemployment and labour unrest, Ursula Bloom and Gilbert Frankau engaged with the threat of political catastrophe and the possibility of redemption through fiction that was highly topical and that proposed solutions. Although Bloom's novel draws on the crucifixion narrative, its emphasis is on the choice faced by the judge over whether to condemn a man he knows to be innocent. The destruction of the class foundations of British society is portrayed as an injustice and catastrophe comparable with the crucifixion, in which the revolutionaries, by implication, would become 'deicides', although the aristocratic landowner Booth is a very different figure from the itinerant preacher that was Jesus. Through the crucifixion/revolution analogy, the narrative implies that the ruling classes are a benign and blameless group, facing martyrdom for the sake of a political ideology. Bloom portrays socialism as an attack on Christianity, and in the conversion of the revolutionary judge, suggests that it is not politics but faith that will counter this threat.

Frankau, on the other hand, appeals to patriotism rather than religious feeling, and explores political solutions to post-war problems. He assigns the right-wing 'Jew' a specific role in the reconstruction of national life, as a means of strengthening and providing leadership for the Tories in the fight against socialism. In this, he is responding to the caricature of the 'Bolshevik Jew' with another construction of 'Jewish' political identity, that of the right-wing, ultra-nationalist 'Jew'.

CONCLUSIONS

As metaphors for military conflict, 'Armageddon' and 'Antichrist', if they are to be effective, rely upon the identification or construction of an enemy that is 'demonic'. Initially, this was 'Prussianism', with the Kaiser as its figurehead, but after the Bolshevik Revolution, the Treaty of Brest-Litovsk and the murder of the Romanovs, much of the hatred previously directed towards the Germans became focused on Russian Jewish immigrants. This group became popularly associated with Bolshevism, which, after 1917, seemed to present a greater threat than Prussian imperialism. Germany was, after all, a Christian nation that had temporarily strayed from the path, whereas the Bolsheviks had attacked the Russian Orthodox Church and killed the tsar. Reports from Britons inside Russia asserted that Jews were at the forefront of the revolution, and the figure of the international revolutionary 'Jew', the enemy of the Christian nations, began to emerge, building upon the pre-war association between eastern European Jews and anarchism, and the sexual anxiety aroused by the pre-war 'white slave traffic'.

Once the 'Jews' had been identified as the 'real' threat, a process that was assisted by the appearance of the *Protocols* in 1920, the rhetoric of apocalypse was transferred onto Bolshevism. In this context, the 'Antichrist' analogy became more coherent than when applied to the Kaiser and Germany, because according to Christian apocalyptic, the followers of Antichrist would come from among the Jews, who would recognise in him their Messiah. For some, Bolshevism became the anti-Christian doctrine that threatened the 'millennium' of a regenerated post-war Britain, and 'Bolshevik Jews' the obstacle to Britain's recovery. Winston Churchill made explicit reference in 1920 to Bolshevism as 'the doctrine of Antichrist', a doctrine that, he suggested, held a particular appeal for Jews, and he urged 'national' Jews to enlist in the fight to defeat it. Nesta Webster, on the other hand, made no distinction between 'national' and 'international' Jews, but regarded all Jews as conspiring against the Christian nations and manipulating events for their own purposes.

Symptomatic of the increase in antisemitism during the immediate post-war years, a number of ultra-nationalist and fascist groups emerged, of which the Britons' Society and the British Fascists are examples. These groups attracted some cross-class support, but ultimately remained marginal because, as Gerry Webber has argued, the revolutionary movement was never large enough to represent a real threat to the parliamentary system or the economic security of the middle classes (membership of the Communist Party in Britain was no higher than 10,000 during the 1920s).[128] There were not, he suggests, enough aliens in Britain for anti-alienism to be exploited, and most antisemites remained in the Conservative Party, which met the needs of the 'radical right' sufficiently to inhibit the success of any far-right political movement in Britain before the 1930s.[129]

The antisemitism that fascist groups tried to mobilise was never far from the surface of British politics, however, and as Home Secretary in Stanley Baldwin's government in 1925, William Joynson-Hicks enthusiastically implemented post-war anti-alien legislation. After successive governments, disillusionment with democracy and admiration for Italian fascism led to calls for strong, autocratic leadership to take Britain out of the war years. But such calls were not confined to the far right. At his Romanes lecture in Oxford in 1930, Churchill discussed the 'failure' of democracy and declared the need for alternative methods of government. Following this, a number of minor aristocrats, facing the loss of their estates through land taxes, called for the temporary disbanding of Parliament in favour of a more authoritarian rule, and proposed Churchill as leader.[130] It was Oswald Mosley, however, who emerged as Britain's fascist leader, forming the British Union of Fascists (BUF) in 1932 after a trip to Mussolini's Italy. BUF ideology incorporated elements of the kind of quasi-feudal society that was portrayed in popular fiction of the period. BUF writers and speakers frequently invoked 'Merrie England', a pre-capitalist 'golden age' loosely imagined as the Elizabethan period, a lost era whose best aspects would, under fascism, be retrieved.

Although the BUF never became a mass movement, the conditions for its emergence can be traced to the secular apocalyptic of the immediate post-war period, in which Bolshevism was identified as a potential cataclysm, orchestrated by 'Jews'. The discourse of the 'world Jewish conspiracy', exemplified in the *Protocols*, entered the mainstream briefly and received coverage in the national press. Once exposed as a fraud, however, the concept became marginalised, and associated with extremist groups such as the Britons' Society. It is, after all, ambivalence that has characterised majority attitudes towards Jews in Britain, as exemplified in Charles Sorley's comment ('I love Jews – of a type'), with which this chapter opened, and in similar distinctions made between 'good' and 'bad' Jews. The antisemitism of the far right did not make such distinctions, but regarded all Jews with suspicion. Mainstream ambivalence was grounded in the perception of the dual nature of 'the Jew', in which the occasional 'outburst of revolting sensuousness' could be overlooked.

NOTES

1   Charles Sorley was born in Scotland in 1895. His father was W. R. Sorley, professor of moral philosophy at Aberdeen, and his grandfather was a minister in the Scottish Church. He joined the 7th battalion of the Suffolk Regiment in December 1914 as a second lieutenant and was killed on 13 October 1915. A collection of his work entitled *Marlborough and Other Poems* was published in 1916.

2   Charles Sorley, letter dated 14 November 1914, in W. R. Sorley (ed.), *The Letters of Charles Sorley* (Cambridge: Cambridge University Press, 1919), p. 238.

3   Sorley was assuming that the Gospel and letters of St John and Revelation were produced by the same Jewish-Christian writer, but this cannot be confirmed. See Introduction to the Gospel and Letters of St John, and Introduction to the Book of Revelation, in Alexander Jones (gen. ed.) *The Jerusalem Bible*, popular edition (London: Darton, Longman & Todd, 1968).

4   For a discussion of the origins of the figure of Antichrist, see Norman Cohn, *The Pursuit of the Millennium* (London: Secker & Warburg, 1957), p. 18.

5   Although as Norman Cohn has pointed out, the view that the Pope was Antichrist developed much earlier than the Reformation period, and circulated during the thirteenth century. See Cohn, *Pursuit* (1957) pp. 65–6.

6   See also Chapter 5 for information on this group and its activities.

7   For a discussion of dispensationalism in the United States, and William Blackstone's Zionist campaign of 1916, see Yaakov Ariel, 'A Neglected Chapter in the History of Christian Zionism in America: William E. Blackstone and the Petition of 1916', in Frankel (ed.), *Prophecy and Politics*, pp. 68–85.

8   See E. A. Bland, 'Babylon, past and future' (1913), and A. R. Habershon, 'The Image of Daniel II, and the Period it Covers' (1913). Both papers were published in pamphlet form, as part of *The Dispensational Series* (London: Alfred Holness, 1913). The Prophecy Investigation Society also regarded wartime developments as 'signs' of the apocalypse, and indeed, some events lent themselves to such interpretation. In 1915 a 'plague' of locusts descended upon Palestine, an account of which is given in Alexander Aaronsohn's book *With the Turks in Palestine*, published in 1917. Alexander Aaronsohn, his brother Aaron and sister Sarah were Palestinian Jews who became spies for the British in Turkish-occupied Palestine. Members of the PIS would doubtless have regarded the 'plague' of locusts as 'evidence' of the fulfilment of scriptural prophecy.

9   For a report on Sir William Willcocks' lecture, see *The Times*, 11 June 1912, p. 5.

10   See, for example, Sir William Willcocks, *al-Arba' basha'ir. The Four Gospels* (Cairo, 1924, 1925), and *Aqwal wa-a'mal Sayyidina al-masih. Sayings and Acts of Jesus Christ. Selections from the Gospels in the spoken dialect of Egypt* (Cairo, 1922).

11   Frank George Jannaway was a prolific writer on religious subjects, and was involved in the Christadelphian movement.

12   Frank G. Jannaway, *Palestine and the Jews: the Zionist Movement and Evidence that the Messiah will soon Appear in Jerusalem to Rule the Whole World Therefrom* (Birmingham: C. C. Walker, 1914), p. 43.

13   Jannaway, *Palestine and the Jews*, p. 70. Pasted onto the flyleaf of the book is a small promotional card, which quotes favourable responses to the book from, amongst others, the editor of *The Zionist*, Dr E. W. G. Masterman of the Palestine Exploration Fund, and Professor Boris Schatz of the Belazel Institute, Jerusalem. Presumably these responses were elicited not by Jannaway's millennial ideas, but the detailed list he gave of all the Jewish settlements he visited (see pp. 28–42).

14   Jannaway, *Palestine and the Jews*, pp. 77–9. In Revelation, Gog and Magog are identified as the servants of Satan, and the leaders of two armies against God's people. See Revelation 20:7–9. In the Old Testament Magog is mentioned in Genesis 10:2 and 1 Chronicles 1:5 as the second son of Japheth and a descendant of Noah. In Ezekiel 39:6 Gog is the leader of a country called Magog, which threatens Israel, and will be punished. It is on Ezekiel that Revelation draws for its portrayal of these figures.

15   G. H. Box and W. O. E. Oesterley (eds), Translations of Early Documents Series, Series I: Palestinian-Jewish Texts (Pre-Rabbinic), and Series II: Hellenistic-Jewish

Texts (London: SPCK). Titles included *I* and *II Esdras* (1912, 1917); *Isaiah* (1917); *The Letter of Aristeas* (1917); *The Testaments of the Twelve Patriarchs* (1917); *The Apocalypse of Abraham* (1918); *The Apocalypse of Baruch* and *The Assumption of Moses* (1918); the Third and Fourth Books of the *Maccabees* (1918); *Joseph and Asenath* (1918); *The Lost Apocrypha of the Old Testament* (1920), and *The Apocalypse of Enoch* (1925).

16   A. F. Winnington-Ingram, *Sermons for the Times No. 4: Sermons on the Holy War* (London: James Clarke, 1914), p. 3, quoted in Wilkinson, *The Church of England*, p. 188.

17   A. F. Winnington-Ingram, *The Church in Time of War*, p. v.

18   Winnington-Ingram, 'The day of the Lord', in *A Day of God*, p. 70.

19   Winnington-Ingram, 'The Day of the Lord', p. 12. The theory of British Israelism was put forward in 1850, by Herbert Armstrong, and argues that the people of the United States and Britain represent the lost tribes of Menasseh and Ephraim respectively, who, along with the other tribes, were scattered after the Assyrian captivity in 721 BCE. The theory is an elaborate argument for Anglo-Saxon supremacy through interpretation of the scriptures and apocrypha, supported by folklore and legend, and attempts to redefine the 'chosen people' as British. Apparently forgetting Cromwell, British Israelism contends that the British monarchy is the only continuous monarchy, and therefore represents the continuation of David's royal lineage referred to in 2 Samuel, 7: 12–13.

20   Winnington-Ingram, 'In Time of War', in *Kaiser or Christ*, p. 6.

21   Winnington-Ingram, 'The Church's call to the soul of the nation', a sermon preached at St Paul's, 25 July 1915, in *The Church in Time of War*, p. 303.

22   Winnington-Ingram, 'The Church's call to the soul of the nation' (1915), p. 308.

23   G. K. A. Bell notes Prime Minister (1906–16) Herbert Asquith's dislike of the Bishop of London's jingoistic speeches, in *Randall Davidson*. For clerical reactions, see comments made by W. R. Inge, then Dean of St Paul's, on the 'un-Christian' nature of some of the Bishop's sermons, in W. R. Inge, *The Diary of a Dean. St. Paul's 1911–1934* (London: Hutchinson, 1949), p. 43.

24   D. Lloyd George, 'Honour and Dishonour', p. 11.

25   Deuteronomy 9:1–6, quoted in Winston Churchill, *The World Crisis 1911–1914* (London: Thornton Butterworth, 1923), p. 68.

26   Winston Churchill, *The World Crisis*, p. 68.

27   See, for example, two papers read to the Women's Branch of the Prophecy Investigation Society in 1916: Hodgkin, 'The firstfruits', and A. R. Habershon, 'The Day of Atonement in its prophetic aspect', a paper read to the Women's Branch of the Prophecy Investigation Society, 11 May 1916. Published in pamphlet form as part of *The Dispensational Series* (London: Alfred Holness, 1916).

28   Churchill, *The World Crisis*, pp. 10–11.

29   Churchill, *The World Crisis*, p. 11.

30   Amy Gordon Grant, *Letters From Armageddon: A Collection Made During the World War* (Boston, MA, and New York: Houghton Mifflin, 1930), p. 147.

31   '"Peeps at the Hidden War": Official Pictures of Armageddon', in *Bioscope*, 23 March 1916, p. 1234.

32   The titles of the films advertised and their release dates were: *Liveliness on the British Front*, 27 March 1916; *Villages in Flanders, the Scenes of Hard Fighting, Now Held by the British*, 3 April 1916; *With the Royal Field Artillery in Action*, 10 April 1916; *The Eyes of the Army: With the RFC at the Front*, 17 April 1916, and *The Battlefield at Neuve Chapelle*, 24 April 1916.

33   A. A. Milne, 'Armageddon', in *Punch*, 5 August 1914, p. 128.

34   See *Punch*, 23 September 1914, p. 262.

35   *The Nation*, 26 December 1914, p. 415.

36   *John Bull*, 5 September 1914, p. 1.

37   In fact they met during the war when, in response to criticism of his sermons in *John Bull*, Winnington-Ingram invited Horatio Bottomley to tea. The meeting ended with Bottomley offering temporary column space in which the bishop would promote the National Mission of Repentance and Hope. See A. F. Winnington-Ingram, *Fifty Years' Work in London, 1889–1939* (London: Longmans, 1940), pp. 126–8.

38   *John Bull*, 12 September 1914, p. 5.

39   The rhetoric of 'good' versus 'evil' is a cliché of war, but the scale of death and destruction in the First World War lent this view an immediacy not found in earlier conflicts.

40   'Mark Seven', *A Subaltern on the Somme*, p. 42.

41   Paul Nash, *Outline, an Autobiography and Other Writings* (London: Faber & Faber, 1949), pp. 210–11.

42   Raymond Savage, *Allenby of Armageddon*, p. 253. The theme of 'Armageddon' in relation to the Great War and Palestine has endured, and a much later account of the role of the cavalry in the campaign was published by Cyril Falls, under the title *Armageddon 1918*, Great Battles of History Series (London: Weidenfeld & Nicolson, 1964).

43   See, for example, the trench journals, in *The Wipers Times* (1918), and Laurence Housman (ed.), *War Letters of Fallen Englishmen*.

44   See Eric Leed, *No Man's Land: Combat and Identity in World War One* (Cambridge: Cambridge University Press, 1979), pp. 200–9.

45   Wilfred Ewart, *Way of Revelation: A Novel of Five Years* (1921, reprinted Gloucester: Alan Sutton, 1986). All further page references for this novel will be given in the text.

46   See Hugh Cecil, *The Flower of Battle: British Fiction Writers of the First World War* (London: Secker & Warburg, 1995), p. 146.

47   Stephen Graham, *With the Russian Pilgrims to Jerusalem* (London: Macmillan, 1914).

48   See *The Times*, 4 December 1918, p. 3.

49   'The Kaiser's God', in *John Bull*, 29 August 1914, p. 14.

50   A. H. T. Clarke, *Anti-Christ and Armageddon: Or, the Passing of Feudalism, Medievalism, and Mahometanism* (London: The Church Book Room, 1916).

51   Clarke, *Anti-Christ and Armageddon*, p. 4.

52   Clarke, *Anti-Christ and Armageddon*, pp. 2–3.

53   Reverend H. C. Beeching, Dean of Norwich, *Armageddon: A Sermon Upon the War Preached at Norwich Cathedral* (London: SPCK, 1914).

54   Beeching, *Armageddon: A Sermon Upon the War*, p. 3.

55   Beeching, *Armageddon: A Sermon Upon the War*, p. 12.

56   Winnington-Ingram, *'Kaiser or Christ?'*.

57   Dr Fort Newton, quoted in *The Times*, 28 December 1917, p. 9.

58   See, for example, the *Morning Post*, '"The Russian Soviet": A Predominance of Germans', 8 October 1917, p. 6, and the series 'Russia To-day', in *The Times*, 20 September–16 October 1917.

59   See Kadish, *Bolsheviks and British Jews*, p. 4.

60   See *A Collection of Reports on Bolshevism in Russia* (London: HMSO, 1919).

61   Telegraph from Sir E. Howard to Arthur Balfour, dated 19 August 1918, in *A Collection of Reports on Bolshevism in Russia*, p. 2. There is no mention of 'Jews' in the reports relating to the tsar's imprisonment and murder at Ekaterinberg; this was a connection supplied by Robert Wilton, British military intelligence agent and reporter for *The Times*.

62   George Nathaniel Curzon (1859–1925) became Baron Curzon in 1898, the same year he was appointed Viceroy of India, a post he held until 1905. He held the office of Lord Privy Seal from 1915 to 1916 in Asquith's coalition government, and Foreign Secretary from 1919 to 1924, under Prime Ministers Lloyd, Bonar Law and Stanley Baldwin.

63   Letter from Reverend B. S. Lombard to Lord Curzon, dated 23 March 1919, in *Reports on Bolshevism in Russia*, p. 67.

64   Telegraph from General Poole to the War Office, received 12 January 1919, in *Reports on Bolshevism in Russia* (1919), p. 32.

65   Report made by General Knox to the War Office, dated 4 March 1919, in *Reports on Bolshevism in Russia*, p. 53.

66   *The Story of Bolshevism: A Warning To British Women* (London: National Publications, 1919), p. 3. This pamphlet was distributed in London by W. H. Smith & Sons, and in Edinburgh by John Menzies. Besides portraying Bolshevism as a sexual threat, the writer used the imagery of contagion and disease, also

associated with Jewish immigrants in the pre-war period. Bolshevism is described as 'a foul far-spreading poison' which would be 'as fatal to the whole Political Body as cancer is to the human body', p. 4.

67   *The Story of Bolshevism*, p. 8.
68   Christabel Pankhurst, *Industrial Salvation* (London: The Women's Party, October 1918).
69   Pankhurst, *Industrial Salvation*, p. 3.
70   Pankhurst, *Industrial Salvation*, p. 11.
71   Pankhurst, *The Lord Cometh*.
72   Pankhurst, *The Lord Cometh*, p. 91.
73   See, for example, the following papers read to the Prophecy Investigation Society during the war, all of which have antisemitic content: A. R. Habershon, *The Dispensations* (London: Alfred Holness, 1912), *The Place of Miracles in the Dispensation* (London: Alfred Holness, 1914), and *The Day of Atonement in its Prophetic Aspect* (London: Alfred Holness, 1916); A. M. Hodgkin, *The Return of the Jews to their Own Land* (London: Alfred Holness, 1914); E. A. Bland, *The Church and the Tribulation* (London: Alfred Holness, 1915).
74   Ernest Peter Cachemaille, MA, attended Gonville and Caius College, Cambridge, and was the secretary of the South American Missionary Society.
75   E. P. Cachemaille, *Palestine and the Warfare of the End*, A paper read to the Prophecy Investigation Society (London: Chas A Thynne, 1921).
76   Cachemaille, *Palestine and the Warfare of the End*, pp. 11–12.
77   Cachemaille, *Palestine and the Warfare of the End*, p. 22.
78   Cachemaille, *Palestine and the Warfare of the End*, p. 15.
79   *Biarritz* was partly a reaction to the impending emancipation of Jews in the North German states, which occurred in 1869, and throughout the entire Reich in 1871.
80   Norman Cohn, *Warrant for Genocide: The Myth of the Jewish World-conspiracy and the Protocols of the Elders of Zion* (London: Eyre & Spottiswoode, 1967), p. 36.
81   Cohn, *Warrant for Genocide*, p. 67.
82   Dr Theodor Herzl was an Austrian Jew who founded the modern political Zionist movement. He wrote the influential *Der Judenstaat* (1896) and led the first Zionist Congress at Basle the following year.
83   Chaim Weizmann, *Trial and Error: the Autobiography of Chaim Weizmann* (London: Hamish Hamilton, 1949), p. 273.
84   Cohn, *Warrant for Genocide*, p. 152.
85   *The Times*, 8 May, 1920, p. 15.
86   *The Spectator*, 15 May 1920, p. 640.
87   Anon, *England Under the Heel of the Jew* (London: C. F. Roworth, 1918). This book was also published by the Britons' Society (London, 1921). Cited in Cohn, *Warrant for Genocide*, p. 149.
88   For press examples, see the *Morning Post*, '"The Russian Soviet": A Predominance of Germans', 8 October 1917, p. 6, and the series 'Russia To-day' in the *Times*, 20 September–16 October 1917. The Foreign Office publication referred to is *Reports on Bolshevism in Russia*.
89   See Cohn, *Pursuit of the Millennium* (1957), pp. 62–3, 310.
90   See Jean-Louis Robert, 'The Image of the Profiteer', pp. 104–32.
91   See Cheyette, *Constructions*, p. 9.
92   Winston Churchill, 'Zionism versus Bolshevism: A struggle for the soul of the Jewish people', *Illustrated Sunday Herald*, 8 February 1920, p. 5.
93   *Jewish Chronicle*, 13 February 1920, p. 8.
94   See 'Peace, War – and Bolshevism', *Jewish Chronicle*, 28 March and 4 April 1919.
95   See Kadish, *Bolsheviks and British Jews* (1992), pp. 120–34 for a full discussion of the 'Letter of the Ten' and its interpretations.
96   Nesta Webster, born Nesta Bevan, grew up in Hertfordshire and was the youngest of 14 children. Her father was a director of Barclays Bank. She worked at supplies depots during the First World War, and afterwards wrote for the *Morning Post* and then as a member of the British Fascists, for the *Fascist Bulletin*.
97   Nesta Webster, *World Revolution: The Plot Against Civilization* (London: Constable, 1921), p. vii.

98   Webster, *World Revolution*, p. 326.
99   Nesta Webster, *Secret Societies and Subversive Movements* (London: Boswell Printing & Publishing, 1924), pp. 369, 402.
100   Webster, *Secret Societies*, p. 374.
101   Webster, *Secret Societies*, pp. 404–5.
102   Pankhurst, 'The Lord Cometh', pp. 100–1.
103   R. A. C. Parker, *Europe 1919–45* (London: Weidenfeld & Nicolson, 1967), p. 116.
104   Women over 21 gained the vote in 1928.
105   Parker, *Europe 1919–45*, p. 123.
106   For a full discussion of Joynson-Hicks' antisemitism, see David Cesarani, 'Joynson-Hicks and the Radical Right in England after the First World War', in Tony Kushner and Kenneth Lunn (eds), *Traditions of Intolerance: Historical Perspectives on Fascism and Race Discourse in Britain* (Manchester & New York: Manchester University Press, 1989), pp. 118–39.
107   Samuel Hynes, *A War Imagined: The First World War and English Culture* (London: The Bodley Head, 1990), p. 356.
108   See Elaine R. Smith, 'Jewish Responses to Political Antisemitism and Fascism in the East End of London, 1920–1939', in Kushner and Lunn (eds), *Traditions of Intolerance*, pp. 53–71.
109   See Kenneth Lunn, 'The Ideology and Impact of the British Fascists in the 1920s', pp. 140–54. British Fascisti membership figures are taken from Home Office memorandum HO144/19069/211-2, cited in Lunn's article, p. 145.
110   Kenneth Lunn, 'The Ideology and Impact of the British Fascists in the 1920s', pp. 146–7.
111   See David Cannadine, *The Decline and Fall of the British Aristocracy* (London: Picador, 1990), p. 546.
112   Gerry C. Webber, for example, argues that the 'radical right' tried and failed to exploit nationalism and anti-alienism, but the economic and political security of the middle classes in particular was not sufficiently threatened to engender their mass support. Tory policies and rhetoric, he suggests, provided sufficient focus and outlet for anti-socialist and antisemitic feeling and the far right groups therefore remained marginal. See G. C. Webber, 'Intolerance and Discretion: Conservatives and British Fascism, 1918–1926', in Kushner and Lunn (eds), *Traditions of Intolerance*, pp. 155–72.
113   See *Punch*, 9 June 1920, p. 457.
114   Paul Rich, 'Imperial Decline and the Resurgence of English National Identity 1918–1979', in Kushner and Lunn (eds), *Traditions of Intolerance*, pp. 33–52, 37.
115   Norman, *Church and Society*, pp,228–9).
116   Norman, *Church and Society*, pp. 221, 235.
117   Norman, *Church and Society*, p. 241.
118   Charles Gore (1853–1932) was Bishop of Oxford from 1911 to 1919, and President of the Christian Social Union from 1902 to 1911.
119   Norman, *Church and Society*, pp. 245–6.
120   Handley Carr Glyn Moule (1841–1920) was Professor of Divinity at Cambridge from 1899 to 1901 and Bishop of Durham from 1901 to 1920.
121   Herbert Hensley Henson (1863–1947) was Dean of Durham from 1912 to 1918 and became Bishop of Durham in 1920, retaining this post until 1939.
122   Norman, *Church and Society*, p. 258.
123   See Wilkinson, *The Church of England*, p. 286.
124   Parker, *Europe 1919–45*, pp. 124–6.
125   Gilbert Frankau, *Masterson. A Story of an English Gentleman*, 4th edn (London: Hutchinson, 1925). All further page references will be included in the text.
126   Ursula Bloom wrote a problem page and film criticism for the *Daily Mail*, and religious articles for the *Sunday Express*. Her first novel, *The Great Beginning*, was published in 1924. See her autobiography, *Mistress of None* (London: Hutchinson, 1933), pp. 26, 30, 139.
127   Ursula Bloom, *The Judge of Jerusalem* (London: George G. Harrap, 1926). All further page references will be given in the text.
128   Webber, 'Intolerance and Discretion', p. 167.

129   Webber, 'Intolerance and Discretion', pp. 161–2.
130   In *The Decline of the British Aristocracy*, pp. 546–7, David Cannadine cites 'declining and embittered landowners', including Sir Henry Fairfax-Lucy, Lord Knebworth, Viscount Lymington and the Duke of Manchester as examples.

8

Conclusion

One of the effects of the First World War was to reveal the instability of the idea of the nation, as demarcations of class, gender and politics that had previously been taken for granted began to shift. Attempts were made to consolidate national identity through the rhetoric of Britain as a Christian nation engaged in a battle against the non-Christian forces of 'evil'. But the idea of a Christian Britain was old-fashioned and inaccurate, a nineteenth-century view that, like the concept of chivalry, was revived during the war. Yet the rhetoric of Christian nationhood was effective, and was widely taken up, as the range of texts discussed above indicates. While the concept of a Christian nation united against non-Christian forces may have provided a sense of cohesion amongst even non-observant Christians, it excluded Jews, both British-born and recent immigrants. Furthermore, the Christian nationalist rhetoric that circulated during the war could not be used selectively: the narrative of crucifixion requires a 'Judas', and 'Antichrist' must have his followers in the battle of the 'last days'. The New Testament model ascribes both roles to Jews, and the wartime uptake of these narratives followed the same pattern, with the rhetoric of 'crucifixion' and 'apocalypse' in particular connecting with pre-existing discourses regarding the nature of 'Jewish' identity. As in the First Crusade, the Christian sense of embattlement during the First World War found partial expression in hostility towards Jews, despite the fact that the enemy was not Jewish.

The war did not generate violence towards Jews on the scale witnessed during the crusades, but there was at least one incident of 'racial' murder, and the case illustrates how popular prejudice could override legal justice. In early September 1917, Lieutenant Douglas Malcolm was charged with the murder of Anton Baumberg, or Count de Borch as he was also known. The incident took place on 14 August, when Malcolm shot Baumberg three times at close range. In his defence, Malcolm argued that Baumberg was 'a White Slave trafficker and a spy', who was luring his wife into dishonour and claimed to have offered Baumberg money to keep away from her.[1] The defence exploited the fact that Malcolm was enlisted and Baumberg was not and the latter was described as a 'Russian', with a false name and a bogus title, who cast 'a black, evil, ugly shadow' over the marital home in Cadogan Square. In summing up, the judge reminded the jury that justice should be available to all, whether foreign or British-born, and that if a 'guilty' verdict was reached the Crown had the power to show mercy in Malcolm's case. Nevertheless, the jury treated what appears to have been a 'racial' murder as a 'crime of passion' and took 20 minutes to find the defendant not guilty.

The 'white slave trafficker' and the 'alien anarchist' were both popularly associated with Jewish immigrants during the early twentieth century, and an expression of the fears associated with this group. Subsequent representations of the 'Jewish' threat combined religious and political anxieties, in a perceived double attack, on Christianity and the liberal partial democracy that existed in Britain at the time. This is clearly seen in the emergence of the figure of the 'Bolshevik Jew', depicted in the press and in popular fiction after the Bolshevik revolution of October 1917. Following the Treaty of Brest–Litovsk and the death of Tsar Nicholas II in 1918, an image that I have termed the 'Bolshevik Judas' took shape, based on the idea of betrayal that was associated with Russia's separate peace with Germany, and on comparisons between the tsar and Jesus, as sacrificial figures. Robert Wilton's book *The Last Days of the Romanovs* (1920), which explicitly compares the tsar to Christ, and claims that Bolsheviks erected a statue to Judas Iscariot in Moscow, is the clearest example of this.

It was in relation to Bolshevism and the fear that it would spread through the Labour movement in Britain, that the imagery of 'apocalypse' became linked to popular antisemitism. The apocalypse as described in the Book of Revelation provided metaphors for the scale of the war and a narrative of redemption that promised deliverance. But Revelation also casts 'unbelievers' as the followers of Antichrist, and in the context described above this threat became identified particularly with 'Jews' and the political left. The concept of 'Antichrist', integral to the Revelation narrative, was identified in various ways during and after the war. Initially it was 'Prussianism' that was most commonly regarded as the force of diabolical 'evil' in the world, but after October 1917 this was replaced by Bolshevism. Modern secular apocalyptic portrayed Bolshevism as the false doctrine of Antichrist, and, drawing on the popular association between Russian Jews and revolutionary politics, cast 'Jews' as its followers. This thinking drew on pre-war associations between Jewish immigrants and anarchism, but was also part of right-wing attempts to discredit the left and the labour movement by appealing to popular antisemitism.

Another important component of the Revelation story is the concept of 'millennium', and in the period described this became linked to both hopes and fears of what post-war reconstruction would bring. Reactions to 'Jewish' Bolshevism and the imagery of the 'Jewish' profiteer and class usurper indicate a fear that the post-war, 'post-apocalyptic' landscape would be dominated by the 'enemies' of Christianity. Again, this anxiety found an outlet in popular fiction as well as in the press and political statements. An example of this appears in a collection of stories written by the journalist Sir Philip Gibbs, based on his experiences as a war correspondent and his visits to post-war Europe. In the preface to this collection, entitled *Little Novels of Nowadays* (1930), Gibbs argued that it was the journalist that was best equipped to write fiction, having travelled widely and witnessed all aspects of human life.[2] Yet Gibbs' stories simply peddled antisemitic rumours from Germany and Russia, and disinformation about 'Jews' that pandered to popular prejudices. One story, 'The Stranger in the Village', tells of the 'resurrection' of the dead Tsar Nicholas II and his sighting in the village of Lubimovka, in the Volga region, in 1920, during the famine. Gibbs claims to have heard the story from Sacha, a poet from Lubimovka, who saw the stranger. The association that Robert Wilton had created between the tsar and Jesus is continued in this story, as the peasant who finds the monarch collapsed in the snow thinks to himself 'He is like a saint ... He is even a little like the good Christ' (p. 15). When the man awakes he identifies himself as 'Nicholas Alexandrovitch, a wandering beggar' (p. 18) and his appearance becomes linked to expectations that Jesus will return to save the village from famine. The discovery is heralded as a miracle by all in the village except 'Braunberg the Jew', secretary of the Bolshevik village council (p. 19). Eventually, after a confrontation with Braunberg and another Bolshevik official, the stranger moves on, leaving only a jewelled cross as evidence of his visit.

Another story, 'The Beggar of Berlin', tells of Gibbs' encounter in the German capital with an ascetic young man who resembled 'John the Baptist in a picture by Titian' (p. 59). After their brief meeting, Gibbs returned to his hotel. He described his fellow guests as 'the international vultures who gather in the capitals of Europe in which there is financial decay and corruption upon which they thrive' (p. 61). The other diners are *déclassé*, overweight figures who speak German with foreign accents, wear a great deal of jewellery and drink liqueurs between courses. They are 'curiously stunted, coarsely-made', and although not specifically identified as 'Jewish', their description is consistent with images of 'the Jew' as an international, vulgar and greedy figure (p. 62). Seeing his interest in the group of 'vultures', the waiter approaches Gibbs and confides his view that 'Most of this crowd...ought to be put in a death chamber with poison gas' (p. 62). Three years after this story was published, Hitler became chancellor of Germany.

Two other examples of popular fiction of the inter-war period shed an interesting light on the relationship between Jesus and Judas in the Christian imagination. John Oxenham's novel *The Hidden Years* (1927) gives an account of the life of Jesus, in which Judas is conspicuously absent, as is Mary Magdalene.[3] The narrative uses the device of several 'eye-witnesses' and members of Jesus' extended family to tell the story, but leaves out Judas altogether, possibly in an attempt to appear unbiased on this matter. The Romans are portrayed as impartial and even sympathetic, through the character of Longinus, a centurion, who provides details of Jesus' audience with Pilate. The scene of the procession to Calvary, however, draws on stock images of the vengeful 'Jew', and exonerates the Romans:

> Jesus had fallen again and lay with his face on the ground. A venomous little Jew, with a most evil face, ran up and began striking him with a stick, till one of the soldiers drove him off with the butt of his spear. (pp. 214–15)

> Round the crosses, some of the High Priest's ruffians hung about jeering and mocking. They looked ready to stone Jesus as he hung there helpless, but the soldiers kept them at a distance. (p. 217)

The novel ends with an affirmation of Jesus' divinity by the narrator, a boyhood friend: 'I knew Jesus and loved him as my dearest friend. And that same Jesus... was in truth The Christ, the Son of the Most High God... So we live in the constant hope of seeing him again sometime' (p. 244).

Two years later, in 1929, the Anglo-Jewish historian Cecil Roth published a novel entitled *Iscariot*,[4] which may, perhaps, be a response to Oxenham's novel *The Hidden Years*, although this cannot be proved. *Iscariot* describes the childhood and early youth of Judas, and frames the betrayal of Jesus as the result of frustrated messianic expectation and sexual rivalry over Mary Magdalene. Roth portrays Judas as in conflict with both Judaism and the sect that would become Christianity, and indicates that Jews, taught to expect a reforming and avenging messiah, were frustrated and disappointed by Jesus' teachings. Judas is a Judaean, of Kerioth ('Iscariot'), who has red hair and blue eyes, and seems 'foreign' even in his own country. His father is Simon, a zealot of the tribe of Reuben who is patriotic rather than religiously devout. Simon's ancestors had fought with the Maccabees, and he himself had fought against the Romans. He named his son after Judas Maccabee and the boy was imbued with a deep messianic hope.

Hearing of a young teacher in Galilee, who is being hailed as the messiah, Judas resolves to join him. In Magdala, he meets the prostitute Mary and becomes infatuated with her, but Mary is fascinated by Jesus, and Judas becomes resentful and increasingly alienated from the group of disciples. The group travels to Jerusalem for the Passover, where Jesus desecrates the Temple by evicting the money-changers, but disappoints the people by advising them to continue to obey Roman law. Judas meets Eliazar, a scribe from his native Kerioth, who doubts that Jesus is the messiah and reminds Judas of the short lineage of the Galileans, saying,

> I have never yet met a Galilean who could trace his ancestry above three generations, or four at the utmost. You know full well that they are for the most part the seed of Gentiles, circumcised by force by the kings of the House of Hasmonaeus. (pp. 135–6)

Judas begins to have doubts about Jesus, and, realising that he will never marry Mary, considers suicide, but instead begins to seek ways of revealing Jesus as an impostor. He approaches Caiaphas and tells him where Jesus and the disciples rest on their way out of the city each evening. Caiaphas asks him what he will have in reward, but, overcome by the enormity of his deed, Judas does not answer. Assuming he wants money, Caiaphas somewhat contemptuously gives him 30 pieces of silver. The next day, Judas reasons to himself that if Jesus is the Messiah, he will know he has been betrayed and will escape the Romans. But he also feels remorse and in the Garden of Gethsemane that evening, is about to confess, but becomes jealous of Mary's attention to Jesus and gives him the kiss that is the signal. He then goes to the Valley of Hinnom, where he finds a dead tree and hangs himself with his girdle. The field, Aceldama, becomes the place where outsiders are buried.

The figure of Judas is significant as an image of rebellion and treachery, and as Hyam Maccoby has observed, the Judas story,

> is part of a larger myth, which gives to the Jews an archetypal role as being people of the Devil...many, perhaps most, people today believe themselves to have outgrown the Christian myth. But it is just at this point in the development of culture, when a myth is renounced on the conscious level, that it can take hold even more strongly on the unconscious level.[5]

One mythic creature that excites the modern imagination and is associated with both anti-Christian 'evil' and the drawing of blood, is the vampire. Vampiric representations of 'the Jewish threat' appeared on front covers of editions of the *Protocols* that were published in numerous countries during the inter-war period. In an example from France in 1934, the threat of 'world Jewish conspiracy' is depicted as a 'Jew' digging his nails into the globe, from which a blood-like substance oozes. Another example from Brazil, which appeared in 1937, symbolises the threat as a snake, with large fangs, while a Spanish edition, dated 1963, shows 'Jewish' vultures perched upon the cross from which Jesus hangs.[6] The association between the 'Jew' and 'Christian blood' is clear.

The image of the vampiric 'Jew' that preys upon Christians has endured even into the twenty-first century. The film *Dracula 2001*, directed by Patrick Lussier, conflates the figures of Dracula and Judas, portraying Judas as the first vampire. Most versions of the Dracula legend trace the vampire's origins to fifteenth-century Transylvania and many link him with Vlad the Impaler. There is a vagueness in the stories, however, which various film-makers have addressed, that relates to Dracula's origins; his motives for feeding on human blood, and whether or not he can actually be killed. In many popular versions of the story, Dracula is not sensitive to light, nor is he frightened of the cross, all of which frustrates traditional methods of bringing about his demise. The stories trade on the fear of the original vampire as an indestructible personification of 'evil' and thus the genre perpetuates itself. This is the fear that *Dracula 2001* both invokes and attempts to assuage.

The action takes place in New Orleans, at the Mardi Gras festival, the traditional pre-Lenten Christian celebration. As a result of an attempted robbery by a gang of black and Hispanic youths, Dracula has escaped from his sealed coffin, held in the vault of the Van Helsing family. Early clues as to his identity include a scene in which the vampire sees Mardi Gras coins falling to the ground, which, in a 'flashback', become Roman silver coins. Another clue is his familiarity with Aramaic script. Like many films in this genre, *Dracula 2001* plunders stock images of horror and 'evil' for sensational effect in its attempt to portray the vampire as a demonic threat that is both familiar and new, and develops the idea of Dracula as a motiveless figure of 'evil' into a sworn enemy of Christianity. There is no 'semitic' imagery in Lussier's screen representation of Dracula/Judas: he is portrayed as more of a religious than a 'racial' threat, but in other respects the film makes an uncritical and unreflective appeal to the racist fears associated with non-white groups in the modern United States. The gang of blacks and Hispanics who attempted to rob the Van Helsing vault become the first vampires created by the newly released Dracula/Judas, and the effect of this is that the forces of 'good' are represented as white and Christian, while those of 'evil' are black, Hispanic, and Jewish, with Dracula/Judas as the treacherous, 'unbelieving' Jew.

In *Dracula 2001*, Dracula/Judas functions as an image of what Hyam Maccoby has termed 'the black Christ'. In *Judas Iscariot and the Myth of Jewish Evil* (1992),[7] Maccoby argues that the figure of Judas developed in accordance with the emotional needs of Christians throughout history. Judas, he suggests, answers the need for a personification of an independent force of 'evil' in the world, and his function is to complete the narrative of human sacrifice and redemption that is central to Christianity.[8] Judas the betrayer plays the role of the 'sacred executioner', the member of the community who performs the appalling but necessary sacrifice that the group believes it needs in order to survive. In this respect, he is both 'holy' and 'evil'. The collective guilt over the necessity of the sacrifice is passed on to Judas, who becomes the 'black Christ' to Jesus' sacrificial 'Lamb', and is himself sacrificed. Depending on the version of the story, Judas hangs himself in remorse at his betrayal of Jesus, or is struck down by God and dies in a field known as 'Blood Acre'. Either way, his sacrifice has no redemptive aspect for the community, but is simply represented as a suitable fate for a traitor.

Yet there is a redemptive aspect to the death of Dracula / Judas in *Dracula 2001*. The film suggests that Judas did not hang himself, as in the legend, but survived, because the rope snapped. It is this that provides the clue to the means of his destruction. The film also provides Dracula / Judas with a motive for drinking blood, albeit an incoherent one: in the final scene, which takes place on the roof of a church, the vampire talks to a neon image of Jesus on the cross, saying: 'You knew that my destiny was to betray you, because you needed me. And now, I drink the blood of your children.' He continues, asserting that he can offer humans 'all the pleasure and freedom you would deny them', and adds 'You made the world in your image – now, I make it in mine'. All this is witnessed by Mary, a young English woman whom Dracula / Judas has kidnapped and fed upon. She realises that the way to destroy him is to re-enact the scene of his death in the legends, and slips a noose around his neck, which she then fastens to the neon cross. This falls forward under his weight, and he hangs from the cross on the roof of the church. His dying act is to release Mary from her own vampire state, and in this he becomes almost Christ-like.

As Maccoby points out, the nature of ritual is that it is repeated, as an assurance against disaster. He argues that in the structure of imagination shaped by the Christian sacrificial narrative, there is a compulsion to enact this ritual of sacrifice and salvation, and that this has historically been enacted upon Jews through pogroms, expulsions, and conversions.[9] But the enactment of ritual in the Jesus / Judas, or Christian / Jew binary has been one-sided: Jesus was crucified once, whereas Jews, as the 'betrayers', or the 'black Christ', have been sacrificed many times. Yet as the historical allegations of ritual murder demonstrate, it is Christians who fear attack by Jews. It was fear of the repetition of persecution that underlay the opposition to the decision by the British Board of Deputies – an organisation that was founded to protect the interests of Jews in

Britain – to auction the Victorian explorer Sir Richard Burton's treatise *Human Sacrifice among the Sephardine or the Eastern Jews* (1877) in 2001. The work refers to the charge of 'blood libel' made in 1840 against 13 Jews in Damascus, who, it was alleged, had carried out the ritual murder of a Capuchin friar named Padre Tomaso and his servant.[10] In order to raise funds for new premises, the Board of Deputies announced that this text, which had been bought in 1911 and suppressed since then, would be auctioned at Christie's in London. Opponents of the board's decision argued that the text could be used by neo-Nazi groups to fuel antisemitism, while representatives of the board felt that sufficient time had elapsed for the document to no longer be considered a threat to Jewry.

Burton's treatise failed to attract bids for its reserve price of 150,000 pounds, and the sale was withdrawn. But the conflation of two figures of anti-Christian 'evil' – Dracula and Judas – in the film *Dracula 2001*, suggests that the suppression of antisemitic historical material cannot in itself prevent the circulation of ancient images of 'evil' in popular culture. I doubt whether Lussier's film is intended to arouse antisemitic feeling: the link between Judas and Dracula seems to have been made for the purpose of introducing 'new blood' into a very familiar genre. Yet in attempting to take a fresh approach to the vampire legend, *Dracula 2001* returns to a very old allegation made against Jews, that of the blood libel, or the ritual murder of Christians. In this most recent version of the vampire story, Dracula's aversion to crosses is explained and Judas attains vampire status. Dracula's creation of fellow-vampires through feeding – always by implication a blasphemous version of the Christian sacrament – gains, through Judas, a more strongly Christian focus, even in a largely secular age. In this respect, just as the narratives of 'crusade', 'crucifixion' and 'apocalypse' found their antisemitic closure in the context of the First World War, so the image of Dracula was completed in *Dracula 2001*, through the figure of Judas, and vice versa. In this latest expression of popular Christian paranoia, Dracula is charged with 'deicide' and Judas becomes the original vampire. Judas provides Dracula with origins and a motive: Dracula provides Judas with a modern significance that simultaneously draws upon ancient representations of 'the Jew', and both are reconstructed and updated, in a new image of anti-Christian malevolence.

Mel Gibson's film *The Passion of the Christ* (2004) reopened the debate over the allegations of deicide that have prompted centuries of violence and persecution against Jews. The cast speak in Latin and

Aramaic, in an attempt to create a sense of historical authenticity, and in the opening sequence, the story is represented uncritically as 'history'. Gibson claims that his film depicts the story as it is told in the New Testament, but the film also uses crude symbolism and juxtaposition to portray the Jews as the aggressors. Satan, reminiscent of the figure of Death in Ingmar Bergman's film *The Seventh Seal* (1957), appears in several scenes and walks among the crowd of Jews, at one point lingering behind Caiaphas, as if to draw a parallel between Judaism and 'evil'. And at Calvary, still walking among the mob of Jews, Satan cradles a demonic child in his arms, as if to suggest an inversion of the iconic Madonna and Child. There is a long history of the portrayal by Christians of Jewish religious practices as an inversion of Christian ritual – in the blood libel, which has provoked allegations and pogroms against Jews into the twentieth century. What is Gibson's purpose in making this film, funded with $25 million of his own money? Is he trying to assert the significance of Christianity in the modern world? Trying to win converts with his graphic representation of the suffering of Jesus? But the violence in this film becomes monotonous, and reminds this viewer, at least, that under imperial occupation, as in war, violence is mundane. The film has been released at a time when tensions between Christians and Muslims are growing. Israel remains a contested territory, and while the Israeli government is clearly not innocent in the Middle East conflict, there is a danger that *The Passion of the Christ* could exacerbate existing anti-Jewish feeling. Gibson's father has made flippant remarks about the Holocaust in public speeches, and Gibson himself funds a traditionalist Catholic group in California that rejects the ruling of the second Vatican Council, in which the Jews were cleared of the charge of 'deicide'. And he has made a film that portrays the last hours of Jesus' life in graphic and monotonous detail, and has presented it as historical 'truth'. Given the way that this biblical narrative has inspired attacks upon Jews in the past, Jewish communities in Britain and elsewhere will no doubt be bracing themselves.

NOTES

1   See *The Times*, 12 September 1917, pp. 4–5.
2   Philip Gibbs, *Little Novels of Nowadays* (London: Hutchinson, 1930). All subsequent references are incorporated into the text.
3   John Oxenham, pseud. (William Arthur Dunkerley), *The Hidden Years* (London: Longmans, Green, 1927). Subsequent references are included in the text.

4   Cecil Roth, *Iscariot* (London: The Mandrake Press, 1929). Subsequent references are included in the text.

5   Hyam Maccoby, *Judas Iscariot and the Myth of Jewish Evil* (London: Peter Halban, 1992), p. 162.

6   These images can be found in Norman Cohn's book *Warrant for Genocide*, between pages 144 and 145.

7   Hyam Maccoby, *Judas Iscariot*.

8   See Maccoby, *Judas Iscariot*, p. 82.

9   See Maccoby, *Judas Iscariot*, pp. 139–40.

10   See *The Times*, 4 June 2001, the *Observer*, 3 June 2001, and the *Guardian*, 7 June 2001.

Bibliography

PRIMARY SOURCES

Aaronsohn, Alexander, *With the Turks in Palestine* (London: Constable, 1917)

Aaronsson, Lazarus, *Poems* (London: Victor Gollancz, 1933)

Adler, Reverend Michael, *The Jews of the Empire and the Great War* (London, New York and Toronto: Hodder & Stoughton, June 1919)

— *A Jewish Chaplain on the Western Front, 1914–1918* (reprinted from *The Jewish Guardian*, Lewes, 1920)

Address of the German Theologians to the Evangelical Christians Abroad. First published in the *Westminster Gazette*, 9 September 1914. Reprinted in *To the Christian Scholars of Europe and America: A Reply from Oxford to the German Address to Evangelical Christians* (London: Oxford University Press, 1914).

Anonymous, *England Under the Heel of the Jew* (London: C. F. Roworth, 1918; London: The Britons' Society, 1921)

Arnold, Matthew, *Culture and Anarchy* (1869, reprinted, Cambridge: Cambridge University Press, 1932).

Beeching, H. C., *Armageddon: A Sermon Upon the War. Preached in Norwich Cathedral* (London: SPCK, 1914).

Bell, G. K. A., *Randall Davidson, Archbishop of Canterbury*, second edition (London, New York & Toronto: Oxford University Press, 1938).

Berman, Hannah, *Melutovna. A Novel* (London: Chapman & Hall, 1913).

Bevan, Edwyn, 'Brothers All: The War and the Race Question', Papers for War Time Series, no. 4 (London: Oxford University Press, 1914).

Birch, William Thomas, *Armageddon and Other Poems* (Manchester and London: John Heywood, 1918).

Bland, E. A., *The Church and the Tribulation* (London: Alfred Holness, 1915).

Bloom, Ursula, *The Judge of Jerusalem* (London: George G. Harrap, 1926).

— *Mistress of None* (London: Hutchinson, 1933).

Blumenfeld, Ralph D., *R.D.B.'s Procession* (London: Ivor Nicholson & Watson, 1935).

Blunden, Edmund (ed.), *The Poems of Wilfred Owen* (London: Chatto & Windus, 1933).

Bourchier, Reverend Basil, *For All We Have and Are* (London: Skeffington & Son, 1915).

Brittain, Vera, *Testament of Youth* (London: Victor Gollancz, 1933, reprinted London: Virago, 1978, 1997).

Brown, William, 'Hypnosis, suggestion and dissociation', *British Medical Journal*, 14 June 1919, pp. 734–6.

Bryce, Viscount, *Neutral Nations and the War* (London: Macmillan, 1914)

Burne, C. S., *'Might Gives Right': The New Gospel of Germany*, Papers for the People Series No. 2 (London: Central Committee of Patriotic Organisations, 1914).

— *'King George or Kaiser Wilhelm': British Freedom against German Despotism*, Papers for the People Series No. 3 (London: Central Committee of Patriotic Organisations, 1914).

Cachemaille, Reverend Ernest Peter, MA, 'Palestine and the warfare of the end', paper read to the Prophecy Investigation Society (London: Chas. J. Thynne, 1921).

Churchill, Winston, 'Zionism versus Bolshevism. A struggle for the soul of the Jewish people', *Illustrated Sunday Herald*, 8 February 1920, p. 5.

— *The World Crisis 1911–1914* (London: Thornton Butterworth, 1923).

— *Great Contemporaries* (London: Thornton Butterworth, 1937)

Coote, William A., *A Vision and Its Fulfilment: Being the History of the Work of the National Vigilance Association for the Suppression of the White Slave Traffic* (London: NVA, 1910).

Coppard, George, *With A Machine Gun to Cambrai: The Tale of A Young Tommy in Kitchener's Army 1914–1918* (London: HMSO, 1969).

Davidson, Randall Thomas, D. D., *The Testing of A Nation* (London: Macmillan, 1919).

Deane, Colonel G. W., CB, *Britannia's Epiphany: Reconciliation of the*

Teaching of Christendom and British Israelism (London: R. Banks & Son, 1919).

Eder, David, 'The psychopathology of war neuroses', in *The Lancet*, 12 August 1916, pp. 264–8.

Epstein, Private Paul, *Diary 1918–1919*, in Rare Books, Parkes Library, University of Southampton, UK, shelfmark MS 1124 AJ15/8.

Ewart, Wilfrid, *Way of Revelation: A Novel of Five Years* (1921, reprinted Gloucester: Alan Sutton Publishing, 1986).

Falls, Captain Cyril, *History of the Great War: Military Operations Egypt and Palestine. Part I: From June 1917 to the End of the War* (London: HMSO, 1930).

Fawcett, Millicent Garrett, *Women's Suffrage: A Short History of a Great Movement* (London: The People's Books Series, T. C. and E. C. Jack, 1911).

Frankau, Gilbert, *Tid'Apa* (London: Chatto & Windus, 1915, reprinted 1921).

— *One of Us: A Novel in Verse* (London: Chatto & Windus, 1912, 1923).

— *One of Them: A Novelette in Verse* (London: Hutchinson, 1918).

— *The City of Fear and Other Poems* (London: Chatto & Windus, 1918).

— *The Judgement of Valhalla* (London: Chatto & Windus, 1918).

— *Peter Jackson, Cigar Merchant. A Romance of Married Life* (London: MacDonald, 1919).

— *Masterson. A Story of an English Gentleman*, fourth edition (London: Hutchinson, Ltd., 1925).

— *Martin Make-Believe: A Romance* (London: Hutchinson, 1930).

— 'An outlier from his tribe', in Joseph Leftwich (ed.), *Yisroel: The First Jewish Omnibus* (London: John Heritage, 1933).

— *Self-Portrait: A Novel of his Own Life* (London: MacDonald, 1944).

Freud, Sigmund, 'Creative writers and day-dreaming', *Standard Edition of the Complete Psychological Works of Sigmund Freud*, trans. James Strachey in collaboration with Anna Freud (London: Hogarth Press, 1955).

— 'Thoughts for the times on war and death', *Standard Edition of the Complete Psychological Works of Sigmund Freud*, trans. James Strachey in collaboration with Anna Freud (London: Hogarth Press, 1955).

Freulich, Roman, *Soldiers in Judea: Stories and Vignettes of the Jewish Legion* (New York: Herzl Press, 1964).

Gibbs, Philip, *The Pageant of the Years: An Autobiography* (London and Toronto: William Heinemann, 1946).

— *Little Novels of Nowadays* (London: Hutchinson, 1930).

Graham, Stephen, *With the Russian Pilgrims to Jerusalem* (London: Macmillan, 1914).

Grant, Amy Gordon, *Letters From Armageddon: A Collection Made During the World War* (Boston & New York: Houghton Mifflin, 1930).

Grant, John Cameron, *The Heart of Hell: A Note Upon the White Slave Traffic* (London: New Constitutional Society for Women's Suffrage, printed by the Women's Printing Society, 1913).

Habershon, Ada R., 'The Dispensations' (London: Alfred Holness, 1912).

— 'The Place of Miracles in the Dispensation' (London: Alfred Holness, 1914).

— 'The Day of Atonement in its Prophetic Aspect', a paper read to the Women's Branch of the Prophecy Investigation Society, 11 May 1916. Published in pamphlet form as part of The Dispensational Series (London: Alfred Holness, 1916).

Hansard Parliamentary Debates, Commons, Vol. LXXI, April 14 to May 19, 1915 (London: Cornelius Buck, 1869).

Hart-Davis, Rupert (ed.), *Siegfried Sassoon Diaries, 1915–1918* (London: Faber & Faber, 1983).

Hay, Ian, *The First Hundred Thousand, being the unofficial chronicle of a unit of "K (1)"* (Edinburgh & London: W. Blackwood & Sons, 1915).

Hobson, J. A., *The War in South Africa: Its Causes and Effects* (London: James Nisbet, 1900).

Hodgkin, A. M., 'The Return of the Jews to their Own Land' (London: Alfred Holness, 1914).

— 'The Firstfruits' (London: Alfred Holness, 1916).

Houghton, Henry D., 'Is the Kaiser Lucifer?' (London: Robert Banks & Son, 1917).

— 'Will Our Dead Soldiers Come Back?: The Evidence of Scripture' (London: Robert Banks & Son, 1919).

Housman, Laurence (ed.), *War Letters of Fallen Englishmen* (London: Victor Gollancz, 1930).

Inge, W. R., *The Diary of a Dean. St. Paul's 1911–1934* (London: Hutchinson, 1949).

Jabotinsky, Vladimir, *The Story of the Jewish Legion*, trans. Samuel Katz (New York: Bernard Ackerman, 1945).

Jannaway, Frank G., *Palestine and the Jews, or, The Zionist Movement an Evidence that the Messiah will soon appear in Jerusalem to rule the whole World therefrom* (Birmingham: C. C. Walker, 1914).

Kenney, Annie, *Memories of a Militant* (London: Edward Arnold, 1924).

Keynes, John Maynard, *The Economic Consequences of the Peace* (London: Macmillan, 1920).

Kingsley, Charles, *The Works of Charles Kingsley, Vol. 1. Poems* (London: Macmillan, 1887).

Kipling, Rudyard, *The Years Between* (London: Methuen, 1919).

— 'An Error in the Fourth Dimension', *The Day's Work* (London: Macmillan & Co., 1898, reprinted 1948).

Kropotkin, Peter, *Memoirs of a Revolutionist* (Gloucester, MA: Peter Smith, 1967).

— *Anarchist Communism: Its Basis and Principles* (London: The New Fellowship Press, 1891).

Leftwich, Jospeh (ed.), *Yisroel: The First Jewish Omnibus* (London: John Heritage, 1933; revised edition London: James Clarke, 1949).

Leslie, Shane, *The End of a Chapter* (London: Constable, 1916).

Levison, Leon, *The Jewish Problem and the World War*, pamphlets for the Great War Series, 1917.

Lloyd George, David, 'Honour and dishonour', a speech by the Rt. Hon. D. Lloyd George, at Queen's Hall, London, 19 September, 1914, in *Pamphlets of the German War* (London: Methuen, 1914).

— *War Memoirs of David Lloyd George*, Volumes I and II (London: Ivor Nicholson & Watson, 1933, reprinted 1936).

Lobagola (Bata Kindai Amgoza ibn), *An African Savage's Own Story* (London: Alfred A. Knopf, 1930).

Lowell, James Russell, *Poems I* (London: Macmillan, 1890).

MacFadyen, Ella, *Songs of the Last Crusade: Verses of the Great War* (North Sydney: Winn & Co., Printers, 1917).

MacNutt, Frederic Brodie *(ed.)*, *The Church in the Furnace: Essays by Seventeen Temporary Church of England Chaplains on Active Service in France and Flanders* (London: Macmillan, 1917)

Marx, Karl, 'On the Jewish question', in David McLellan (ed.), *Karl Marx: Selected Writings* (Oxford: Oxford University Press, 1977, reprinted 1990).

Maxwell, Donald, *The Last Crusade* (New York and London: John Lane, 1920).

Meinertzhagen, Colonel R., *Middle East Diary, 1917 to 1956* (London:

The Cressnet Press, 1959).

Meynell, Alice, *Collected Poems of Alice Meynell* (London: Burns and Oates, 1914).

Meynell, Viola, *Alice Meynell. A Memoir* (London: Jonathan Cape, 1929, reprinted 1947).

Montague, C. E., *Disenchantment* (London: Chatto & Windus, 1922)

Nash, Paul, *Outline, An Autobiography and Other Writings* (London: Faber & Faber, 1949).

Nicholson, C. A., *The First Good Joy* (London: Hutchinson, 1923).

— *Their Chosen People* (London: Hutchinson, 1925).

Nietzsche, Friedrich, *The Portable Nietzsche*, ed. Walter Kaufmann (Harmondsworth: Penguin, 1978).

Nilus, Sergey, *Protocols of the Meetings of the Learned Elders of Zion*, trans. Victor E. Marsden (London: Hamish Hamilton, 1949).

Orchard, W. E., DD, 'The Real War', Papers for War Time Series No. 10 (London: Oxford University Press, 1914).

Oved, Moshe, *Visions and Jewels: Autobiographic in Three Parts* (London: Faber & Faber, 1925, reprinted 1952).

Owen, Harold, and Joan Bell, eds, *Wilfred Owen: Collected Letters* (London: Oxford University Press, 1967).

Owen, Wilfred Edward Salter, *Poems*, with an introduction by Siegfried Sassoon (London: Chatto & Windus, 1920).

Pankhurst, Christabel, 'The great war', a speech at Carnegie Hall, New York, 24 October 1914 (London: Women's Social and Political Union, 1914).

— *Industrial Salvation* (London: The Women's Party, October 1918).

— *'The Lord Cometh': The World Crisis Explained* (London: Morgan & Scott, 1923)

— *Unshackled: The Story of How We Won the Vote* (London: Hutchinson, 1959).

Pankhurst, Emmeline, *The Suffragette Movement: An Intimate Account of Persons and Ideals* (London, New York, Toronto: Longmans Green, 1931).

Patterson, J. H., Lieutenant Colonel, DSO, *With the Zionists in Gallipoli* (London: Hutchinson, 1916).

— *With the Judaeans in the Palestine Campaign* (London: Hutchinson, 1922).

Phillips, Stephen, *Armageddon: A Modern Epic Drama in a Prologue Series of Scenes and Epilogue Written Partly in Prose and Partly in Verse* (London: John Lane, The Bodley Head, 1915).

Ponsonby, Arthur, MP, *Falsehood in War-Time: Containing an*

Assortment of Lies Circulated Throughout the Nations during the Great War (London: George Allen & Unwin, 1928).

Raphael, Chaim (Chaim Pruss), *A Coat of Many Colours: Memoirs of a Jewish Experience* (London: Chatto & Windus, 1979).

Redivivus, Junius (pseud.), *The Holy War/ Diabolus/ Extremes: Generosity and Avarice* (London: John Bale, Sons and Danielsson, 1915).

Reilly, Sidney, *The Adventures of Sidney Reilly, Britain's Master Spy* (London: Elkin Matthews & Marrot, 1931).

Richards, Private Frank, *Old Soldiers Never Die* (London: Faber & Faber, 1933, reprinted 1964).

Rivers, W. H. R., 'The repression of war experience', in *The Lancet*, 2 February 1918, pp. 173–7.

Roback, A. A., 'Is psychoanalysis Jewish?', *Jewish Influence in Modern Thought* (Cambridge, MA: Sci-Art Publishers, 1929).

Robertson, J. A., *The Spiritual Pilgrimage of Jesus*, The Bruce Lectures, 1917, fifth edition (London: James Clarke, 1921).

Rocker, Rudolf, *The London Years*, trans. Joseph Leftwich (London: Robert Anscombe, 1956).

Rosenberg, Isaac, *The Collected Works of Isaac Rosenberg*, ed. Ian Parsons, (London: Chatto & Windus, 1979).

Rubinstein, H. F., Halcott Glover, *Exodus: A Dramatic Sequence in Five Episodes* (London: Ernest Benn, 1923).

Russell, G. W. E., 'The Jewish Regiment', *Daily News*, 17 September, 1917; reprinted as pamphlet, 1917.

Samuel, Horace B., *Unholy Memories of the Holy Land* (London: Hogarth Press, 1930).

Sassoon, Siegfried, *Collected Poems* (London: Faber, 1947).

Savage, Raymond, *Allenby of Armageddon* (London: Hodder & Stoughton, 1926).

Smith, Guy Vernon, *The Bishop of London's Visit to the Front* (London: Longmans, Green, 1915).

Sorley, W. R. (ed.), *The Letters of Charles Sorley* (Cambridge: Cambridge University Press, 1919).

Stern, G. B., *Pantomime. A Novel* (London: Hutchinson, 1914).

— *Twos and Threes* (London: Nisbet, 1916).

— *Children of No Man's Land* (London: Duckworth, 1919).

— *Monogram* (London: Chapman & Hall, 1936).

Talbot, Neville S., *Religion Behind the Front and After the War* (London: Macmillan, 1918).

Tatlow, Tissington, *The Story of the Student Christian Movement of*

Great Britain and Ireland (London: Student Christian Movement Press, 1933).

Thieberger, Frederick, *The Great Rabbi Loew of Prague: His Life and Work and the Legend of the Golem: With Extracts from his Writings and a Collection of the Old Legends* (London: East and West Library, 1955).

Treitschke, Heinrich von, *Politics*, Vols I & II, trans. Blanche Dugdale and Torben de Bille (London: Constable, 1916).

Webster, Nesta H., *World Revolution. The Plot Against Civilization* (London: Constable, 1921).

— *Secret Societies and Subversive Movements* (London: Boswell Printing & Publishing, 1924).

Weininger, Otto, *Sex and Character*, authorised translation for the sixth German edition, (London: William Heinemann; New York: G.P. Putnam's Sons, 1906).

Weizmann, Chaim, *Trial and Error. The Autobiography of Chaim Weizmann* (London: Hamish Hamilton, 1949).

Wilde, Oscar, *De Profundis. The Complete Test* (1905, reprint, London: Methuen, 1949).

Williams, A. Lukyn, *The Hebrew-Christian Messiah: or the Presentation of the Messiah to the Jews in the Gospel according to St Matthew* (London: SPCK, 1916).

Willink, Margaret Dorothea Rose, *Utopia According to Moses. A Study in the Social Teachings of the Old Testament* (London: SPCK, 1919).

Willis, Irene Cooper, *England's Holy War: A Study of English Liberal Idealism During the Great War* (New York: Alfred Knopf, 1928).

Wilson, William E., BD, *Christ and War: The Reasonableness of Disarmament on Christian, Humanitarian and Economic Grounds*, second edition (London: James Clarke, November 1914).

Wilton, Robert, *Russia's Agony* (London: Edward Arnold, 1918).

— *The Last Days of the Romanovs* (London: Thornton Butterworth, 1920).

Winnington-Ingram, A. F., 'A call to arms', address on 31 August from a waggon to 5,000 British Territorials at Bulwater Camp (London: Wells Gardner, Darton, 1914).

— 'Kaiser or Christ?', *The War and its Issues* (London: James Clarke, 1914).

— *Sermons for the Times No. 4: Sermons on the Holy War* (1914).

— *A Day of God: Being Five Addresses on the Subject of the Present War* (London: Wells Gardner, Darton, 1914).

— 'The Eyes of Flame' (London: Wells Gardner, Darton, 1914)

— *The Church in Time of War: Sermons and Addresses, 1914–15*

(London: Wells Gardner, Darton, 1915).

— 'The soul of a nation', sermon preached from the steps of St Paul's Cathedral, 25 July 1915 (London: C. Arthur Pearson, 1915)

— 'They shall not pass', sermon preached in St Paul's Cathedral, Easter Day 1918 (London: Wells Gardner, Darton, 1918).

— *Fifty Years' Work in London, 1889–1939* (London: Longmans, 1940).

Woolf, Leonard S., 'The three Jews', in Leonard S. Woolf and Virginia Woolf, *Two Stories* (Hogarth, Richmond, 1917).

'X', 'The Witness of the Church in the Present Crisis', Papers for War Time Series No. 9 (London: Oxford University Press, 1914).

Zangwill, Israel, *Children of the Ghetto: A Study of a Peculiar People* (1892, reprinted Philadelphia: Jewish Publication Society of America, 1938).

NEWSPAPERS AND PERIODICALS

Bioscope
Christian Challenge
Church Guardian
Commonwealth
Daily Chronicle
Daily Graphic (London)
Daily News
East London Advertiser
Illustrated Sunday Herald
Jewish Chronicle
John Bull
Manchester Guardian
Morning Post
The Nation
The Times
Suffragette
The Wipers Times: a complete facsimile of the famous World War One trench newspaper, incorporating the 'New Church' Times, The Kemmel Times, The Somme Times, the BEF Times, and the 'Better Times' (London & Basingstoke: Papermac, Macmillan, 1988)

PUBLIC RECORDS

British Army Officer's File for Gilbert Frankau, PRO WO 339/11211

REPORTS

Official Report of the Jewish International Conference on the Suppression of the Traffic in Girls and Women, (London, 1910).

GB War Office, *Report of the War Office Committee of Enquiry into 'Shell-shock'*, (London: HMSO, 1922).

League of Nations, *Report of the Special Body of Experts on Traffic in Women and Children*, Parts 1 and 2 (Geneva, 1927).

A Collection of Reports on Bolshevism in Russia (London: HMSO, 1919).

DICTIONARIES AND CONCORDANCES

The New International Dictionary of the Christian Church, gen. ed. J. D. Douglas (Exeter: Paternoster Press, 1974).

Illustrated Dictionary and Concordance of the Bible, gen. ed. Geoffrey Wigoder (London: Collier Macmillan Publishers; New York: Macmillan Publishing, 1986).

The Jerusalem Bible, gen. ed. Alexander Jones (London: Darton, Longman & Todd, 1968).

Drabble, Margaret (ed.), *The Oxford Companion to English Literature*, 5th edition, (Oxford, New York, Tokyo, Melbourne: Oxford University Press, 1985).

SECONDARY SOURCES

Abrahams, Israel, *Campaigns in Palestine from Alexander the Great* (London: Humphrey Milford, Oxford University Press, 1927).

Ariel, Yaakov, 'A neglected chapter in the history of Christian Zionism in America: William E. Blackstone and the Petition of 1916', in Jonathan Frankel (ed.), *Jews and Messianism in the Modern Era: Metaphor and Meaning*, Studies in Contemporary Jewry Series, VII (New York & Oxford: Oxford University Press, 1991), pp. 68–85.

Armstrong, Karen, *Holy War: The Crusades and their Impact on Today's World* (London: Macmillan, 1988).

Ashworth, A. E., 'The sociology of trench warfare', *British Journal of Sociology*, 19, (1968), pp. 407–23

Atkinson, Diane, *The Suffragettes in Pictures* (Museum of London:

Sutton Publishing, 1996).

— *Votes For Women* (Women in History Series, Cambridge: Cambridge University Press, 1988, reprinted 1989).

Avineri, Shlomo, *Moses Hess: Prophet of Communism and Zionism* (New York and London: New York University Press, 1995).

Barczeweski, Stephanie L., *Myth and National Identity in Nineteenth-Century Britain: the Legends of King Arthur and Robin Hood* (Oxford: Oxford University Press, 2000).

Berkowitz, Michael, *Western Jewry and the Zionist Project 1914–1933* (Cambridge: Cambridge University Press, 1997).

Bew, Paul, *Ideology and the Irish Question: Ulster Unionism and Irish Nationalism 1912–1916* (Oxford: Clarendon Press, 1994).

Bourke, Joanna, *Dismembering the Male: Men's Bodies, Britain and the Great War* (London: Reaktion Books, 1996).

Bridgwater, Patrick, *Nietzsche in Anglosaxony: A Study of Nietzsche's Impact on English and American Literature* (Leicester: Leicester University Press, 1972).

Bristow, Edward J., *Vice and Vigilance: Purity Movements in Britain since 1700* (Dublin: Gill & Macmillan, Rowman & Littlefield, 1977).

— *Prostitution and Prejudice: The Jewish Fight Against White Slavery 1870–1939* (Oxford: Clarendon Press, 1982).

Buitenhuis, Peter, *The Great War of Words: British, American, and Canadian Propaganda and Fiction, 1914–1933* (Vancouver: University of British Columbia Press, 1987).

Cannadine, David, *Aspects of Aristocracy: Grandeur and Decline in Modern Britain* (New Haven, CT and London: Yale University Press, 1994)

— *The Decline and Fall of the British Aristocracy* (New Haven, CT and London: Yale University Press, 1990).

Cecil, Hugh, *The Flower of Battle: British Fiction Writers of the First World War* (London: Secker & Warburg, 1995).

Cesarani, David (ed.), *The Making of Modern Anglo-Jewry* (Oxford: Basil Blackwell, 1990).

— 'Joynson-Hicks and the radical right in England after the First World War', in Tony Kushner and Kenneth Lunn, eds, *Traditions of Intolerance: Historical Perspectives on Fascism and Race Discourse in Britain* (Manchester and New York: Manchester University Press, 1989), pp. 118–39.

— *The Jewish Chronicle and Anglo-Jewry 1841–1991* (Cambridge: Cambridge University Press, 1994).

Cesarani, David and Tony Kushner, eds, *The Internment of Aliens in Twentieth Century Britain* (London: Frank Cass, 1993).

Cheyette, Bryan, 'Jewish stereotyping and English literature, 1875–1920: towards a political analysis', in Tony Kushner and Kenneth Lunn, eds, *Traditions of Intolerance: Historical Perspectives on Fascism and Race Discourse in Britain* (Manchester and New York: Manchester University Press, 1989).

— 'The other self: Anglo-Jewish fiction and the representation of Jews in England, 1875–1905', in David Cesarani, ed., *The Making of Modern Anglo-Jewry* (Oxford: Basil Blackwell, 1990), pp. 97–111.

— *Constructions of 'the Jew' in English Literature and Society: Racial Representations, 1875–1945* (Cambridge University Press, 1993).

Cheyette, Bryan and Laura Marcus, eds, *Modernity, Culture and 'the Jew'* (Oxford: Polity Press, 1998).

Cohen, Joseph, *Journey to the Trenches: The Life of Isaac Rosenberg 1890–1918* (London: Robson Books, 1975).

Cohen, Michael J., *Churchill and the Jews* (London: Frank Cass, 1985).

Cohen, Stuart A., *English Zionists and British Jews: The Communal Politics of Anglo Jewry, 1895–1920* (Princeton, NJ: Princeton University Press, 1982).

Cohn, Norman, *The Pursuit of the Millennium* (London: Secker & Warburg, 1957).

— *Warrant for Genocide. The Myth of the Jewish World-conspiracy and the Protocols of the Elders of Zion* (London: Eyre & Spottiswoode, 1967).

Cunningham, Valentine, *British Writers of the Thirties* (Oxford and New York: Oxford University Press, 1988).

Eksteins, Modris, *Rites of Spring: The Great War and the Birth of the Modern Age* (London: Black Swan, 1990).

Endelman, Todd M., *Radical Assimilation in English Jewish History, 1656–1945* (Bloomington and Indianapolis, Indiana University Press, 1990).

— 'The Frankaus of London: a study in radical assimilation, 1837–1967', *Jewish History*, Vol. 8, Nos. 1–2, 1994, pp. 117–54.

Erdmann, Carl, *The Origin of the Idea of Crusade* (Princeton, NJ: Princeton University Press, 1977).

Feldman, David, *Englishmen and Jews: Social Relations and Political Culture 1840–1914* (New Haven, CT and London: Yale University Press, 1994).

Ferris, A. J., *The Throne of David Found in Britain* (private publication by author, London, undated).

Ferris, Paul, *Sex and the British: A Twentieth-Century History* (London: Michael Joseph, 1993).

Frankel, Jonathan, *Prophecy and Politics: Socialism, Nationalism, and the Russian Jews, 1862–1917* (Cambridge: Cambridge University Press, 1981).

— (ed.), *Jews and Messianism in the Modern Era: Metaphor and Meaning*, Studies in Contemporary Jewry Series, VII (New York and Oxford: Oxford University Press, 1991).

Friedman, O. Michael, *Origins of the British Israelites: The Lost Tribes* (San Francisco: Mellen Research University Press, 1993).

Gardner, Brian, *Allenby* (London: Cassell, 1965).

Gartner, Lloyd P., *The Jewish Immigrant in England, 1870–1914* (London: George Allen & Unwin, 1960).

Gay, Peter, ed., *The Freud Reader* (London: Vintage, 1995).

Gilman, Sander L., *Jewish Self-Hatred: Anti-Semitism and the Hidden Language of the Jews* (Baltimore, MD and London: Johns Hopkins University Press, 1986).

— *The Jew's Body* (New York: Routledge, 1991).

Girouard, Mark, *The Return to Camelot: Chivalry and the English Gentleman* (New Haven, CT and London: Yale University Press, 1981).

Glover, David, *Vampires, Mummies, and Liberals: Bram Stoker and the Politics of Popular Fiction* (Durham, NC and London: Duke University Press, 1996).

Golomb, Jacob, ed., *Nietzsche and Jewish Culture* (London and New York: Routledge, 1997).

Gottlieb, Julie V., *Feminine Fascism: Women in Britain's Fascist Movement 1923–1945* (London: I. B. Tauris, 2000).

Green, Jeffrey, *Black Edwardians: Black People in Britain, 1901–1914* (London: Frank Cass, 1998).

Harrison, J. F. C., *The Second Coming: Popular Millenarianism, 1780–1850* (London and Henley: Routledge & Kegan Paul, 1979).

Hine, Edward, *Forty-Seven Identifications of the British Nation with the Lost Ten Tribes of Israel Founded Upon Five Hundred Scripture Proofs* (London: R. Banks & Son, undated, but *ca*. 1902).

Holmes, Colin, *Anti-Semitism in British Society, 1876–1939* (London: Edward Arnold, 1979).

Holton, Sandra Stanley, *Suffrage Days: Stories from the Women's Suffrage Movement* (London and New York: Routledge, 1996).

Horsman, Reginald, 'Racial Anglo-Saxonism before 1850', *Journal of the History of Ideas*, Vol. 37, No. 3, July–September 1976, pp. 387–410.

Hynes, Samuel, *A War Imagined: The First World War and English Culture* (London: The Bodley Head, 1990).

Jorgenson-Earp, Cheryl, *The Transfiguring Sword': The Just War of the Women's Social and Political Union* (Tuscaloosa and London: University of Alabama Press, 1997).

Kadish, Sharman, *Bolsheviks and British Jews: The Anglo-Jewish Community, Britain and the Russian Revolution* (London: Frank Cass, 1992).

— *'A Good Jew and a Good Englishman': The Jewish Lads' and Girls' Brigade 1895–1995* (London: Valentine Mitchell, 1995).

Katz, David S., *Philo-Semitism and the Readmission of the Jews to England 1603–1655* (Oxford: Clarendon Press, 1982).

Katz, Shmuel, *Lone Wolf: A Biography of Vladimir (Ze'ev) Jabotinsky*, Volume One, (New York: Barricade Books, 1996).

Kennedy, Paul and Anthony Nicholls, eds, *Nationalist and Racialist Movements in Britain and Germany Before 1914* (London and Basingstoke: Macmillan, 1981).

Kermode, Frank, *The Genesis of Secrecy: On the Interpretation of Narrative* (Cambridge, MA and London: Harvard University Press, 1979).

Killingray, David, 'LoBagola and the making of "An African Savage's Own Story"', in Bernth Lindfors (ed.), *Africans On Stage* (Bloomington: Indiana University Press, 1998)

Kinder, Hermann and Werner Hilgemann, *The Anchor Atlas of World History*, Vols 1 and 2 (New York, London, Toronto and Sydney: Anchor Press, 1978).

Knightley, Phillip, *The Second Oldest Profession: The Spy as Bureaucrat, Patriot, Fantasist and Whore* (London: André Deutsch, 1986, reprinted 1987).

Kushner, Tony, *The Persistence of Prejudice: Antisemitism in British Society during the Second World War* (Manchester and New York: Manchester University Press, 1989).

Kuzmack, Linda Gordon, *Woman's Cause: The Jewish Woman's Movement in England and the United States, 1881–1933* (Columbus, OH: Ohio State University Press, 1990).

Langmuir, Gavin I., *Towards a Definition of Antisemitism* (Berkeley, Los Angeles and Oxford: University of California Press, 1990).

— *History, Religion and Antisemitism* (London and New York: I. B. Tauris, 1990).

Leed, Eric, *No Man's Land: Combat and Identity in World War One* (Cambridge: Cambridge University Press, 1979).

Levene, Mark, War, Jews, and the New Europe: The Diplomacy of Lucien Wolf 1914–1919 (Oxford: Oxford University Press, 1992).

— 'The Balfour Declaration: a case of mistaken identity', English Historical Review, Vol. CVII, 1992, pp. 54–77.

Liddington, Jill and Jill Norris, One Hand Tied Behind Us: The Rise of the Women's Suffrage Movement (London: Virago, 1978).

Loughlin, James, Ulster Unionism and British National Identity Since 1885 (London and New York: Pinter, 1995).

Lunn, Kenneth, 'The ideology and impact of the British Fascists in the 1920s', in Tony Kushner and Kenneth Lunn, eds, Traditions of Intolerance: Historical Perspectives on Fascism and Race Discourse in Britain (Manchester and New York: Manchester University Press, 1989), pp. 140–54.

Maccoby, Hyam, The Mythmaker: Paul and the Invention of Christianity (London: Weidenfeld & Nicolson, 1986).

— Judas Iscariot and the Myth of Jewish Evil (London: Peter Halban, 1992).

— A Pariah People: The Anthropology of Antisemitism (London: Constable, 1996).

MacDougall, Hugh A., Racial Myth in English History: Trojans, Teutons, and Anglo-Saxons (Montreal: Harvest House; Hanover, NH and London: University Press of New England, 1982).

Marrin, Albert, The Last Crusade: The Church of England in the First World War (Durham, NC: Duke University Press, 1974).

Marwick, Arthur, The Deluge: British Society and the First World War (London: The Bodley Head, 1965).

Mayhall, Laura E. Nym, 'The rhetorics of slavery and citizenship: suffragist discourse and canonical texts in Britain, 1880–1914', Gender and History, Vol. 13, No. 3, November 2001, pp. 481–97.

McDermid, Jane, Midwives of the Revolution: Female Bolsheviks and Women Workers in 1917 (London: UCL Press, 1999).

Melinkoff, Ruth, The Horned Moses in Medieval Art and Thought (Berkeley: University of California Press, 1970).

— The Mark of Cain (Berkeley, Los Angeles and London: University of California Press, 1981).

Moeyes, Paul, Siegfried Sassoon: Scorched Glory. A Critical Study (Basingstoke: Macmillan, 1997).

Myers, Jody Elizabeth, 'The Messianic Idea and Zionist Ideologies', in Jonathan Frankel (ed.), Jews and Messianism in the Modern Era: Metaphor and Meaning, Studies in Contemporary Jewry, Vol. VII (New York and Oxford: Oxford University Press, 1991), pp. 3–13.

Nelson, G. K., *Spiritualism and Society* (London: Routledge & Kegan Paul, 1969).

Nochlin, Linda and Tamar Garb, *The Jew in the Text* (London: Thames & Hudson, 1995).

Norman, E. R., *Church and Society in England 1770–1970: A Historical Study* (Oxford: Clarendon Press, 1976).

Norquay, Glenda, *Voices and Votes: A Literary Anthology of the Women's Suffrage Campaign* (Manchester and New York: Manchester University Press, 1995).

Parker, R. A. C., *Europe 1919–45* (London: Weidenfeld & Nicolson, 1967).

Parry, J. P., *Democracy and Religion: Gladstone and the Liberal Party, 1867–1875* (Cambridge: Cambridge University Press, 1986, reprinted 1989).

Parsons, Ian, ed., *The Collected Works of Isaac Rosenberg* (London: Chatto & Windus, 1979).

Pearsall, Ronald, *The Worm in the Bud: The World of Victorian Sexuality* (London: Weidenfeld & Nicolson, 1969; London: Pimlico, 1993).

Pick, Daniel, *Faces of Degeneration: A European Disorder, c. 1848–c. 1918* (Cambridge: Cambridge University Press, 1989).

Price, Richard, *An Imperial War and the British Working Class: Working-Class Attitudes and Reactions to the Boer War 1899–1902* (London: Routledge & Kegan Paul, 1972).

— *War Machine: The Rationalisation of Slaughter in the Modern Age* (New Haven, CT and London: Yale University Press, 1993).

Porter, Roy and Lesley Hall, *The Facts of Life: The Creation of Sexual Knowledge in Britain, 1650–1950* (New Haven, CT and London: Yale University Press, 1995).

Ragussis, Michael, *Figures of Conversion: 'The Jewish Question' and English National Identity* (Durham, NC and London: Duke University Press, 1995).

Read, Donald, ed., *Documents from Edwardian England 1901–1915* (London: Harrap, 1973).

Rich, Paul B., *Race and Empire in British Politics* (Cambridge: Cambridge University Press, 1986).

Rich, Paul, 'Imperial decline and the resurgence of English national identity 1918–1979', in Tony Kushner and Kenneth Lunn, eds, *Traditions of Intolerance: Historical Perspectives on Fascism and Race Discourse in Britain* (Manchester and New York: Manchester University Press, 1989), pp. 33–52.

Riley-Smith, Jonathan, 'The first crusade and the persecution of the Jews', in W. J. Shields, ed., *Persecution and Toleration: Papers read at the twenty-second summer meeting and the twenty-third winter meeting of the Ecclesiastical History Society* (Oxford: Blackwell for the Ecclesiastical Society, 1984), pp. 51–72.

Rosen, Andrew, *Rise Up Women! The Militant Campaign of the Women's Social and Political Union 1903–1914* (London: Routledge & Kegan Paul, 1974).

Rubinstein, W. D., *A History of the Jews in the English-Speaking World: Great Britain* (Basingstoke: Macmillan, 1996).

Scult, Mel, *Millennial Expectations and Jewish Liberties: A Study of the Efforts to Convert the Jews in Britain, up to the Mid Nineteenth Century* (Leiden: E. J. Brill, 1978).

Schweitzer, Albert, *The Quest of the Historical Jesus: A Critical Study of its Progress from Reimarus to Wrede*, third edition (London: Adam & Charles Black, 1954).

Searle, G. R., *Eugenics and Politics in Britain 1900–1914* (Leyden: Noordhoff International Publishing, 1976).

Shepherd, Naomi, *A Price Below Rubies: Jewish Women as Rebels and Radicals* (Cambridge, MA: Harvard University Press, 1993).

Showalter, Nathan D., *The End of A Crusade: The Student Volunteer Movement for Foreign Missions and the Great War* (Lanham, MD and London: The Scaremongers Press, 1998).

Smith, Colin, *The Last Crusade* (London: Sinclair-Stevenson, 1991).

Smith, Elaine R., 'Jewish responses to political antisemitism and fascism in the East End of London, 1920–1939', in Tony Kushner and Kenneth Lunn, eds, *Traditions of Intolerance: Historical Perspectives on Fascism and Race Discourse in Britain* (Manchester and New York: Manchester University Press, 1989), pp. 53–71.

Spater, George and Ian Parsons, *A Marriage of True Minds: An Intimate Portrait of Leonard and Virginia Woolf* (London: Jonathan Cape and Hogarth Press, 1977).

Stein, Leonard, *The Balfour Declaration Declaration* (London: Vallentine, Mitchell, 1961, reprinted Jerusalem: The Magnes Press, the Hebrew University and London: Jewish Chronicle Publications, 1983).

Stone, Martin, 'Shellshock and the Psychologists', chapter 11, Roy Porter and Michael Shepherd, eds, *The Anatomy of Madness: Essays in the History of Psychology. Volume II: Institutions and Society* (London and New York: Tavistock, 1985), pp. 242–71.

Tate, Trudi, *Modernism, History and the First World War* (Manchester:

Manchester University Press, 1998).

Theweleit, Klaus, *Male Fantasies, Volume 1: Women, Floods, Bodies, History* (Minneapolis: University of Minnesota Press, 1987).

Tickner, Lisa, *The Spectacle of Women: Imagery of the Suffrage Campaign 1907–14* (London: Chatto & Windus, 1987).

Verrier, Anthony (ed.), *Agents of Empire: Anglo-Zionist Intelligence Operation 1915–1919. Brigadier Walter Gribbon, Aaron Aaronsohn and the NILI Ring* (London and Washington: Brassey's (UK), 1995).

Vital, David, *Zionism: The Formative Years* (Oxford: Clarendon Press, 1982).

Walkowitz, Judith, *Prostitution and Victorian Society: Women, Class and the State* (Cambridge: Cambridge University Press, 1980).

Warner, Marina, *Joan of Arc* (London: Vintage Books, 1981).

Webber, G. C., 'Intolerance and discretion: Conservatives and British fascism, 1918-1926', in Tony Kushner and Kenneth Lunn, eds, *Traditions of Intolerance: Historical Perspectives on Fascism and Race Discourse in Britain* (Manchester and New York: Manchester University Press, 1989), pp. 155–72.

Webbington, D. W., *Evangelicalism in Modern Britain: A History from the 1730s to the 1980s* (London: Unwin Hyman, 1989).

Wilkinson, Alan, *The Church of England and the First World War* (London: SPCK, 1978).

— *Dissent or Conform? War, Peace and the English Churches 1900–1945* (London: SCM Press, 1986).

Wilson, John, 'British Israelism: The ideological restraints on sect organisation', in Bryan R. Wilson, ed., *Patterns of Sectarianism: Organisation and Ideology in Social and Religious Movements* (London: Heinemann, 1967, pp. 345–76).

Wilson, Duncan, *Leonard Woolf: A Political Biography* (London: Hogarth, 1978).

Wilson, Trevor, *The Myriad Faces of War: Britain and the Great War, 1914–1918* (Cambridge: Polity Press, 1986).

Wilson, Jean Moorcroft, *Siegfried Sassoon. The Making of a War Poet: A Biography (1886–1918)* (London: Gerald Duckworth, 1999).

Winter, J. M., *The Great War and the British People* (London: Macmillan, 1985).

— *Sites of Memory, Sites of Mourning: The Great War in European Cultural History* (Cambridge: Cambridge University Press, 1995).

Winter, Jay, and Jean-Louis Robert, eds, *Capital Cities at War: Paris, London, Berlin 1914–1919* (Cambridge: Cambridge University

Press, 1997).

Wolffe, John, *The Protestant Crusade in Great Britain 1829–1860* (Oxford: Clarendon Press, 1991).

Woodcock, George, *Anarchism: A History of Libertarian Ideas and Movements* (Harmondsworth: Penguin, 1962, reprinted 1979).

Woods, Oliver, and James Bishop, *The Story of the Times: Bicentenary Edition 1785–1985* (London: Michael Joseph, 1983, reprinted 1985).

Yerushalmi, Yosef H., *Zakhor: Jewish History and Jewish Memory* (Seattle and London: University of Washington Press, 1982, reprinted 1996).

Index

Recently published by Vallentine Mitchell

Anglo-Jewish Poetry
from Isaac Rosenberg to Elaine Feinstein
Peter Lawson, University of Southampton

This is the first book-length study to survey the phenomenon of twentieth-century Anglo-Jewish poetry. It proceeds by reading established Anglo-Jewish poets against the grain of conventional thinking about English verse. For example, rather than understanding Isaac Rosenberg and Siegfried Sassoon as simply First World War poets, it approaches them as minority Anglo-Jewish poets as well. A similar challenge to the notion of an undifferentiated English literature is made with respect to four other major writers: John Rodker (1894–1955), Jon Silkin (1930–97), Elaine Feinstein (1930–) and Karen Gershon (1923–93). All these poets share a peripheral relationship with English and Jewish culture, together with a common attachment to the disaporic narrative of exile and deferred return to a textually imagined homeland.

'Peter Lawson generously considers the work of six Anglo-Jewish poets and persuades us that their marginality in relation to the central English literary tradition is a blessing.'
Dannie Abse

'To American readers, "Anglo-Jewish poetry" might seem an oxymoron. The delight of Lawson's ground-breaking study is not that it introduces us to new writers, but that it helps readers understand and identify with six British poets who are an essential part of modern Jewish literature. Clear and cogent, provocative and persuasive, this volume is long overdue.'
Rochelle Ratner, Executive Editor,
American Book Review